JESUS AFTER
THE
CRUCIFIXION

JESUS AFTER THE CRUCIFIXION

From Jerusalem to Rennes-le-Château

Graham Simmans

Bear & Company
Rochester, Vermont

Bear & Company
One Park Street
Rochester, Vermont 05767
www.BearandCompanyBooks.com

Bear & Company is a division of Inner Traditions International

Library of Congress Cataloging-in-Publication Data
Simmans, Graham.
  Jesus after the Crucifixion : from Jerusalem to Rennes-le-Chateau / Graham Simmans.
    p. cm.
  Includes bibliographical references and index.
  ISBN-13: 978-1-59143-071-1 (pbk.)
  ISBN-10: 1-59143-071-2 (pbk.)
  1. Jesus Christ—Miscellanea. 2. Rennes-le-Chateau (France) I. Title.

BT295.S45 2007
232.9—dc22

                              2006103552

Printed and bound in the United States by Lake Book Manufacturing
10 9 8 7 6 5 4 3 2 1

Text design and layout by Jon Desautels
This book was typeset in Sabon with Charlemagne used as the display typeface

CONTENTS

ACKNOWLEDGMENTS

To Ingrid Riedel-Karp I give thanks and appreciation for her excavation work in Egypt, research at Rennes-le-Château, and the completing of this book. I give much appreciation to my friend, agent, and editor, Tuvia Fogel, for his broad vision, help, and support.

I express my grateful appreciation for the work of Mr. Paul Remeysen in making extensive examination of the text draft and cross-checking with original source material during a period of many weeks.

I am grateful for the encouragement and help from my many friends and helpers during my fifteen years of research work in Rennes-le-Château, Egypt, Israel, and Jordan. In particular, I thank my close and valued friend and archaeological partner Professor Bastian Van Elderen, who died at his home in August 2004 and is here remembered with gratitude for the close collaboration in Egypt.

INTRODUCTION

There is a desperate need among many people today, especially the young, for a sense of purpose and direction, for a way to give more meaning to their life. It is my belief that the whole world, and Christians in particular, have a burning desire for new spiritual truths.

A thousand years ago, the Christian world expected the Second Coming of Christ, for that was how it had interpreted the prophecies in the Bible. It did not happen. Today again, as we enter the third millennium, many people of Christian belief expect a Parousìa—that is, for Christ to come again. The orthodox version of this Second Coming, firmly believed in the Middle Ages, was that he would arrive astride the clouds of heaven. Then there is the idea that he survived the cross and is buried somewhere from whence, at the right time, he will rise again as a living being of power and wisdom. But many Christians today have come to a new, different understanding. To them the Second Coming means the Spirit of Jesus will enter every human mind, thus enabling a new heaven and a new world—a more divine form of life—to come into being.

If we want to know which of these eschatological visions of the Second Coming is more likely to come about, nothing can help us more than a greater knowledge of the events of the beginning. Archaeological

1

discoveries such as the Dead Sea Scrolls at Qumran and the gnostic gospels at Nag Hammadi have brought those times and people closer to us. I feel sure that new document finds are still to come that will further strengthen our understanding of the origins of Christianity. In fact, one understanding of the Second Coming could be the appearance of something that, as though coming directly from Jesus, will explain exactly what he taught and meant. If such a thing appears, the new era of enlightenment could be closer than we think.

But let's begin at the beginning. Early Christianity was still very much rooted in the cultures of the region where it was born. The geographical proximity of Palestine and Egypt made it inevitable for the people in these regions to exert cultural and religious influences on each other over centuries. We are told that Moses was raised as an Egyptian prince. Certainly at the royal court of the pharaoh, ideas about leadership of a nation, law, and order would have formed in his mind at an early age. He would have witnessed the Temple worship, the magic of the priests, and the deep mysticism of Egyptian religion. In fact, all this was present in the makeup of Judaism. Psalms in the Bible carry traces of Egyptian hymns to the sun god Ra (Amun/Aton).

The religious ideas of Mesopotamia, Phoenicia, and other countries also penetrated into the Jewish faith. It is important to note that the first five books of the Hebrew scriptures, attributed to Moses, were actually written at least six hundred years after his time, during and after the Babylonian captivity. Early Jewish Law was greatly influenced by the law of Babylon.

Thus the wisdom and insight of many centuries and people went into the scriptures of the "Law and the Prophets" of Israel, which the young Jesus studied to become a rabbi. His background and education were entirely Jewish and his disciples were Jewish. His intention was not to create a new faith or change the basic Jewish creed, but rather to use this creed as a vehicle of enlightenment and love. We in the West tend to forget this. He was a teacher rather than a redeemer.

Then, with the conversion of Saul/Paul of Tarsus, early Christian teaching blossomed into the Greco-Roman world. Paul's theological skill was to integrate aspects of non-Jewish thinking into what he thought to be the message of Christ. The Hellenistic-Roman Empire, extended eastward by Alexander the Great, was the ideal medium through which to spread the new creed all over what was then the whole known world.

Alexander's dream may appear unrelated to early Christians, but it was in fact the first conscious attempt at globalization, and Christianity's universal project (*catholic* comes from the Greek *katholicos,* meaning "universal")—though this may surprise some—was more political than spiritual in its profound nature. In spite of initial resistance, including terrible persecution of Christians, Rome's great empire of mixed races, cultures, and religions eventually embraced the Christian message of charity, redemption, and access to Paradise after death. Christianity spread ever wider and became the cradle of European civilization.

For the most part, the Fathers of the Church of early centuries never met, and it is not surprising that differences in interpretation and dogma soon developed. Each of the four canonical gospels was written for its own locality; the four were not intended to be read side by side, as we encounter them today. It is now certain that the gospels we have were written not by the apostles themselves, but by others in their name.

The early Fathers were determined that theirs should become the supreme religion, but they could not possibly have guessed that it would achieve such astounding success so widely and so fast. St. Mark sparked amazingly rapid growth in Christianity between AD 45 and 55 in Egypt, as did others in Rome and Greece. This book will, among much else, attempt to show part of this startling progress.

Few people realize that in the early days there were many forms of Christianity, whose followers I like to call the forgotten Christians. During the long period of their repression and torture and of the destruction of so-called heretical Christian writings (roughly from the late second to the late fourth century), thousands of these other Christians (perhaps the original Christians?) fled to the desert, moved by deep faith and a search for direct communion with God. Today, many wrongly believe that this was an abdication of responsibility. In fact, the desert was for them a place of temptation and of devils, and great courage was required to live there.

Important new finds of a large (one mile by one mile) Christian community of the early centuries of this millennium have been traced in the Wadi Natrun Desert in western Egypt. More than one hundred buildings, some partly intact and each about forty yards square, are hidden in the sand, as are about eight large mud-brick constructions. This site was never completely lost, but knowledge of its true extent is totally new.

There is a striking similarity between the beliefs of the first- and second-century Christian gnostics of Egypt and those of the Cathars of southern France in the twelfth and thirteenth centuries. So far no proof of a direct link has come to light, but such identical thinking seems too strong for chance. Most scholars suggest Cathar beliefs originated with another heretical sect, the Bogomils, first written about in tenth-century Bulgaria, but during years of research, I have developed a different scenario. The idea that Cathar gnosticism came from the East, traveling first from the Paulicians of Cappadocia to the Bogomils of Bulgaria, and from there spreading through Lombardy and Provence to the Languedoc, is more far-fetched, I believe, than the notion of the existence of a local tradition from antiquity and late antiquity.

I see this cultural continuity as tied to the undisputed presence of Jewish communities in Gaul from before the destruction of the Temple in AD 70. Monks are known to have traveled between Europe and Egypt in the second, third, and fourth centuries. In his book *Through the Lands of the Bible,* scholar H. V. Morton mentions ancient records of many Irishmen who traveled to Egypt in the first six centuries of the millennium and of Egyptian monks visiting Hibernia, as Ireland was then known. In fact, seven Coptic monks are said to be buried at Disert Ulidh in Ireland, which we shall learn more about later.

I intend to show that in many different strands of historical and archaeological research, a remarkable connection can be shown to have existed among Jerusalem, Egypt, and the south of France. Here at Rennes-le-Château, where I have lived for fifteen years, there is a unique concentration of about ten layers of history. The story of the priest Bérenger Saunière is the superficial "sugar layer" on the cake, but truly it is relatively unimportant to what lies beneath. There can be no doubt that Saunière came into the possession of a huge amount of money, whether by finding something in the church here and selling it or through payments made to him. Much has been written about this mystery, but most stories are based on conjecture and none has been proved. Certainly, however, *something* was found here! I've spent many years on the site, and while I tend to discount the tales of buried treasure here, gripping as they are, I believe the hilltop area contains Christian secrets.

There is an explosive link between new discoveries on the beginnings of Christianity in Egypt—in which I have had the good fortune to take part—and the strange history of Rennes-le-Château. This book is intended to stimulate and challenge readers in their conception of the roots and original meaning of Christianity, and thereby promote progress in Christian thinking. Soon, I trust, we shall achieve a complete understanding of the real Jesus, his message, and his life's purpose.

Yet we should remember that God's love and compassion for this world and the yearning of the human soul to reach enlightenment and eternal life are the main themes of all great religions. Jesus' words "There are many mansions in my father's house" are sometimes interpreted as the many paths to heaven available to humanity. When I was very young, I made the firm resolve to study the early writings and spiritual beginnings of Christianity. In approaching other cultures on my travels all over the world, I have always tried to observe the principles of respect and understanding for different views of God and the universe.

Written in the French village to which my studies have eventually led me, this is the story of my search.

✝

Part 1

RENNES-LE-CHÂTEAU: A NEW APPROACH

I

A GENERAL HISTORY
OF RHEDAE
(RENNES-LE-CHÂTEAU)

For about fifteen years now I have been living in Rennes-le-Château, and the attraction this village holds for me grows with every year. The people here are kind, with a warm welcome for all visitors, who come in large numbers from all over the world, fascinated by the mystery of the place. From 2000 through 2003, there were almost fifty thousand visitors a year, but the phenomenal success of the novel *The Da Vinci Code* brought 120,000 people to the village in 2004. Rennes also embodies a stimulating energy level, something that innumerable sensitive individuals have experienced here. I suppose in my life I've always looked for a sort of Shangri-La, a faraway hidden city of enlightenment like the one so brilliantly portrayed by James Hilton in his novel *Lost Horizon*. For me, Rennes is a superb place, and I have found happiness here.

There has been a constant flow of visitors to my house, and many come to discuss what they have found here and their concept of the future. They have read all the books on the famous Abbé Saunière and his great secret and they know every new hypothesis about where Saunière's riches came from and what the secret could be. Treasure seekers of all kinds have come and gone, yet no one ever found anything valuable. Then there are others who have approached more seriously what Saunière may have discovered and what the real mystery of the place may be.

Rennes-le-Château—or Rhedae, as it was called in ancient times—has a long history. In the sixth century BC, Celts, later known as Gauls, lived nearby. According to the accounts of Posedonius (ca. 135–50 BC), who traveled widely in France and northern Spain, their leaders and holy men, the Druids, had high status and sophisticated nature wisdom. They worshipped their god Bram and had a sanctuary on nearby Bugarach Mountain. Little is known of Celtic rites, though an ancient offering stone was found in a cave south of Rennes, near the Stream of Colors. This massive block, weighing several tons, now stands in a sheltered place in the middle of the village. Some ten Celtic crosses can be seen carved on the surface of the stone, together with a dug-out depression, probably there to hold the blood of sacrifices. The stone is believed to date from sometime between 2000 and 1000 BC.

Some say that the ancient name of Rennes—Rhedae—derives from the Celtic tribe of the Redones, who occupied the southeast of France in the third century BC. They originated in what is today Belgium and also founded the other Rennes, in the north of France. Tectosages was another name given to the Celtic tribes of the area. Rennes might even be the fabulous Celtic city described by Herodotus in 420 BC as "a treasure city south of Carcassonne."

Greek colonization of the south of France started in about 600 BC and continued until about 200 BC. Greek coins have been found from this period on the hilltop itself, as well as in the fields below. Other Greek cities in the area were Marseille, Les-Saintes-Maries-de-la-Mer (where the ruins of a Greek temple to Aphrodite were found on the seashore), Lattes, Agde, Glanum, and Avignon, all of which formed a chain of occupation by the early Greeks. Several places in the south of France still reveal their Greek origin by their names, as in the case of Agde (from the Greek Agathe Tyche).

Here there was also a thriving community in Roman times, from 100 BC to AD 300, with a town at Alet and hot-spring baths at Rennes-les-Bains. There were extensive gold mines in the area, and traces of Roman mining tunnels—at one time much frequented by treasure hunters—still exist. At around the time of Jesus' life there was a mixed population of Celts, Greeks, Romans, and Jews living in Rhedae.

THE VISIGOTHS AND ALARIC I

The name Rhedae may also have come from the Visigoth word for "traveling chariots." Before the Visigoths surrounded Rennes with walls, ravines, and entrenchments, these great wheeled chariots, made of wood and roofed with leather hides, were also used, Far West–style, for defense. Rennes was of great strategic importance near the end of the time of the Roman Empire. It commanded the crossroads of two important routes that intersected at the foot of the hill at what is today the village of Couiza: one route from Paradise Pass leading to Narbonne and the other from St. Louis Pass leading to Bugarach and to Perpignan and, eventually, to Spain.

It must be noted that while Frankish tribes led by Merovingian kings already controlled most of present-day France in the sixth and seventh centuries, from AD 412 to 711 the Visigoths controlled both Spain and a fingerlike protrusion into France along the Mediterranean coast, a sliver of land known as Septimania, which includes Rennes and about which we shall soon learn more. The period of the Visigoth kings in this region began with Alaric I and lasted until early in the eighth century. Only then was it followed by the Merovingian and Carolingian Frankish dynasties

Many people confuse Alaric I, king of the Visigoths (Western Goths), with Attila the Hun, a brutal barbarian whose tribe hailed from the Siberian steppes, possibly because the two were near contemporaries and because Alaric sacked Rome, which is what people believe Attila to have done. (He would have, of course, but Pope Leo I pointed out that Alaric had died right after his sacking, and Attila relented.) Alaric, born in AD 364 near the mouth of the Danube, was an attractive personality of considerable ability and was well educated as a Christian in Constantinople at the court of the Eastern emperor Theodosius. His brother-in-law married Theodosius's famous daughter Galla Placidia, whose magnificent tomb in Ravenna, with its blue and gold mosaics, remains one of the great surviving works of art of the fifth century.

Alaric conquered Rome in AD 410 with the help of rebellious slaves, of whom there were forty thousand inside the city. As with many fortified cities in the past that were captured not by force but by a traitor who opened the gates to an enemy, Rome's Salarian gate was opened to Alaric's troops by slaves. Although there was pillaging, Alaric respected the churches and spared the lives of those who did not resist. The slaves, however, took every opportunity to avenge themselves and filled the streets with dead. Alaric in fact treated his foes and the city itself in a far more Christian manner than did those self-styled defenders of Christendom, the Crusaders, in Jerusalem seven centuries later, when they massacred every single inhabitant of that Eastern city. Actually, though the Romans did not know this at the time, Alaric was a Christian himself, but an Arian Christian—that is, a follower of the so-called heresy named after Bishop Arius of Alexandria.

There are conflicting reports of the rest of his life. What is known (and recorded by the Roman historian Procopius) is that the treasure of the Second Temple of Jerusalem (Herod's Temple), which Titus had taken to Rome in AD 70 after the sack of Jerusalem, was carried away by Alaric the Visigoth in AD 410. His army marched out along the Appian Way toward the southern tip of Italy, loaded with gold and silver. His dream was to conquer Sicily and then North Africa, but when he tried to embark, most of his ships sank in a storm. He returned to Cosenza, about fifty miles from Sybaris, in the south of Italy, where he suddenly died and was buried. Alaric's tomb is said to contain the spoils of Rome, including the famous candelabrum of Solomon's Temple (the menorah), though none of these treasures has ever been found.

We have a fascinating description of how Alaric was buried in the bed of the Busento River: In his *Decline and Fall of the Roman Empire*, Gibbon quotes extensively from a book by Jordanes, the first historian to write about the Goths, in AD 551, and whose account of Alaric's burial is almost certainly correct. Jordanes relates that Alaric met an untimely death and his people mourned him with the utmost affection.

They turned the Busento River from its course near the city of Cosenza and then led a band of captives into the middle of the riverbed to dig out a place for the ruler's grave. In this pit they buried Alaric with many of his treasures, and then turned the water back into the former channel. So that no one would ever know the place, they then put to death all the gravediggers.

The site of the tomb is undiscovered to this day. I have spent much time searching this area in southern Italy with Italian archaeologists. The only river here is dry for much of the year. Cosenza lies inland, above the toe of Italy, and aerial photographs of the Busento River valley reveal nothing. In Alaric's day, the river meandered through the quiet countryside with a small village situated on its bank. Today, a modern city rises by a stream running between stone embankments. Alaric might lie underneath any of a dozen modern buildings. The course of the river as it ran sixteen hundred years ago has not been found and probably never will be.

After his death, Alaric's brother-in-law Ataulphus led the Visigoths to southern France, where the Roman emperor Constantius III agreed to settle them in Aquitania Secunda. Then, in 415, they moved on and took over much of Spain, with their first capital being Toledo, which they later lost. Ataulphus was succeeded by Theodoric, who died in 451. In 507 they possessed Septimania—which included Carcassonne—and fortified the twin hills of Rhedae, today's Rennes-le-Château. The map still shows the Mountain of Alaric about twelve miles east of Carcassonne, on the south side of the motorway. The name Rhedae, the city of the chariot, may well have come down to us as a memory of Alaric's army of wagons. It is interesting to note that the horseshoe arches so typical of Visigothic architecture can still be seen in Rennes's church of Mary Magdalene, originally an Arian church.

SEPTIMANIA

The province of Septimania was created by the emperor Augustus, who settled the veterans of his Seventh (Septima) Legion in the Narbonne area as a reward upon their retirement. The name Septimania continued to be used through early medieval times, when the Visigoths settled there on and off from 440 to 759. During the sixth and seventh centuries, the large Jewish population in the region had close relations with the Visigoths, who, being Arian Christians, believed Jesus to have been fully human and were thus more inclined to get on with Jews than with Catholics.

Some historians claim that traces still exist of a Jewish princedom that existed on territory on both sides of the Pyrenees, around Pamplona and Barcelona and in the Languedoc. The Visigoth kings later converted to Catholicism and new laws were made to harass and convert the Jews, so much so that when the Muslims conquered parts of Visigoth Spain, the Jews welcomed them and were given charge of Córdoba, Toledo, and Granada by the Muslims for their gracious treatment. At the turn of the ninth century, the Jewish princes in Narbonne enjoyed recognition as the "Seed of the House of David" by the caliph of Baghdad, the same Harun al-Rashid who sent an elephant as a gift to Charlemagne. Truly, today's antagonistic Muslims and Jews seem to have come from another planet.

The Arabs entered Septimania in stages between 720 and 759, reaching almost to Lyon until checked by Charles Martel, whose son took the region under his control. After defeating the Arabs at Poitiers in 732 (and thus preventing a Muslim Europe), Charles Martel laid siege to Narbonne in 738, defeating Jews and Arabs fighting together. In 759, with Narbonne once more in Muslim hands, the Jews traitorously turned on their Arab allies and surrendered the city. As a reward for this betrayal, they were given nominal autonomy. The Jews prospered greatly and their wealth included much land. It must be noted that deliberate attempts were made to obliterate this Jewish period from the history of the region, and very little corroboration of these traditions can be found today.

MEROVINGIANS AND CAROLINGIANS

Despite much work by medievalists to define them, the Merovingians remain a great mystery. Much of what is mysterious about the village of Rennes-le-Château and the most outrageous claims made by people researching its history revolve around these strange, charismatic, long-haired leaders who became kings in Gaul four hundred years after the death of Jesus. The Merovingians derived from the Sicambrians, a Germanic people and one of the many tribes collectively known as the Franks. The Sicambrians were pagan but got on well with the newly Christianized Romans.

The Merovingians claimed descent from ancient Troy and, like other tribes, were driven west into Gaul and the Ardennes in the mass migrations caused by the invasion of the Huns in the early fifth century. They were literate and enjoyed a reasonable standard of living. The kings were polygamous and accumulated great wealth, mainly in gold coins. They were priest-kings with long hair and, like Samson in the Bible (and certain consecrated Jewish sectarians known as Nazirites), they attributed special power to their uncut hair. In fact, in their burials they practiced ritual skull incisions. Though some historians hold that France went through a truly dark age during the reign of these peripatetic, superstitious kings, these rulers somehow retain the aura of shamanlike mystical figures whose secrets went underground when their dynasty was trodden on by the wheels of history.

Mérovée, founder of the dynasty, was a supernatural figure of whom nothing is known apart from myths. He became king in 417 and died in 438. Childeric I, son of Merovée and father of Clovis, was born in 408, reigned for twenty-four years (457–481), and was known as a learned man. In 1653 his tomb was found containing regalia, arms, and treasure worthy of a royal tomb, including a severed horse's head, a golden bull's head, and a crystal ball. Found there were also three hundred bees made of pure gold. Charmed by this ancient regal symbol, Napoleon later had similar emblems fixed onto his coronation robes. Clovis I reigned from 481 to 511, and through him, Rome set up for the first time its undisputed supremacy in Europe. By 496 the Roman Catholic Church was dangerously weak, its very existence threatened. The bishop of Rome at the time was busy fighting heresies such as Arianism, which was very popular and spreading rapidly. In this milieu, Rome decided to seek a champion. By 486 Clovis had greatly extended his kingdom, and seemed very much the man of destiny. His conversion to Catholicism was brought on by his wife, Clothilde, but not before the king had held some secret meetings with St. Remy. Clovis was ultimately baptized by St. Remy at Rheims in 496.

A subsequent accord with the Church provided him with authority equal to that of the Greek Orthodox Church. Clovis received the title of New Constantine, becoming a de facto Western emperor. The pact binding Clovis and the Church "insolubly in perpetuity" was of momentous consequence to Christianity and to the future history of France (to the point that in 1996 the fifteen-hundredth anniversary of his conversion was celebrated as the birth of the French nation).

Clovis immediately attacked the Visigoths, the Arian heretics then straddling the Pyrenees as far north as Toulouse, defeating them at the battle of Vouille in 507. The Visigoth colony north of the Pyrenees collapsed and the Visigoths fell back to Carcassonne. Their last remaining bastion in the Razès (the region around Rhedae) was Rhedae itself.

When Clovis died in 511, his empire, in accordance with Merovingian custom, was divided among his four sons. One hundred and forty years (and several Merovingian kings and queens) later, in 651, we come to a crucial turn of events in our story. Dagobert II, heir to the kingdom of Austrasia, was kidnapped but managed to escape to exile in Ireland, where he was brought to the monastery of Slane, near Dublin. There he obtained a much higher education than he could have achieved in Gaul, and he married Mathilda, a Celtic princess, and later moved to England to live at York. It was there that he formed a close spiritual friendship with the bishop of York, St. Wilfred.

At this time, the Irish Church still refused to accept the authority of Rome. We shall discover more about Celtic Christianity, an important piece of the puzzle, further on. Suffice it to say that Bishop Wilfred was keen to bring the Irish Church into the Roman fold, something he finally accomplished at the Council of Whitby in 664. He also hoped to see Dagobert return to Gaul and eventually reclaim his kingdom of Austrasia, fulfilling the terms of Clovis's pact with Rome 170 years earlier. Thus, when Dagobert's wife died, in 670, Wilfred arranged a dynastic match: Dagobert's new wife would be Giselle of Razès, daughter of the count of Rhazès and niece of the Visigoth king. The Merovingian and Visigoth bloodlines would thus be allied, providing a basis for the unification of most of France from the Pyrenees to the Ardennes. It would be a partly Visigoth realm, and Arian thinking was still strong among Visigoths, but it would be under Rome's control. The marriage took place at the bride's official residence at Rhedae, in fact at the very church of St. Magdalene, the original building on the site, which later became the medieval church next to my cottage.

The marriage produced three children, with the last one—a son born in 676—being the future Sigisbert IV. By this time, Dagobert II was king and had to deal with anarchy among various rebellious nobles and with accumulating vast wealth to finance the recapture of Aquitaine, which had become independent. What's more, his inclination toward Arianism very probably upset the Catholic Church. Thus, on December 23, 679, when Dagobert went hunting at the royal palace at Stenay and lay down at midday for a rest by a stream near a tree, one of his servants stole up to him and, acting under enemy orders, pierced him through the eye with a lance, killing him. The murderer then rode back to Stenay with his accomplices, planning to wipe out the rest of the family there. Whether they succeeded in doing so is not known, but the reign of Dagobert and his family came to an immediate end. The Church not only associated with the king's assassins; it also went as far as justifying the murder.

One story has it that in 681 Sigisbert IV, Dagobert's son and still a little boy, was smuggled by his sister to his mother in the Languedoc, where he later became the duke of Rhedae (nicknamed Plantard), but the veracity of this story is doubtful, for it seems to derive from Priory of Sion sources (which we shall explore soon). No official records exist about him, but maybe this is the result of his enemies' understandable efforts to prove the end of the Merovingian bloodline. Dagobert's body was buried in the royal chapel of St. Remy. Two centuries later, in 872, it was moved to another church, which became the church of St. Dagobert. (In the same year, he also became a saint, though it's not clear why.) During the French Revolution, the church and the relics of

St. Dagobert were destroyed, and today only an incised skull said to be that of Dagobert II is in the hands of a convent at Mons. All other relics of the saint have disappeared.

In 725, Arab forces, which had come from North Africa via Spain, quickly beat back the Visigoths in Septimania. Rhedae was built up into a great stronghold with a citadel at each end and two sets of battlements surrounding the city. Shortly afterward, power effectively passed into the hands of the Carolingians. The first of these was Charles Martel, who stopped the Moorish invasion at the Battle of Poitiers in 732. But Martel did not take the throne. It was the pope who declared that Childeric III should be deposed in favor of Pepin III, thus openly breaking the Church's pact with Clovis. This betrayal by the Church was extraordinary. A document was produced known as the Donation of Constantine (which would be proved to be a forgery in the fifteenth century), which attested not just to the Church's spiritual authority over all of Christianity, but also to its power to make kings!

A complex, unclear period followed, with some sources speaking of a Sigisbert VI, also referred to as Prince Ursus, surviving the betrayal and continuing the Merovingian bloodline. The Franks eventually pushed both Visigoths and Arabs out to Spain for good. This was the time of Charlemagne's piece-by-piece assembly of his immense empire. On Christmas Eve in 800 he was proclaimed Holy Roman Emperor by Pope Leo III in Rome, a title that three hundred years earlier had been solemnly reserved for the Merovingian line. Both Pepin III and Charlemagne married Merovingian princesses, as if to strengthen the legitimacy of their dynasty. It should be noted that the betrayal of the Merovingians by the Catholic Church was never forgotten and is at the root of many apparently inexplicable events in later centuries, perhaps right down to the present.

The walled city of Rhedae, a dependency of Carcassonne, reached its peak in the eleventh century. When Amalric married Clothilde in 1062, it had two towers and two sets of battlements, with similar fortifications upon the nearby twin hill that formed part of the royal city. It had thirty thousand inhabitants, two churches—the church of St. Pierre and the church of Mary Magdalene—a monastery inside the village and another one outside, and many shops and craftsmen.

The language of the Occitan, quite different from medieval French, was spoken everywhere. (In the Languedoc the word for "yes" is *oc*, not *oui*.) The royal city was famous for the music and poetry contests in the splendor of its court. Christians, Muslims, and Jews, as well as countless heretics of all descriptions, lived in "Alexandrian" harmony within its walls.

After losing its royal status, however, Rhedae began its decline. In the twelfth century, now called Rhedesium, it changed hands many times: first belonging to the viscounts of Béziers; then to Alfonso, king of Barcelona; then to the Trencavels. In 1170 Afonso attacked the badly defended city and destroyed the hilltop defenses and the lower village; only the main citadel with its tower remained. In the time of the Great Cathar heresy, vast destruction and killing also took place. During the Albigensian crusade of 1209, Simon de Montfort took Rhedae and Coustaussa easily, given that they were practically defenseless, and all remaining walls were removed. Simon then destroyed the whole area to prevent its possible reuse as a Cathar stronghold. His heirs, the lords of Voisins, however, rebuilt double-walled battlements, strengthened the castle at the top of the hill, and restored the two churches. Rennes once more became the principal town of the region.

In the years around 1360, the people of Rennes were cut down by the plague and were almost destroyed by roving Catalan bandits, the so-called Routiers. Near anarchy prevailed, a terrible period of merciless killing, fires, and pillage by armed adventurers. In 1361 the plague killed most remaining survivors, and subsequently, Count Henri de Trestamare, a feared bandit from Spain, attempted to override the city by siege. The Voisinses put up a fight, but in 1362 all walls were destroyed once again, as well as the monastery and the church of St. Pierre.

This was the end of Rhedae. The town, even the names Rhedae and Rhedesium, disappeared forever. Only the church of Mary Magdalene and the name Rennes-le-Château remained. The house of Voisins ended when Jeanne married the Spanish nobleman Marquefave. His descendant Blanche de Marquefave married Pierre d'Hautpoul in 1422, bringing as her dowry the baronry of Rennes-le-Château. Henri, baron of Hautpoul, later decided to take up the title of Blanchefort, a branch of the family that in the twelfth century had produced two grand masters of the Knights Templar, Bertrand and Hugues. The last marchioness of Blanchefort was Marie de Nègre d'Ables, a descendant of an important family from the Sault Plateau. She married the last marquis of Blanchefort in 1732 and thirty years later became his widow without a male heir. On January 17, 1781, Marie died at the age of sixty-seven, and the family name died with her.

Exactly one hundred years later, exhibiting elusive and fascinating connections to every stage of the history I have outlined, the legendary tale of the parish priest Bérenger Saunière began to unfold.

2

THE MYSTERY OF ABBÉ SAUNIÈRE

As is well known, the main elements of this story formed the basis of the best seller *Holy Blood, Holy Grail,* by Henry Lincoln, Michael Baigent, and Richard Leigh, first published in 1982. Their presentation followed on the heels of three successful BBC documentaries: *The Lost Treasures of Jerusalem* (1971), *The Painter and the Devil* (1974), and *Shadow of the Templars* (1979).

The enormous success of the book was due to the resurfacing into public awareness, for the first time since the Cathar heresy, of the tradition concerning the marriage of Jesus and Mary Magdalene and the fate of their offspring. Many books—more than four hundred, perhaps—have now been published claiming to know the great secret of Rennes-le-Château. Some of these are sheer fantasy, some are based on honest research work, and most of them are a mixture of these two.

I became interested in these ideas because they seemed an extension of my own historical research, begun long before I became aware of them. Since discovering the tradition of Jesus and Mary Magdalene, my work was carried out mostly on-site in Rennes, and eventually I simply moved to the village itself. Over the years I have come to believe that the most likely explanation of the Rennes story and its various mysteries is different from the one put forth in *Holy Blood, Holy Grail,* but I will let the reader be the judge. Before returning to the mystery of the village in depth, however, we shall take a detour through the early centuries of Christianity, but first I will provide here a brief outline of the story of Rennes and of my interpretation of the available clues.

Of all the researchers I have corresponded with, I am most indebted to Tatiana Kletzky-Pradere, author of *Rennes-le-Château: Guide du Visiteur.* With her consent, I present the mystery through a summary of the results of her work, interspersed with my own comments in brackets. I must say at the outset that the following account reflects only the way in which Madame Kletzky-Pradere and I propose that events likely developed.

MARIE DE NÈGRE D'ABLES, DAME D'HAUTPOUL DE BLANCHEFORT ET DE RAZÈS-RHEDAE

At the time of her death, in 1781, Dame d'Hautpoul de Blanchefort was the keeper of a very great secret that had been passed on from generation to generation of her family. Because she had no son, when she realized that she didn't have long to live, she decided to entrust her secret to her confessor, the curé of Rennes-le-Château, Antoine Bigou.

She confided to him the secret and presented for his safekeeping vitally important documents. She died on January 17, 1781, but not before making the priest promise that before his own death, he would entrust her secret to someone worthy.

What the priest heard frightened him considerably, particularly as France was in the midst of great political upheavals that before long would lead to the Revolution of 1789 and the destruction of the king and noble families of France. After much thought, he decided to hide the documents in the Visigoth altar pillar in the church of Mary Magdalene in Rennes. Fearing for his life in those difficult times, he decided to entrust a stone slab with what was to be passed on to future generations. The slab was engraved with Latin inscriptions, and in 1791 it was laid upon the grave of the marchioness. One of the inscriptions, written partly in Greek letters, reads ET IN ARCADIA EGO. Bigou had this stone lifted from the vaults of Arques (a castle exactly on the original zero meridian), between the parishes of Peyrolles and Serres near Pontils. At the head of the grave he had erected another flagstone bearing conspicuous anomalies in the epitaph. And all of this Bigou accomplished because he believed the correct interpretation of this script would lead to the hiding place of the secret [which in fact it did]. Finally, inside the church he decided to place facedown at the foot of the altar a very old sculptured slab depicting a knight and a small child riding the same horse. [The source of this slab is not known, but it probably came from a Merovingian tomb in the churchyard.]

Very soon after, in 1792, Curé Bigou was declared an insubordinate priest and fled to Sabadell, in the Catalan region of Spain. There he died eighteen months later, but not before he had entrusted the great secret to Curé Cauneille, an exile like himself. Cauneille carried out his own sacred mission by writing two books, *The Golden Ray* and *The Line of Sight*. He also transmitted the secret by word-of-mouth to two other priests: Curé Jean Vie, vicar of Rennes les Bains from 1841 to 1872, and Curé Emile-François Cayron, vicar of St.-Laurent-de-la-Cabrerisse at about the same time.

I believe that all three priests knew that a huge treasure of untold value was buried somewhere around Rennes-le-Château and Rennes-les-Bains, hidden in twelve different hiding places that had been pointed out to Curé Bigou by Marchioness de Blanchefort. These hiding places were indicated by Curé Bigou by means of a coded message, with its key cut into the epitaphs on the stones erected to mark the grave of the marchioness.

The priests also must have known of the existence of several parchments of great historic value containing proof relating to the lineage of the royal families of Europe. This fact is important in light of the relationship Abbé Saunière developed with Johann von Hapsburg.

Saunière and another priest, Boudet, were later clever enough to make the most of these documents. Curé Henri Boudet, a poor boy from Quillan, was taught by Curé Cayron, who had himself been a disciple of the curé of Rennes-les-Bains, Jean Vie. It is known that Boudet was a man of high education and knowledge of history, Greek, Latin, English, and Saxon. Curé François Bérenger Saunière, born in Montazels, a small village near Rennes-le-Château, was appointed priest at Rennes in 1885 with the task of looking after a decrepit church which at that time had a very small congregation. Together, these two priests lived out their great adventure.

Less than six months after his installation as priest of Rennes-le-Château, Saunière was visited by the archduke Johann von Hapsburg, a cousin of the powerful emperor of Austria-Hungary, Franz Joseph. Someone, probably Boudet, had suggested he visit Saunière. The archduke introduced himself as Monsieur Guillaume, stating that he had come on behalf of the countess of Chambord, who had been born a Hapsburg and had been a widow for two years. Her late husband, Henri de Bourbon, count of Chambord, a direct descendant of Louis XIV and a grandson of Charles X, had been the legitimate pretender to the crown of France and could have reigned under the name Henri V. He had died childless, however, and this was where one of the branches of the royal lineage of Louis XIV had disappeared forever.

The archduke, a most refined man, offered the country priest the sum of three thousand francs, a considerable amount in those days, to look for precious parchments—which Bigou had deemed of immense importance at the time—hidden somewhere inside the church. For several years the archduke returned regularly to check Saunière's progress, and provided compensation totaling twenty thousand francs, which would now be about fifty thousand euros. [We know that Saunière and Johann von Hapsburg had accounts at the same bank in Perpignan and that Saunière received many letters from a bank in Budapest as well.]

At about the same time, in 1886, Henri Boudet published his most peculiar book *The True Celtic Language and the Stone Circle at Rennes-les-Bains*. When it was published, experts regarded it with disdain, though some researchers still believe the book contains encoded secrets, including the location of twelve hidden boxes, each to be opened in its proper, numbered turn—but the key to deciphering the supposed secrets in the text has yet to be found.

Boudet was greatly disappointed by the reception scholars gave his book, so he had a rather clever idea: He decided to immortalize his message in stone through the coded symbolic decoration of the church of St. Magdalene in Rennes. He reached an agreement with Saunière that he, Boudet, would pay for all restoration work on the church and would remain the absolute unquestioned supervisor of planning while leaving Saunière the role of very highly paid overseer of the work required.

Some believe that Boudet imposed upon Saunière his eighteen-year-old servant, Marie Denarnaud, known as Marinette, as a collaborator who would also play the role of treasurer. She came to live in Rennes in the now roofless house beside the Saunière garden. Restoration work soon started, with large sums of money arriving to Marinette's account. Boudet's account book shows that in fifteen years she received the sum of 4,516,691 francs in gold coins, an unbelievable fortune then and quite a sum even now.

Under the stone slab sculpted with knights, which Bigou had placed facedown at the foot of the altar, Saunière's workers discovered a grave containing three skeletons and a ceramic pot filled with ancient coins and jewels. In 1891 the documents hidden by Antoine Bigou inside the pillar a hundred years earlier were found, and they consisted of two authenticated deeds, an ancient document from the crown of France bearing the seal of Blanche de Castille and a more recent manuscript, which was deciphered by Henri Boudet and revealed an anagram of the epitaph:

BERGERE PAS DE TENTATION—QUE POUSSIN, TENIERS TIENNENT LA CLEF PAX 681—PAR LA CROIX ET CE CHE-VAL DE DIEU, J'ACHEVE CE DEMON DE GARDIEN A MIDI POMMES BLEUES

[SHEPHERDESS NO TEMPTATION—THAT POUSSIN, TENIERS HOLD THE KEY PEACE 681—BY THE CROSS AND THIS HORSE OF GOD, I COMPLETE (OR DESTROY) THIS DEMON OF GUARDIAN AT NOON BLUE APPLES.]

It is believed this message refers to St. Sulpice Church in Paris, in the land of St.-Germain-des-Prés, where Merovingian kings were buried until the construction of the basilica of St. Denis. St. Sulpice is based upon the design of the Temple of Solomon and was completed at the time the marchioness died. It is also believed that the message recommends that the person who can interpret it refrain from undertaking anything before 1891 unless ordered to do so by superior authorities. The marchioness's epitaph clearly points to 1891, and researchers have been puzzled why that date had been chosen. She died in 1781, so the inscription should have read January 17, 1781 (MDCCLXXXI), but Bigou had insisted on engraving XVII JANVIER MDCOLXXXI, substituting an O for the second C. But because O does not appear in Roman numerals, it can be ignored and the date can be read MDCLXXXI, or 1681. If we now take the O—which reminds us of the zero meridian that runs through both St. Sulpice in Paris and Rennes-les-Bains—as a pivot point, we can turn the date around so that 1681 becomes 1891.

Curé Boudet decided to follow this instruction by sending Saunière to St. Sulpice for orders. According to records in the church, Saunière was there during five days in March 1892 and came in contact with Émile Hoffet, a famous occultist and author of many essays on esoteric works, and Emma Calvé, the opera singer and a close friend of Joseph Peladan, who in 1891 had founded the Order of the Rose Cross of the Temple and Grail.

He also met Charles Plantard, who claimed to be a descendant of the royal branch of the Merovingians. Saunière later lavishly entertained these and other people in high authority at Rennes-le-Château. Interestingly, a number of symbolic decorations in St. Sulpice portray the landscape around Rennes-les-Bains and Rennes-le-Château and the secrets that are hidden there. Saunière is said to have brought back from Paris three reproductions of paintings [but there exists no proof to support this story]: *The Temptation of St. Anthony,* by David Teniers (St. Anthony's day is January 17, the day of the marchioness's death); *The Shepherds of Arcadia,* by Nicolas Poussin, showing the landscape around Blanchefort castle and the famous inscription ET IN ARCADIA EGO; and a portrait of Pope Celestin V (artist unknown).

On Saunière's return to Rennes, he and Boudet opened in darkness Marchioness de Blanchefort's tomb vault in the graveyard of the church of Mary Magdalene and went to quite a lot of trouble to chisel away the engraving upon it. [Infrared photography has since shown what the engraving was.]

Thereafter, Saunière traveled widely through France and abroad, but never stayed away very long. Apparently much correspondence came to him. The redecoration of the church continued on a grand scale, with Boudet investing considerable sums of money. The smallest details were continually corrected at high cost by Italian artists and a secret room was built behind the vestry to which there was access through a false cupboard.

In 1897 the church was finally finished and inaugurated. Contractors' records show the expenditure of extremely large sums of money. In addition, land was purchased in the name of Marie Denarnaud and buildings were constructed, including Villa Bethany and the Magdala Tower, a semicircular gallery on the edge of a cliff with a greenhouse and an orangery. Also constructed was a garden with trees and a fountain. Bérenger Saunière also spent money lavishly on high-ranking people, much to the anger of Curé Boudet, who quarreled with him about this. Yet even after repeated disagreements with his bishop, Saunière appeared to think he had some kind of immunity.

Curé Gelis, of Coustaussa, was found murdered in his vestry on All Saints Day 1897. Neither the murderer nor any motive was ever found. [Nothing had been disturbed and the body was laid out in a reverent position, so it seems the killer must have been known by Curé Gelis.] In 1903, after suspecting Saunière of intimidating Curé Gelis, Boudet became very upset by Saunière's behavior. He suspended all payments to Marie Denarnaud and ceased contact with Saunière.

Deprived of Boudet's flow of donations, Saunière found himself in financial difficulties and he was thus compelled to sell some valuable furniture, silverware, and collections. Because Boudet had cut off his gifts to the new bishop as well, the bishop decided he was no longer going to condone Saunière's behavior. On the bishop's recommendation, the Vatican forbade Saunière to hold Mass in the church. Being greatly distressed by this, the priest constructed his own altar on the veranda of Villa Bethany so that he could continue to offer Mass to any parishioner who wanted to attend. [The Vatican accused him of simony—that is, selling Masses and pardons—and some researchers believe that to have been the sole source of his wealth.]

Saunière's diaries show that he continued to have serious money problems until Curé Boudet, on his deathbed, revealed to him the source and hiding place of the great fortune. After thirty years of this turbulent life, Saunière was at last sole master of Rennes's secret. He continued spending substantial sums on several strange projects. For example, he signed a large contract with his building contractor in Couiza, saying he would pay cash for construction of another tower below the existing Magdala Tower. Certainly Saunière found wealth from some source, but it may not have been treasure as such. More likely, it was a secret of vital importance. Perhaps there were secret documents of lineage, proof favoring one or the other of the competing branches of French royalty or the Hapsburgs. These could have been vital for many members of the European nobility of the time.

Why did Saunière receive money from the Hapsburg archduke Johann von Hapsburg using the pseudonym of Jean Orth? The archduke first came to Rennes not long after he had renounced all rights and titles in 1889 and was banished from all Austrian empire territories. Officially he was said to have died in 1890, but in fact he died in Argentina in 1911. On the face of it, the most likely and credible explanation for Saunière's sudden wealth would seem to be payments from the archduke for archaeological services. Other clues in Saunière's life, however, point to his possessing some kind of powerful information. Why was he admitted so readily to the Hoffet elite circle in Paris? How was he able to flout the authority of his bishop and later secure exoneration from the Vatican without too much difficulty (although this was formally given only after his death)? We shall probably never know. In the end, Saunière outlived Boudet by only a couple of years. On January 17, 1917, he was found by Marie Denarnaud at the Magdala Tower, the victim of a stroke.

He is believed to have passed his secret to his friend Curé Rivière, from Esperaza, sometime in the five days before his death on January 22, 1917. True to his word, Curé Rivière passed the great secret to another member of the clergy, who is so far not identified. The Church is said to have then pressured Marie Denarnaud to sell her property and made every effort to hush up the whole matter.

Fifty years later, an extraordinary event occurred: A British newspaper suddenly published three of the parchments belonging to Marchioness d'Hautpoul de Blanchefort. The documents had considerable historic value and had been bequeathed by will to a niece of Saunière who lived in Montazels. She seemed to have sold them very cheaply in 1965 to Captain Rowland Stanmore and Sir Thomas Frazer, two Englishmen representing the International League of Ancient Books. The whereabouts of the documents at present are not known, but it is believed that they were placed in a safe deposit box in a Lloyd's Bank vault in London. Investigation to verify has been fruitless. No confirmation could be obtained from Lloyd's Bank, the International League of Ancient Books, or the Englishmen concerned. All denied knowledge of the transaction. The story was finally dismissed as having no foundation. The three published parchments contained:

1. A genealogy of the counts of Rhedae, the first descendants of the Merovingian kings, from Mérovée until 1244. The documents bore the seal of Blanche de Castille, queen of France in that year, and were written in the form of litanies to Notre Dame. They were countersigned by Raymond Y. A. Niort, the man who had negotiated the conditions of surrender of the last surviving Cathar fortress at Montségur, which fell in that same year. Blanche de Castille is said to have given the Cathars these documents in exchange for the location of a Visigoth treasure of gold hidden in the Razès. These documents are said to have been

secretly carried out of Montségur by the last four men to escape the siege by being lowered with ropes at night. I believe they were then handed over by the Cathars to the Knights Templar, to whom they were absolutely vital.

2. The will of François-Pierre d'Hautpoul, lord of Rennes and Bézu, drawn up by Captier, a solicitor at Esperaza, on November 23, 1644. This includes the descendants of the genealogy of the first document from 1244 to 1644 together with six lines in Latin about St. Vincent de Paul of Alet.

3. The will of Henri d'Hautpoul drawn up on April 24, 1695, with his seal and signature and a Latin invocation to five saints, including Mary Magdalene.

These, then, are the documents that Saunière found in the graveyard tomb of Marchioness d'Hautpoul de Blanchefort, who had believed them to be vital. She said they had to be deciphered in order to know what belonged to the family because they bear the crucial evidence of the survival of the Merovingian dynasty.

Dagobert II was assassinated in 679 in the forest of Woevre, now in Belgium, on the orders of Pepin the Fat. Because this is seen by many as the betrayal by the Church of Rome of a dynasty who should reign over the Holy Roman Empire to this day, the question of whether Dagobert's son, Sigisbert IV, survived the assassination has been a potent mystery for centuries among the nobility of Europe. The parchment shows that he did indeed survive, secretly hidden by his mother, the countess of Rhedae. He succeeded his grandfather Béra as count of Razès, continuing the Merovingian line with his wife, Magdala. It was probably the count's, his wife's, and his successor's skeletons that Saunière excavated in the the church of Mary Magdalene in Rennes.

This is the story of Abbé Saunière as it is told in the village of Rennes and as it was recorded by Madame Kletzky-Pradere. There are many more riddles connected to it, however, of which I shall mention but a few in the following text, for they may throw some light on the secret—or perhaps make it even more mysterious.

RIDDLES IN THE CHURCH

When Saunière restored the church of Mary Magdalene, he left numerous strange "clues." Over the porch he carved the curious inscription: TERRIBILIS EST LOCUS ISTE (this place is terrible or, better, "this place is awesome"). The phrase is actually a carefully selected part of Genesis 28:16–17 in which, after dreaming the ladder to heaven with angels going up and down it, Jacob "awaked out of his sleep and said, 'Surely the Lord is in this place; and I knew it not.' And he was afraid, and said, *'How dreadful is this place!'* [my italics] This is none other but the house of God, and this is the gate of heaven." The words in Saunière's inscription sound sinister out of context, but on the entrance to a house of God they are not actually out of place.

The inside of the church is also full of mysteries and coded messages:

1. In the picture relief at the western end of the church showing the Sermon on the Mount, inexplicably there is a bag of gold at Jesus' feet.

2. Just inside the entrance of the church, holding up the baptismal font, Saunière set up a statue of the demon (or *djinn*) Asmodeus, who, in Jewish legend, is the guardian of ancient secrets and of the treasure of Solomon's Temple.

3. The church contains many unusual Christian statues and unorthodox pictures of the Stations of the Cross. These include a strange representation of station six of the Via Dolorosa, in which the centurion holds his shield high to conceal Simon the Cyrene, who substituted himself for Jesus, as believed by Muslims and by many heretical Christians in medieval times. Did Saunière also believe that it was not Jesus who was nailed to the cross?

   The strangest station is undoubtedly the fourteenth, in which a small white circle of paint turns out to be a true provocation: A full moon looks on the disciples as they apparently take Jesus' body into the sepulchre. Yet Jesus died at three o'clock in the afternoon. If this scene is taking place at night, perhaps the disciples are *removing* the body from the tomb rather than taking it there.

4. Below the altar, in a depiction of Mary Magdalene kneeling in contemplation, the landscape in the background is the same as that in the Teniers painting *The Temptation of St. Anthony.*

5. The five principal statues in the nave of the church form a sequence that, using the initials of the saints they represent—St. Germaine, St. Roch, St. Anthony the Hermit, St. Anthony of Padua, and St. Luke—spells out the word *graal.* Some have noted, however, that the "statue" depicting Luke is not, in fact, a statue in a niche on the walls like the others. Instead, it is one of the four bas-reliefs that surround the pulpit.

6. The two statues at the east end of the nave show Joseph and Mary, mother of Jesus, both holding in their arms what would appear to be the infant Jesus. But those statues could also represent, as many believe, Jesus and Mary Magdalene holding *their* child.

Was Saunière trying to communicate something that, as a Catholic priest, he couldn't say more directly?

Saunière's Riddles

Along with the church's riddles, there are also "mysteries" about Saunière himself that can be quickly debunked. It has been alleged by some scholars that Saunière's coffin was ordered one week before his death from a stroke he suffered on January 17, 1917, but this is quite untrue. In fact, I have a copy of the receipt of the payment Marie Denarnaud made for the coffin (see plate 3), and it is dated June 12, 1917, five months after the priest's death. It seems that the month of June *(juin)* has been misread as Jan (as in *janvier*), which some see as in keeping with the habit, in those days, of paying invoices up to six months after the job was carried out.

As the story goes, during the five days that Saunière lay dying, a priest was called from another parish to hear his final confession and to administer Last Rites. It is said that the priest arrived and retired to the sickroom. According to others present, he emerged not long after, visibly upset. It is also said that the priest actually refused to administer the Rites, though I consider this to be unlikely and untrue. Catholic priests I know have confirmed and emphasized this. Saunière died, as stated earlier, on January 22, 1917, and his body, wrapped in red plaid edged with scarlet tassels, was placed upright in a chair in the entrance hall of Villa Bethany. One by one, the mourners passed him, each taking a tassel from the garment as a remembrance.

The "Blue Apples" Church Glass

Another curiosity in the Magdalene church that still remains unsolved has become known as the "blue apples" glass. We now know that the coded documents said to have been found by Saunière, including one ending with the words *blue apples,* were forgeries by the marquis de Chérisey, an eccentric friend of Pierre Plantard (1920–2000; grandson of Charles Plantard). But this does not in itself eliminate the possibility that de Chérisey himself knew something more. This highly gifted and cultured Frenchman liked to mix reliable material with misleading deviation. There could be truth behind the forgery, but it's unlikely ever to become known.

Here is an example: With remarkable skill, the makers of the windows for the church inserted on the south side a very special stained glass. Actually, the original glass was smashed by vandals some years ago—or at least that was the official version of its removal, though I have since discovered that the mayor, fed up with tourists and treasure hunters, did away with it. The replacement for the glass never reached the original quality. It is said that the light shining through the glass at midday on about January 17 projected onto the north wall of the church an image of three trees bearing colored apples, including a group of three blue ones. A short time after noon, as the sun moved on, the red apples disappeared and only the blue apples remained. What does this story really mean? Certainly the apples were not projected by mere chance. This curiosity might have an importance not yet known, and as such it was recorded by Madame Kletzky-Pradere, for the question springs to mind: If de Chérisey made up both the code and the message, which came first—the glass or the code?

Engravings on the Base of the Stone Calvary

The calvary in the garden of the church has the following words carved on its four sides: CHRISTUS VINCIT (Christ conquers), CHRISTUS REGNAT (Christ reigns), CHRISTUS IMPERAT (Christ rules), and CHRISTUS A.O.M.P.S. DEFENDIT (Christ defends AOMPS).

A.O.M.P.S. is believed to stand for Antiquus Ordo Mysticusque Prioratus Sionis—the Ancient and Mystic Order of the Priory of Sion. If this interpretation of the letters is correct, it would imply that the name Priory of Sion was in use in Saunière's time and is not an invention of Pierre Plantard and de Chérisey. Others, however, claim that this acrostic is quite common in Catholic liturgy and stands for Ab Omni Malo Populum Suum, which, with the words carved before and after it, would simply read "Christ defends his people from all evil."

The Tombstones of Marie de Nègre d'Ables and the Stone of Coumesourde

Here we return to the tombstones of Marie de Nègre, last marchioness of Blanchefort. Why did Saunière take so much effort to deface the inscriptions? Most researchers are grateful to Eugène Stublein's 1884 book, *Pierres gravées du Languedoc,* in which the inscriptions erased by Saunière are faithfully reproduced, though some people claim that the book is a forgery because Stublein's signature in it is different from that in another book written by him.

Ernest Cros, a local historian who carried out research in the region near Rennes from 1920 to 1943, discovered in 1928 another engraved stone near the hamlet of Coumesourde, in the immediate neighborhood of Rennes. This stone's inscription, a triangular diagram and Templar crosses, could well have belonged to the destroyed church of St. Pierre. When Ernest Cros came to know of the Blanchefort tombstones half destroyed by Saunière, he accused the dead priest of vandalism and reconstructed the text of the stones with the help of knowledgeable villagers. There has been a great deal of conjecture about the meaning of the obviously coded messages of these stones—and astonishingly, there are remarkable similarities in the code of the stone of Coumesourde and the tombstones in the Rennes cemetery. The letters *PS* are carved on the horizontal tombstone as well as on the Coumesourde stone, as are the words PRAE-CUM.

The Strange Story of the Arab Spirit or Djinn

To emphasize the fact that in Rennes there are hidden ancient and powerful secrets that many gnostics—that is, knowers—through the ages have sought to protect, here is the story of a mystery within a mystery: the tale of Saunière's talisman.

Early in 1993, I had the privilege of staying with Henri Buthion at Villa Bethany while I was buying my current home and property. One day we noticed that the wooden skirting board on the right side of the second-floor landing had become loose, but on closer examination, we found that someone had concealed a small book behind it.

It was was a three-inch by three-inch hardback volume with a thin red cardboard cover, and it contained seventy pages of Arabic handwriting. I have color photographs of each page of the original manuscript, with each notarized as authentic. It was obviously old, though not more than one hundred or two hundred years, for the pages were bound with white string, which seemed a more modern method of binding. It has not been possible to establish its exact age, but the text was handwritten in medieval Arabic, so it could have been copied from an ancient original. I later learned from the director of the Cairo Islamic Museum that binding with string is a very ancient tradition in the Orient and that the work looked about eight hundred years old.

This translation caused much difficulty, even with the help of Islamic scholars at Al-Azhar University and several mosques in Cairo, which I consulted during my many archaeological trips to Egypt. Very few people today, even in Arab countries, have knowledge of this period of Islamic writing, and they all seem reluctant to give Christians access to the contents and full meaning of these texts. It took me some time to find out why no Muslim would help with translation. The following article, which appeared in the Cairo press a few years ago, illustrates well the dangers facing scholars studying the Muslim faith or translating documents such as the one I found:

PROFESSOR'S MARRIAGE FALLS FOUL OF DEVIL

An Egyptian professor was ordered to separate from his wife because he did not believe in angels, devils, and genies. An appeals court in Cairo found that Nasr Hamed Abu Zaid of Cairo University had disputed verses in the Quran about "magic and the evil eye." The ruling said he believed that angels, devils, and genies were legends; had denied "that the Quran is the word of God"; and had called on Muslims not to apply shar'ia law because it is "no longer appropriate." Nasr Hamed Abu Zaid was ordered to separate from his wife because a Muslim woman cannot be married to an apostate. The couple will appeal.

I now know how widespread the belief in djinns, or dark spirits, still is in the Muslim world. Hotel staff, shopkeepers, and taxi drivers in Egypt talk frankly about their total belief in and experiences with these forces. The booklet I found contains many symbols of the most powerful and dreaded djinns and demons, and I have been told not to repeat these verbally, because repetition of their names is said to increase their power. I have also been advised that the document should never be made public because it contains material sensitive to the Muslim faith and includes black magic symbols.

The authorities at the Muslim Museum eventually told me that the book was a *tiwas,* or talisman, written in Arabic, and that it probably originated in Cairo at the time of the Crusades. A tiwas is actually a religious prayer document invoking the help of Allah and Muhammad to alleviate the complaint of an ill person or, more often, to protect someone from danger, and it is usually kept in the vicinity of the person in need of protection.

The pages of the book certainly seemed to be set out in the form of prayers, with much repetition for chanting. In total, three years and a fee of one thousand dollars were required to secure its translation. The work was carried out by an Arab Christian scholar, but I am advised by Muslim and other authorities that it would be unwise to publish the contents at this time. I can, however, say that it proved indeed to be a tiwas, a talisman, which gave protection not only to the place but also to the holder. This may have been the reason why Saunière kept it in his house, Villa Bethany, near to him.

Henri Buthion and I thought it must have been hidden by Saunière himself. When I found it, inside there was a loosely inserted picture of the archangel Michael, rendered in the pious Catholic style of Saunière's time. He may have hidden the book in Villa Bethany because by that time he had become aware of his own poor health. Or was it because he needed direct protection from some danger? At the time when Buthion and I discussed the book and postulated its purpose, no complete translation had yet been made. Now that I have read its contents, it seems to me that it may have been prepared with more important intentions, which I shall expand upon later on.

There is one more piece to this spirit puzzle: A well-known healer and sensitive from Germany visited me in Rennes for a period in June 1993. Along with spending much time walking alone on the hilltop, he spent time in the church, the old church graveyard, and the garden beside the calvary memorial. During this time and to his great astonishment, he perceived in the garden the presence of what he described as "the powerful evil force of a djinn, or demon, of great age and of ancient Egyptian origin." He eventually came to the conclusion that this was Asmodeus, the demon protector of ancient treasure and tombs, whose effigy Saunière had set at the entrance of the church supposedly to protect the secrets of the place.

The German sensitive told me that he had carried out what in Christian terms is called an exorcism, because it was part of his task to free human environments from evil influences and spirits. He said it had required considerable effort to overcome this strong spirit, which had been there, it seemed, for a very long time.

As this chapter's short outline of the Rennes riddles makes clear, the mystery of this place is complex, with many trails leading into it. Those who fall into its labyrinth of clues, allusions, symbologies, and chronological tricks seldom find their way out again. But if not actual treasure—which needs no explanation—what exactly is it they all hope to find?

3

RENNES-LE-CHÂTEAU:
WHAT COULD BE
DISCOVERED?

There have always been and there will always be riddles and mysteries, codes and forgeries, treasure hunters and mystics. At the height of the madness in Rennes in the 1970s, people were using explosives to blow holes all over the hill and the surroundings. They climbed into the sewers, dug into burial areas, and smashed through stone walls. Some of the tales still related by witnesses in the village are truly exhilarating, like that of a French resident (and notorious treasure hunter) who emerged from under a grave slab in the cemetery just as a grieving widow was laying some flowers on it. She ran screaming down the street and he was all but driven from the village at gunpoint. This story is still told with much mirth over glasses of the local Corbière red.

Recently, there was even an attempt to plan a proper archaeological dig under the church of Mary Magdalene. In April 2001, an American-Italian team carried out extensive probes with Ground Penetrating Radar (GPR) equipment. A year later, with the mayor's consent, they filed a request with the regional director of Cultural Affairs to dig in the church. All digging in Rennes-le-Château was forbidden by a municipal decree of 1965, so the mayor must suspend this ruling in order for a dig to take place. Yet though the current mayor lifted the ban for the request presented by the American-Italian team, in April 2003 its formal request was rejected. Confidential sources in Montpellier claim that the Inter-regional Committee for Archaeology prompted the rejection because of "the absence of a proper scientific project, a strategy for digging the site, and a competent team."

The team's application was signed by well-known maverick scholar Robert Eisenman of the University of California at Long Beach, whose books on the Dead Sea Scrolls and on James, the brother of Jesus, have made him a controversial figure in biblical studies. Yet why was a biblical scholar and historian of the first century requesting permission to dig up a medieval church in the French Pyrenees? What did this expert on the Essene community at Qumran think he might find in the crypt under Abbé Saunière's church?

In this chapter, we shall learn what could be found in Rennes, from both the archaeological and the esoteric points of view. There are many fascinating possibilities but, as we shall see, they all boil down to the underlying hope of a single, unique find. First, however, let's survey the as yet uninvestigated features in and around the village—that is, apart from the church of Mary Magdalene, about which rivers of ink have already been poured.

THE CHÂTEAU AT RENNES

This fine building of considerable age in the center of Rennes-le-Château is in poor condition. On the northern side, parts of the walls, floors, and rooms have suffered substantial damage, but on the ground floor of the south side there are important rooms still intact. These were probably kitchens: Fire cooking areas with original chimneys, large ancient iron spits, and turning gear for roasting can still be seen. The most splendid structure is the great banquet hall, which also served as a communal living room. Here the superb curved ceiling is still intact and traces of decoration can be seen. Above the hall is a flat floor area for storage and possibly for minstrels. All this is almost certainly Merovingian, dating perhaps to the sixth or seventh century.

In this building there is also a high domed roof over a large circular room, which may have been a meat-storage chamber stacked with ice and snow for food preservation in winter. The banquet and food-storage rooms may be among the oldest in France and indeed the rest of Europe. Interestingly, there are many Templar markings above interior doorways and arches, and iron doorlocks remain in place.

According to traditional belief, there are also secret stairs hidden in the foundation walls of the building and leading to a passage under the village, though this has not been proved so far. The castle underwent reconstruction work in the sixteenth century. Today, because it is partly in ruin and in danger of collapse in some sections, visitors are not allowed in the structure, though I have had the great fortune of visiting there several times before this decree.

ST.-PIERRE (ST. PETER'S CHURCH)

The existence of a second church in Rennes-le-Château in medieval times is well known. First mentioned in AD 798, it was destroyed in 1361 by the Aragon Routiers under Count Trestamare.

There are various theories about this structure, one claiming that the church of St.-Pierre was the main church for a long time, while the church of Mary Magdalene was merely the château's house chapel. Others believe that St.-Pierre became too small for the growing number of inhabitants in Rennes and was abandoned for the bigger church of Mary Magdalene.

St.-Pierre is located close to the still existing Place St.-Pierre and was erected above ancient Celtic cave sanctuaries. Traces of the foundation have been found, covered by various occupation levels of the village. Parts of the church itself became integrated into other buildings, though this is not easy to recognize. Some stones of the church have been reused in other buildings, like the one used upside down and recognizable by its reversed cross. There is hope that the crypt of this church is intact and that it will be possible to obtain official approval to excavate it. It almost certainly would hold tombs of knights and noblemen—and perhaps other clues to Rennes's secrets are waiting there to be discovered.

UNDERGROUND PASSAGES IN THE VILLAGE

According to some scholars, local tradition, and my own research, there are five ancient and deep stone passages under the village to be found in the following places:

1. A passage from the destroyed church of St.-Pierre at the south face of Rennes near the water tower
2. A passage from below the church of Mary Magdalene
3. A passage from the bottom of a secret stairway in the Hautpoul château
4. The so-called wet passage of Visigoth times, below the ancient water-storage area on the east side of Rennes
5. The west-side passage from due west of Villa Bethany's belvedere

These are all dangerous and unstable structures due to the poor quality of the rock adjacent to each passage. Near the château there is also an old water tunnel used to provide water from a source outside the ramparts in case of a siege. In fact, such water reservoirs are found in many ancient fortified places.

Interestingly, French scholar Pierre Simon developed a complex method of deciphering the Coumesourde stone, which led him to draw out a whole system of underground passages through the village. Because of the strong local belief that Saunière found his treasure underground, many residents have, at various times, made holes in their houses in search of such passages. As an example, the hole in the museum office floor, which tourists must circumnavigate to reach the desk and purchase their tickets, was made with explosives. There is another such hole in the garage floor beside the ruined Denarnaud house. The existence of tunnel four, some 322 to 427 feet long, was recently revealed to the mayor of the village, though it filled up with water and had to be pumped out before a party led by the mayor could enter it. In this passage there were clear signs of manual shaping, and stalactites there indicated an age of one thousand to two thousand years.

THE CHURCH GRAVEYARD
AND THE OSSUARY

It is interesting to note that no tombs more than one hundred years old exist in the graveyard today. It is known that Saunière excavated many of the tombs and may well have cleared all of them. In earlier times, to prevent overcrowding of the dead, it was the custom to store bones removed from the graves in an ossuary, which still exists. In times of greater population, Rennes was served by another cemetery, together with a chapel, in the lower town on the hillside.

THE FIELDS

The fields south of Rennes-le-Château stretch from the old ramparts down to the Stream of Colors. My own research, based on aerial photographs, clearly shows outlines of Celtic and Greco-Roman settlements on these fields. It is said that ramparts were erected along the cliffs of the Stream of Colors by the Visigoth king Eric (470–75). Down by the stream, large stone blocks can still be seen, probably parts of the rampart thrown from the cliff by their destroyers.

During my early days at Rennes, I searched the entire area and found strange features, such as an oval outline about 213 feet by 108 feet in a field below the village. This outline can also be seen in an aerial photograph at the Phototeque of the Institut Géographique National. Several theories on the origin of this outline have been put forward, some suggesting that it was an ancient temple or sanctuary that is now under the surface of the earth. One scholar, Monsieur Sipra, believes it to be a mausoleum in Byzantine style. I must also report—though I am aware that this will not seem significant to all of my readers—that sensitive people feel a strong energy radiating from this place. The owner of the land, Mrs. Elizabeth van Buren, calls it the "sacred heart" and has built a little well and rose garden there.

In the same field I also discovered the foundations of three stone and mud buildings probably dating from Visigoth times, which I called the palace due to its prime location in what I believe to be the Visigoth-era town. I took my own aerial photographs of the area, which confirmed this. Given that the surface of the field has been plowed continually for perhaps one thousand years since the town stood here, I could not understand how it was possible for me to trace all this. Much later, I used surface methods to trace roadways and the outlines of houses in the ancient village. It seems that when land is plowed and becomes partially dry after a rain, these can be seen, as my photographs attest.

A field that recently came into my possession, situated just below the village on the south side, includes part of the ancient lower village with ramparts, houses, a well, a chapel, and a cemetery. After clearing the land of thorns, shrubs, and small trees, I could trace the outlines of ancient stone buildings, with some foundation walls still standing. French archaeologists have suggested that these buildings were originally Celtic stone huts used and rebuilt throughout the Middle Ages, until their final destruction in 1361. Many corpses, people slaughtered by their attackers, are believed to lie under these ruins. A well located here may reveal some interesting clues to the history of that period. In this field there is also a ruined tower that evidently had been used as a mill but may have been a defensive watchtower in earlier times. I would dearly love to clear and restore this ancient settlement, a vital part of the history of Rennes-le-Château.

THE POSSIBLE TREASURES

The first hypothesis regarding treasure in the area concerns pre-Christian loot. Celtic tribes considered this a sacred area, and it is also known that Celts and Romans excavated for gold on a large scale here. According to tradition, the two hills of Rhedae, the Rennes hilltop and the twin hill south of the village, were each crowned with a temple or sanctuary to Celtic deities. When the Romans arrived, they built a temple to Vesta, goddess of hearth and fire, over the ancient sanctuary on the Rennes hilltop —in fact, on the very site where the church of Mary Magdalene now stands.

Another tradition has it that there was a Roman temple to Isis on this hilltop and another to Osiris on the hill opposite. I have traced a Roman foundation near the church at Rennes and aerial photographs show clear outlines of rectangular buildings on the flat top of Rhedae's twin hill, now called Casteillas. I have also found two ancient lookout posts, but these are probably from Merovingian times. Coins dating from 100 BC to AD 200 have been found in the fields below Rennes, proving the presence of Greco-Roman communities.

A former resident once showed me his research concerning a strange story: A huge treasure—looted by the Romans from a hoard held by the Celts at Toulouse and being transported under strong Roman military protection—passed near Rennes en route for Rome via Perpignan. The escort was attacked and done in, however, and the stolen treasure disappeared. The source of this Celtic wealth is not certain, but the raid is recorded in Roman accounts.

THE VISIGOTH TREASURE OF ROME AND JERUSALEM

When Titus sacked the Temple of Jerusalem in AD 70, it is recorded that he took the Temple treasure back with him to Rome. In the Forum area in Rome is Titus's victory arch commemorating this attack. On the inner left face of the arch, soldiers are shown carrying the treasure of the Temple, including the seven-armed candleholder, or menorah, and other important pieces. Procopius records that when Alaric had Rome at his mercy in AD 410, he took its treasures—including that of the Temple of Jerusalem—but spared the churches. It should be noted, however, that the Ark of the Covenant ceases to be mentioned in the Hebrew scriptures after the eighth century BC and is not depicted on Titus's arch, so it is unlikely to have been brought to Rome.

Alaric's successor constructed hundreds of leather-covered six- and eight-wheel wagons as fighting cover for his army in order to transfer the huge amount of gold and treasure. He later ringed the defense wall on the south side of Rennes with large wagons, surrounding his city, and the treasure was hidden in Rennes and also dispersed between

Toledo and Carcassonne. Much later, after the Visigoths withdrew from Toledo, the treasure was hidden in natural caves and Roman gold passages that were long abandoned but known to Alaric and impossible to discover. Procopius, Frédégaire, Makkari, Roderic of Toulouse, and Edward Gibbon all wrote about the treasures of the Visigoths. Among other famous objects they possessed were the Missorium, a one-hundred-pound gold plate with inlaid precious stones, and the Emerald Table—a single piece of emerald lined with three rows of pearls and held up by sixty strands of solid gold inlaid with precious stones—which probably originated in the Temple of Jerusalem and was taken from Rome in 410. The Arabs later took the Emerald Table from Toledo and probably sent it to the Middle East.

The Visigoths' amazing wealth first became known at the wedding of King Athaulphus and Princess Gallia Placida (daughter of the emperor Theodosius), who was given one hundred basins filled with pieces of gold and precious stones. After the Visigoth defeat at Vouillé and Clovis's attack on Toulouse, the widow of Alaric II fled to Septimania with the royal treasure and nothing more was ever heard of it. It is quite likely, of course, that Visigoth and Merovingian kings remain buried in the hilltop of Rennes-le-Château, which should in itself be considered a treasure of inestimable value.

THE TREASURE OF THE TEMPLARS AND CATHARS

It is my estimation that both Templars and Cathars made Rennes a stronghold, a depository of documents and treasure, and a school for their religious thinking. Unsupported traditions claim that special Templar protection was provided to nearby Bezu. The Cathars possessed substantial treasure, which was never found by those who destroyed them. Certainly they spent great sums on weapons, the hire of mercenaries, and fortifications over the forty years of the wars against them. Documents vital to these remarkable people would never have been allowed to fall into the hands of their attackers, and might have been buried at Rennes.

Could the Cathars have possessed some Christian secret that caused the frenzied Catholic desire to exterminate them? Rennes-le-Château may well contain several Christian secrets, one of which is likely Cathar documents and sacred ritual objects.

Some scholars have even postulated that the two great Christian secrets concealed in Rennes-le-Château and protected by Templars and Cathars were no less than the Ark of the Covenant and the Holy Grail, both originally brought here from Rome. These legendary objects are known to have inspired much writing of knightly stories and romances, all the way to Richard Wagner, whose *Parsifal* was inspired by the Grail story. In the 1930s, SS Lieutenant Otto Rahn carried out research in the region for the Nazis, probably on behalf of Heinrich Himmler, who was obsessed, no less than his Fuhrer, with the Ark of the Covenant, the Grail, and objects of power of any kind. During World War II, in 1945, the SS was known to have undertaken actual excavations in the area. Rahn later died in a mountain expedition, but rumors are still rife that the Nazis eliminated him.

As with the Cathar treasure, no Templar treasure has ever been found. The Templar grand master Bertrand de Blanchefort is said to have ordered near Rennes secret excavations carried out by a group of German-speaking miners brought in for special building work belowground. Centuries later, excavations by treasure hunters in the area proved beyond doubt that this earlier Templar work had indeed been undertaken.

THE RANSOM PAID BY BLANCHE DE CASTILE

Blanche, wife of Louis VIII and mother of Louis IX—later to be made St. Louis—was queen of France until her son came of age in 1226. In 1248 she became regent again, during Louis's absence on the ill-fated Seventh Crusade, a project she had strongly opposed. Louis was defeated and captured with his retinue at Mansoura, in the Nile Delta, in March 1250. In the midst of that disaster, Blanche cool-headedly and efficiently drained the land of money to raise the ransom the sultan had put on her son's head. The Arab historian Al-Makrisi writes:

The king paid four hundred thousand pieces of gold for his own ransom as well as that of the queen, his brother, and the other lords that accompanied him. All the Franks that had been made prisoner obtained their liberty: They amounted to twelve thousand one hundred men and ten women. The king, with all the French, crossed to the western branch of the Nile and embarked on a Saturday for Acre.

Louis stayed in Syria for another four years, not returning to France even upon Blanche's death in 1252 and thus never thanking his mother for all that she'd done to obtain his freedom. (This was less than saintly behavior on Louis's part.)

Some historians claim that the Templars were involved in the ransom episode and that Blanche was forced to rob her subjects of the necessary gold only after the Crown's own riches, entrusted to the Temple, had inexplicably disappeared. Sixty years later, Louis's grandson Philip the Fair literally destroyed the Order of the Temple to lay his hands on its fabulous wealth, which he sorely needed to fix the Crown's near bankrupt finances. From his point of view, I suppose, he was only taking back what those arrogant fighter- and banker-monks had stolen from his family. If that was true, the eighteenth-century stories of shepherd boys in this area finding "Louis d'or"—gold coins from the thirteenth and fourteenth centuries—could well be tied to the vanished ransom that Blanche had sent to Egypt.

Could Saunière also have found part of the Templar loot? He certainly found wealth from some source, but it may not have been treasure as such. More likely it was a secret of vital importance. We might conclude that the Hapsburgs selected Saunière while he was still in seminary to carry out in Rennes-le-Château searches of great importance to them. It seems there was a defect in the known lineage of the Hapsburgs, and the priest was required to examine and excavate all tombs in the cemetery in Rennes. Upon doing this, he found the untouched tomb of the last marchioness of Blanchefort, and the documents he discovered in the grave proved invaluable to the Hapsburg family, who periodically provided the large sums of money that would become known as the Rennes treasure.

Even if the only unexplained part of the story, the source of a local parish priest's sudden wealth, turned out to be no mystery at all—either because he was only selling Masses to Parisian widows at inflated prices or because the Hapsburgs were happy to bankroll him, or in fact for any other reason obeying the rule of Occam's razor (the principle that forbids the adoption of complex explanations when simple ones are available)—this would mean only that there is no *material* treasure to be found. It would not explain, however, the mystique and legends that have become associated with the village over the centuries, long before Saunière and his exploits brought the treasure hunters and the tourists.

If debunking the Saunière mystery serves to demotivate and drive away all those people who are looking for Visigoth, Judaean, Roman, Cathar, or Templar *gold,* then I'll be the first to support it, for there is plenty of mystery in Rennes even without Abbé Saunière. What could be found here could make all of humanity richer, though not in gold.

4

THE DEBUNKING OF WHICH MYSTERY?

In recent years, many works have been published challenging the thesis put forward in *Holy Blood, Holy Grail* that the Grail actually refers to a bloodline descended from Jesus. As we have seen, that best seller suggested that Jesus and Mary Magdalene had children and that their descendants gave rise to the Merovingian dynasty, which ruled France from the fifth century to the eighth. The new studies claim that well-intentioned readers have been deceived by a hoax, mistaking it for the revelation of a suppressed history. According to researchers such as Paul Smith, Robert Richardson, and others, the false story originated in fraudulent documents created by an extreme right-wing French sect known as the Priory of Sion, which claims to have kept its ancient esoteric lineage and its authentic history carefully hidden. But its background reveals much murkier political motivations. Let's try to see what these may be.

In the years of Saunière's restoration of his little church, Paris was in the grip of a culture war. The great esoteric and occultist revival and the political struggle between nostalgic "royalists" and Masonic-influenced republican lobbies made it difficult to be sure that anyone was what he or she seemed to be. In this climate, the French far right formed its own seemingly esoteric groups, which were actually front organizations pretending to have Masonic and esoteric affiliations in order to draw support away from the Masons. This trend continued through the years of World War I, and in the fiercely anti-Semitic 1920s and 1930s, new groups (such as the Alpha Galates, founded in 1934) dabbled in esoteric traditions, using the language of "chivalry" and "honor" and speaking of "purifying" and "renewing" France. A central character in these ambiguous new orders was the precocious Pierre Plantard, who by the mid-1950s had begun to promote himself in Catholic circles as the Merovingian pretender to the throne of France.

THE PRIORY OF SION

In 1956, Pierre Plantard and others created a group called the Priory of Sion. It had statutes remarkably similar to those of the Alpha Galates and published a magazine called *Circuit*. Disinformation about what would eventually become the Rennes-le-Château affair also began to appear, starting in the newspaper *La Dépêche du Midi* in early 1956. Claiming to be an inside source, the Priory alleged that an underground chapel of St. Anne in Gisors, Normandy, contained the lost treasure of the Knights Templar. No treasure materialized; however, the story gave the Priory the chance to successfully promote in books and articles its false history of France, complete with descendants of Jesus and esoteric orders.

Here is a synthesis of the most recent research on the Priory of Sion.

1. The real Priory of Sion was an authentic Catholic monastic order. Sion, or Zion, is the ancient name for Jerusalem, where the order was based at the monastery of Our Lady of Mount Zion. In 1617 it was absorbed into the Jesuit order and ceased to exist. It was never a cabal of esoteric and political interests, never exercised any influence over the Templars or any other order, and does not exist today. It has been appropriated, like many other authentic esoteric traditions and orders, to create a false history.

2. Plantard alleged his "real" last name was St. Clair, though no shred of proof supports this claim. The Sinclairs (originally St. Clair), hereditary heads of Scottish Rite Freemasonry, were related

by marriage to Templar founder Hugues de Payen. In alleging a connection with the St. Clairs, the Priory sought to imply that it had an ancient and leading role in Freemasonry. Appropriating honored names associated with the esoteric tradition was a tactic often used by prewar, anti-Masonic French rightists. The Priory constructed its fiction of the bloodline of Jesus by placing fabricated histories in libraries and by falsely associating itself with ancient esoteric groups. It mostly plagiarized the Order of the Rose Cross of the Temple and the Grail, founded by Joséphin Péladan in 1891. These sources, twisted and distorted, were used to create the fiction that a special bloodline, supported by an age-old esoteric society, lay behind most key political events and mysteries of French history and behind the Holy Grail itself.

3. There are many associations between the prewar activities of Plantard and his partners and the postwar Priory of Sion. It is likely that Alpha Galates continued on, implementing a plan carried out under the guise of the Priory of Sion. Their first objective was to position themselves in the mind of an unknowing public as the supreme Western esoteric organization. They then planned to promote their hybrid agenda of right-wing politics and turn-of-the-century esoteric teachings. The Priory, say researchers, does not represent the teachings of any esoteric order. It is materialistic and obsessed with attaining power, and it fabricated documents with no regard for ethical considerations. Its program is to manipulate people through lies in order to promote itself.

So where does all this leave the intellectually honest truth seeker? Something still doesn't add up. If there is no need of any ancient treasures to explain Saunière's sudden wealth and the Priory of Sion is a fraud, then why does talk of a secret that could shake the foundations of Christianity emerge so often—in fact, in every century of this alleged conspiracy so many have investigated? Why, for example, did the brother of Nicolas Fouquet, finance minister to Louis XIV, write to him from Rome in 1656: "Monsieur Poussin could provide you with advantages that *kings* would have great pains to get from him and that, after him, perhaps no one in the world could recover in the centuries to come. These are things so hard to discover that no one, no matter who, upon this earth today could even dream of doing so."

I find it difficult to debunk the old belief that there is a secret hidden in these hills that has excited, intrigued, and frightened (sometimes, indeed, horrified) all those who have discovered it, protected it, or transmitted it. Perhaps the most explicit attempt to expose the nature of this secret was a book by Paul Schellenberger and Richard Andrews, published in 1996: *The Tomb of God*. The authors admitted that some of their material derived from *Holy Blood, Holy Grail* and *The Messianic Legacy*, the two works by Lincoln, Baigent, and Leigh. The reaction to their suggestion that Jesus' mortal remains were buried somewhere in the Rennes area was virulent, to say the least.

Later in 1996, the BBC produced a *Time Watch* program called "The History of a Mystery." Schellenberger and Andrews were invited to explain their theories and present their supporting evidence. The program was a major step in the debunking process, for it made available important information:

- Sacred geometries, triangulations, and pentacle projections from paintings such as Poussin's *The Shepherds of Arcadia* are entirely without foundation.
- It is doubtful that Saunière ever went to Paris or brought back the three copies of the paintings *The Shepherds of Arcadia*, *The Temptation of St. Anthony*, and the portrait of Pope Celestin V. *Time Watch* established that there is no record in the Louvre of any purchases of copies of those paintings at that time.
- Key documents described in Lincoln's writings (some for BBC programs) and in *The Tomb of God* are now known to be forgeries created by the marquis de Chérisey, a brilliant, eccentric actor and friend of Plantard. In particular, the two Merovingian pillar parchments were shown to be false and the geographical interpretation of the code by the authors was shown to be incorrect.

- Monsieur Plantard's claim that his lineage derived from the Merovingian kings, as well as his claim of wartime activities in the French Resistance, was shown to be false.

At the end of 1996, Schellenberger and Andrews produced a rebuttal document to counter the BBC comments, but the narrating voices of television documentaries have an uncanny way of creating, in the eyes of their audience, a sort of scientific legitimacy for the views they support. The idea of Jesus' tomb being somewhere in southern France was declared cranky, and that's how it stayed.

But the fact is that traditions about Mary Magdalene coming to France after the Crucifixion are far too ancient and widespread in all of Provence and the Languedoc to be the result of a nineteenth- or twentieth-century hoax. Further, it is historically attested that at the time of the Roman persecution in Palestine—about AD 50 to 70—Judeo-Christian refugees came to the south of France. The legend of two women named Mary, of the entourage of Jesus, with a "black" girl named Sarah, beaching their boat at Les-Saintes-Maries-de-la-Mer on the shores of the Camargue indicates that the ground must have been prepared by Jewish inhabitants so that their kinsmen fleeing Roman persecution could find refuge in Gallia in spite of Roman rule there.

Here I must digress briefly to address the role of gnosticism in the birth of the Jewish movement we now call Christianity. Gnosticism is the teaching based on *gnosis,* the "knowledge" of transcendence arrived at by way of interior, intuitive means. Gnosticism rests on personal religious experience, which does not lend itself to the language of theology or of philosophy, but instead expresses itself through the medium of myth. Indeed, we find that most gnostic scriptures take the form of myths. The gnostic cosmogony is nearly always dualistic in that it conceives of a supreme, invisible deity and a lesser demiurge, creator of matter and false God. The demiurge keeps the divine sparks that are human souls imprisoned in their bodies and in the material world, and gnosis is the only key that can free them and allow them to return to the true spirit of which they are a part.

As I mentioned in the introduction, I believe that Jesus was a gnostic teacher and not a divine being, and that the words attributed to him in the gnostic gospels recovered at Nag Hammadi are probably as close as we can get—at least at the present time—to his true teachings. Contrary to what was believed until the middle of the twentieth century, gnosticism was not a Christian heresy. It existed as a philosophical school well before Jesus' time in both Hellenistic and Jewish circles and was probably espoused by the Essenes of Qumran, among others. Instead of viewing Christian gnostics as a kind of dualistic opposition to orthodox Christianity—which is just what the Fathers of the Church would like us to do—we might view them as the true, original Christians.

Not surprisingly, the gnostic tradition is the oldest, most tenacious opposition to Catholicism (at least in the West—excluding the "outside" opposition from Islam). The fury of the Church Fathers against the promoters of a Christianity that had no need for bishops requires no explanation. By most accounts, Catholic bishops had succeeded in uprooting the heresy by the late fourth century, the same epoch in which the Nag Hammadi scrolls were buried for safety (surely not a coincidence). Pauline Christianity, the official religion of the Roman Empire from the days of Constantine early in the same century, had finally won that war.

Among the more unpleasant consequences of the Council of Nicaea (AD 325), which had excommunicated all Christians who didn't subscribe to the Pauline view of Christ, was the ferocious persecution of heretics all around the eastern Mediterranean—and most harshly in Alexandria—in the last two decades of that century. Several gnostic churches and many traditions that didn't believe in the divinity of Jesus—Nazarenes (Nazoreans), Nestorians, Ebionites, Elchasites, Johannites, Arians, Mandeans—somehow survived in the folds of a mainly Greek Orthodox and Eastern Christianity, but in the West they vanished almost completely except in a few lands far from Rome's influence, such as Portugal, Ireland, and Scotland.

These peripheral areas saw the spread of a peculiar form of Christianity that historians call Celtic Christianity, which, like early Judeo-Christianity, refused the divinity of Christ, the Virgin Birth, and the

Trinity and had much in common with the Arianism embraced by most "barbarians" on the Continent. In fact, what most distinguishes Celtic Christianity from Arianism are its monastic elements and its monophysitism,* both traits that are clearly of Egyptian origin. Yet even before we consider these characteristics, geographical and chronological considerations make it very likely that these non-Pauline Christians on the edges of the Roman Empire came from the sea and were probably the escaping remnants of the thriving gnostic Judeo-Christian communities that had their center in Alexandria from the earliest days of St. Mark's preaching in Egypt.

We know that gnostic, dualistic, and anti-trinitarian views resurfaced with unexpected vigor in twelfth-century Europe, especially in the deep south of France. It is hard not to wonder where these ideas had been hiding for seven centuries. The current explanation of Cathar dualism is that it had come from the East in the eleventh century, moving westward from the Paulicians of Cappadocia to the Bogomils of Bulgaria and from there to Lombardy and Provence. As I've stated earlier, in my opinion this scenario is nowhere near as plausible as the suggestion that they instead adopted in from an existing local tradition, a cultural continuity tied to the presence in Gaul of numerous Jewish communities dating from before the destruction of Jerusalem in AD 70. During these fateful early decades of the millennium, while Paul was preaching all over the Mediterranean and causing a near schism with the Church of Jerusalem led by James, the brother of Jesus, these diaspora centers would have received a steady influx of refugees, both Jewish and Judeo-Christian.

In the coming chapters, we shall see that some gnostic Jews and Gentiles who believed that Jesus was the Christ (to them the Anointed or the Messiah meant the "bringer of gnosis," not the Son of God) came here because they had somehow heard the rumor that their teacher and Messiah had survived the cross—and had moved to these southern mountains.

Monophysitism (from the Greek *monos,* meaning "one," and *physis,* meaning "nature") is the theological position that Christ has only one nature, as opposed to the position that Christ has two natures, one divine and one human. The Syrian and Coptic Orthodox Churches are Monophysite to this day.

5

THE LIFE OF JESUS: WHAT WE KNOW AND WHAT WE DON'T KNOW

C an we today, after two thousand years, come to know anything certain about Jesus' life?

Until very recently, all we knew of Jesus was the written testimony of the gospels and some mention in the writings of the Jewish and Roman historian Josephus. Paul's writings make no reference to where and when Jesus was born and lived or to his parentage, nor do they mention any miracles or parables or the trial by Pilate. Paul never met Jesus, or at least the Bible does not tell us that he did. The apostle's whole faith was rooted in his vision of Jesus after resurrection.

But in the mid-twentieth century, the Dead Sea Scrolls and the Nag Hammadi codices were discovered, and these introduced completely new ideas of what the background and life of Jesus must have been. European and American, Christian and Jewish scholars continue to study these fascinating sources, and the work of some of them has greatly influenced my personal thinking.

Throughout my life I have also met many mystics, some very gifted as healers and sensitives, and a few of them have claimed to have spiritual sources for their knowledge of the life of Christ. I started out as a skeptic, but eventually came to believe that some of these claims may well be true. Obviously, no hard evidence can be found for these ideas, and all need to decide for themselves whether they can accept these sources. Here I shall present parts of this account of the life of Jesus and will attempt to back them up with circumstantial evidence that may lead to conclusions similar to those of these psychics, whether retrieved from a collective unconscious, memories of previous lives, or some other obscure source. You may be the judge of which version, or which Jesus, is more credible.

But first, let us consider the evidence for the so-called historical Jesus.

THE HISTORY OF JESUS

The remarkable history written by Flavius Josephus provides the most valuable evidence for Jesus' historical existence. Josephus was born in AD 37, the son of a Jewish priest. He was educated as a Pharisee and helped defend Galilee against the Romans during the Jewish revolt that started in AD 66. He was captured but took the step of defecting to the Romans, which was much resented by the Jews, but he later endeavored to persuade his Jewish friends that resistance against such mighty forces was useless. In AD 70 he acted as Titus's interpreter during the siege of Jerusalem, afterward moving to Rome, where he lived in comfort.

From about AD 77 on, he wrote two important works: *The Antiquities of the Jews* and *The Jewish War,* our main and most reliable sources for the history of the Jews in the first century. In them, for example, he quotes details of the siege and fall of Masada that archaeology has since shown to be accurate. Yet the reference he makes to Jesus in *The Antiquities* is disputed.

Around this time lived Jesus, a wise man, if one might call him a man, for he accomplished surprising feats and was a teacher to such people as are eager for novelties. He won over many Jews and many Greeks. He was the Messiah. When Pilate, upon an indictment brought by the principal men among us, condemned him to the cross, those who loved him from the very first did not cease to be attached to him. On the third day he appeared to them restored to life, as the holy prophets had foretold, and myriad other marvels are told concerning him. The brotherhood of the Christians, so called after him, has to this day still not disappeared.

It seems quite certain that this is a later Christian interpolation. We might well ask if the original text mentioned Jesus at all. Fortunately, as Ian Wilson points out, Josephus's *Antiquities* provides an invaluable reference to the unjust execution in AD 62 of James the Righteous, the brother of Christ. This reference must have been present in Josephus's original works, because the Christian author Origen, writing in the early third century, expresses great surprise that Josephus, though disputing that Jesus was the Messiah, should have written with such respect of his brother. Origen thus provides us with proof that Josephus referred to Jesus before any Christian copyist could have had a chance of altering his text.

In the second century, the Roman historian Tacitus referred in his *Annals* to

> . . . a class of men, loathed for their vices, whom the crowd styled Christians. Christus, the founder of that name, had undergone the death penalty in the reign of Tiberius, by sentence of the procurator Pontius Pilate, and the pernicious superstition was checked for a moment, only to break out once more not merely in Judaea, home of the disease, but in the capital itself.

Suetonius says only that during Claudius's reign (AD 41–54) some Roman Jews rebelled in the name of Christ. Pliny the Younger wrote in about AD 112 that the Christians were harmless and sang hymns to their Messiah at daybreak. It must be said that he also detected in them "depraved and excessive superstition."

Jewish references to Jesus are minimal but do at least confirm his existence. It would be interesting to delve into the medieval libelous tract

Toledoth Jeshu, which was the cause of much denunciation and persecution of the Talmud by Dominican friars, but it would lead us too far
astray. In any case, Jewish research continues to look for mentions of
Jesus in their oldest manuscripts.

Finally, the writings of the tenth-century Arab-Christian Agapius
include this passage: "His disciples reported that he had appeared to
them three days after his crucifixion and that he was alive, therefore he
was perhaps the Messiah, whose wonders the prophets had recounted."
These words more or less correspond to the writings of Josephus.

The exact day, month, and year of Jesus' birth are unknown and
perhaps unknowable (and it certainly isn't December 25). In the sixth
century, the monk Dionysius Exiguus fixed his date of birth at AD 1,
but we now know that this cannot be right. In addition, while Mark and
John give no account of his birth, Matthew and Luke substantially contradict each other. Matthew also illogically traces Jesus' ancestry back
to the royal line of David through his earthly father, Joseph, which is
embarrassingly difficult to reconcile with the Virgin Birth.

The star of Bethlehem at his birth (Matthew 2:2–11) may have been
a conjunction between Saturn and Jupiter that occurred in the constel-
lation of Pisces in 7 BC (as calculated by Kepler, who saw the same conjunction in 1603). It could also have been Halley's comet, flying past in
12 BC. A third candidate is a nova visible for more than seventy days in
5 BC and recorded by astronomers of the Chinese Han dynasty. In the
end, the consensus of scholars is that the most likely date of Jesus' birth
is 5 BC, due mainly to the fact of Herod's death in 4 BC.

Of course, no historical record has yet been found to confirm the
slaughter of children ordered by Herod, but the census in Judaea did
take place under Quirinius's governorship of Syria: "At this time, Caesar
Augustus issued a decree for a census to be taken of the whole world . . .
and everyone went to his home town to be registered" (Luke 2:1–3). It
was the first of its kind and is recorded by Flavius Josephus as occurring in
the year AD 6. It couldn't, of course, have happened before AD 6, because
this was the first year of direct Roman rule over Judaea. Again, the most
likely date of Jesus' birth would therefore seem to be either 5 or 6 BC.

As for his childhood, few people are aware that no archaeological evidence has so far been found of the existence of Nazareth at the time of Jesus. The strata exposed in the digs there show the location was inhabited before and after but not during the first century. In fact the growth of the Byzantine town corresponds nicely with the start of pilgrimages to the place the gospels had declared to be Jesus' hometown, as if Nazareth had been called into existence by the cult of Jesus itself. What's more, Josephus, who was in command of Galilee during the Jewish revolt, lists in his writings all the region's towns and villages but makes no reference to Nazareth, which doesn't appear in Jewish literature until the seventh century. If there was no Nazareth, then where did the real Jesus grow up? I suggest that he spent his childhood and youth in Egypt, and shall presently set out my reasons for this hunch.

The Bible is strangely silent concerning Jesus' life between the ages of twelve and thirty. The last incident of his childhood is mentioned Luke 2, when he goes missing and is found sitting in the midst of the teachers at the Temple. The last mention of the boy Jesus is in Luke 2:52, which simply states: "And Jesus increased in wisdom and stature, and in favor with God and men." After this there is a gap of eighteen years in his life—and the Christian scriptures are silent about the activities and whereabouts of the growing Jesus during this time.

Most people think he lived in Nazareth, working as a carpenter until he embarked on his mission at the age of thirty. Yet a number of clues indicate otherwise—that he was in fact outside the confines of Judaea during those years. For example, Luke 4:16–22 says: "So he came to Nazareth, where he had been brought up. And as was his custom, he went into the synagogue on the Sabbath, and stood up to read . . . And the eyes of all who were in the synagogue were fixed on him . . . So all bore witness to him, and marveled at the gracious words which proceeded out of his mouth. And they said, 'Is this not Joseph's son?' "

Two things stand out here: First, the phrase "where he had been brought up" seems to imply that while Jesus had spent his childhood in Nazareth, he had not continued to live there, or, at the very least, that he had not lived there for some time. This impression is reinforced by the question his hearers ask in the synagogue: "Is this not Joseph's son?"—almost as if they are in doubt regarding his identity.

The same incident in Matthew 13 includes more questions of the synagogue worshippers: "Is this not the carpenter's son? Is not his mother called Mary? And his brothers James, Joses, Simon, and Judas? And his sisters, are they not all with us? Where then did this man get all these things?" Clearly, they were not familiar with Jesus. In fact, he was such a stranger to them that they referred to him by not by name, but instead by his relationship to the members of his family, whom they knew. "Where then did this man get all these things?" surely implies that Jesus did not receive his knowledge in Nazareth.

There is another passage in the gospels (Matthew 17:24) that implies Jesus' absence from the region: "After they arrived in Capernaum, the men collecting the two drachmas [tax] approached Peter and said: 'Does your teacher not pay the two drachmas?' He said: 'Yes.' " A number of translations call the two drachmas "Temple tax"; however, the Temple tax was paid with a Jewish half shekel—a coin especially minted for that purpose. In the above passage, Jesus is being asked about his liability to pay the two drachmas of the "strangers' tax," a Roman poll tax levied against foreign visitors to Capernaum, usually merchants and traders conducting business there. Evidently the tax collector considered Jesus a stranger or a foreign visitor. This, again, would make sense only if Jesus had been absent from Palestine for a considerable time.

The same conclusion could be drawn from John the Baptist's reaction to Jesus. When Jesus appears upon the banks of the Jordan, John seems scarcely able to recognize him, even though they were first cousins and must have known each other in their childhood. Finally, John recognizes who the stranger is and exclaims: "Behold, the Lamb of God!" If Jesus had been living in Nazareth all those years, surely John would have had no doubts as to his identity. Further indication of John's lack of familiarity occurs later when he sends two disciples to ask Jesus: "Are you he who should come or look we for another?" Clearly the two had not met for years, or John would not be so lacking in knowledge of the one he was proclaiming.

There is more. In the Gospel of John we read:

Philip found Nathanael and said to him, "We have found him of whom Moses in the Law and also the prophets wrote—Jesus of Nazareth, the son of Joseph." And Nathanael said to him, "Can anything good come out of Nazareth?" Philip said "Come and see." Jesus saw Nathanael coming toward him, and said of him, "Behold, an Israelite indeed in whom is no guile!" Nathanael said to him, "How do you know me?" Jesus answered him, "Before Philip called you, when you were under the fig tree, I saw you."

Nathanael lived in Cana of Galilee, about five miles from Nazareth. Again, if Jesus had been living in Nazareth all those years, it is likely that Nathanael would have known him. The implication can be only that Jesus had not been in Palestine for a long time.

Concerning the next stage of his life as told in the gospels, Luke dates Jesus' baptism by John in the fifteenth year of Tiberius's reign, which is calculable to AD 29. The synoptic gospels suggest that Jesus' public ministry lasted for one year after the baptism, placing the Crucifixion in AD 30. But John says that Jesus' ministry occupied three years after his baptism, thus placing the Crucifixion in AD 32.

All four canonical gospels and the Roman historian Tacitus say that the Crucifixion took place during the governorship of Pontius Pilate—that is, between AD 27 and 36. The consensus is that the likeliest date for the Crucifixion is between AD 30 and 33. Hugh Schonfield, though, about whom I shall have more to say later, places it in AD 36. If the real date of Jesus' birth is 6 BC, that would mean that he underwent the Passion at forty two years of age—not a young man any more, especially in those times.

THE FAMILY OF JESUS: SOURCES AND INDICATIONS

The sources that follow seem to make clear that Jesus had brothers and sisters. Many early writers, such as Hegesippus and Tertullian, confirm this, yet some Christian teaching declared these to be cousins and not literally brothers (or else that they were children of Joseph by an earlier marriage). The gospels claim that Jesus was the eldest son of Joseph and Mary and that Joseph, his earthly father, was of David's royal line.

> Matthew 1:16, And Jacob begat Joseph the husband of Mary, of whom was born Jesus, who is called Christ.
>
> Luke 2:4, And Joseph also went up from Galilee, out of the city of Nazareth, into Judaea, unto the city of David, which is called Bethlehem; because he was of the house and lineage of David.
>
> Luke 4:22, And all bore him witness, and wondered at the gracious words which proceeded out of his mouth. And they said, "Is not this Joseph's son?"

Jesus was followed by a brother called James (the Younger), who later, as James the Righteous, became head of the Church of Jerusalem, and three more brothers (Galatians 1:19, "But others of the apostles saw I none, save James, the Lord's brother"). In his work *James, the Brother of Jesus,* Robert Eisenman writes that James was regarded as the successor of Jesus and that he was deeply involved in the revolt of the Jews against the Romans. It also seems probable that James was the companion of Cleophas on the road to Emmaus (Luke 24:13–32).

The earliest Christian schism (though it's actually premature to refer to them as Christians at this early stage) was between the followers of James the Righteous, who believed that the teachings of Jesus should be confined to Jews, and Pauline Christians, who were convinced that Jesus' teaching should be available to all.

There is an astonishing parallel, says Eisenman, between James the Righteous and the Dead Sea Scrolls' figure of the Teacher of Righteousness, who could be seen as the adversary of Paul and his ideas of a divine Christ and of a worldwide—and not necessarily Jewish—Christianity. Eisenman has in fact convinced himself that James and the Teacher of Righteousness were one and the same person.

Mark and Matthew mention sisters (one or two) and brothers—
James, Joses, Judas, and Simon:

> Mark 6:3, Is not this the carpenter, the son of Mary, the brother of
> James, and Joses, and of Juda, and Simon? And are not his sis-
> ters here with us? And they were offended at him.
> Matthew 13:55, Is not this the carpenter's son? Is not his mother
> called Mary? And his brethren, James, and Joses, and Simon,
> and Judas? And his sisters, are they not all with us?
> Mark 15:40, There were also women looking on afar off, among
> whom was Mary Magdalene, and Mary the mother of James the
> less, and of Joses, and Salome.

Other relatives such as Cleophas, brother of Joseph, are possible but
not proved. Simeon, son of Cleophas, became a martyr in AD 106–7.
He was the head of the Jerusalem church after Christ's brother James the
Righteous. According to Eisenman, Peter (Simon Petrus) is probably an
amalgam of several people, especially Simeon bar Cleophas and Simon,
the cousin of Jesus.

Though Catholics still mostly balk at the very idea, it is now accepted
by a growing number of scholars that Jesus was probably married to
Mary Magdalene. This would be entirely logical and in accordance with
Jewish tradition: A religious teacher, a rabbi, had to be married. Further,
his descent from the line of David had to be continued. Therefore, his
bride would have been a virgin of a noble family, specially educated and
prepared for her task of becoming the wife of the heir apparent of the
royal line. By no means could Mary Magdalene have been a sinning pros-
titute (of which there is no evidence in the gospels anway). Her anointing
of Jesus is today regarded as the required ceremony for the king of Israel.
Yet there is no evidence of the marriage, except indirectly in the Gospel
of Philip from the Nag Hammadi codices, which reads: "The companion
of the [Savior] is Mary Magdalene. [Christ] loved her more than [all] the
disciples [and used to] kiss her often on her [mouth]. The rest of [the dis-
ciples] were offended. They said to him: 'Why do you love her more than

all of us?' The savior answered and said to them, 'Why do I not love you like her?'" Some writers also suggest that the wedding at Cana was that of Jesus himself, for his behavior at the wedding is that of a bridegroom and not of a host, but no real evidence has been produced for this.

As for those who knew and heard Jesus and still remained within the Jewish Law, what became of them? Were they wiped out? Were they the Ebionites, destroyed by the Romans like the Essenes in the years between the Crucifixion and the Jewish Revolt? According to Eisenman, Ebionim was the name given to the community headed by James in Jerusalem. We now know the Romans sought out and destroyed many of the early followers of Jesus, especially his relatives and their families.

THE UNKNOWN YEARS OF JESUS' LIFE THROUGH THE RESURRECTION AND AFTER

The following is based entirely on statements by a number of mystics who claim to have knowledge of Jesus' life either from the universal memory of humankind (the Akashic record) or by regressions—that is, stepping back mentally into a former life. There is no evidence whatsoever for this information, but I find it nevertheless worth examining as a possible life story for Jesus in those years about which nothing is known through his days after the Crucifixion.

Jesus was in Egypt as a child for eleven and a half years, until about age twelve, in a settlement of Essenes, known there by their Greek name Therapeutae. The place seems almost certainly to have been Scetis (Wadi Natrun). After this time, he was taken back to the Temple in Jerusalem and to Beth Shean, where he lived with his parents, who were Essenes. His father, Joseph, was not a carpenter (the result of a misunderstanding of the Aramaic word), but rather a teacher.

Jesus then went to Mount Carmel, an important teaching center for Essenes of the Zadokite orientation, enforcing the high standard needed to produce the most learned spiritual leaders. The Essenes were masters of kabbalistic meditation techniques, which involve the use of certain sounds and words that release a powerful energy when they are spoken.

It was by the vibration of these sounds that, for example, the vibrations of a sick body could be corrected and an illness cured.

His instruction completed, Jesus commenced his mission in Judaea for a period of between one and three years (according to the Christian scriptures). He married Mary Magdalene, and their daughter was born in Israel and a son was later born in France.

Jesus was imprisoned in Jerusalem when he was thirty-three. He was of the line of David and the real king of Israel. The Romans were anxious that he might declare himself the rightful king of Israel and that the people would follow him, causing serious unrest. Major riots were expected in the city, so he was taken by a large force, consisting of one section of a Roman legion and Temple guards—that is, five hundred and sixty soldiers and three hundred guards. Jesus had entered Jerusalem along the traditional route on Palm Sunday. He had refused to lead certain groups in a riot, and because most of these groups were disappointed, they soon considered him an obstacle to their cause. Thus many extremist Jews wanted him dead.

On Palm Sunday this radical mob, which mingled with the great number of Jesus' followers, demanded his death. Some scholars claim there is evidence that a number of such Messiahs appeared every year, causing serious problems for Roman authorities. The extremists against him went to the Sanhedrin, who accepted that Jesus must die for his misdeeds and preaching, which was, in their view, contrary to the Jewish creed. They decided, however, that they would need Roman approval for his death. As stated in the Bible, Pilatus did not agree, for he did not consider Jesus to have committed any wrong. Thus it was that Jesus was in prison for three months.

Because they would not accept this decision, the Sanhedrin sent a message to Caesar (Tiberius) in Rome, who ordered Pilatus to carry out the sentence demanded by the Sanhedrin. Terrible death by crucifixion was reserved for enemies of the Roman state, though it is not certain why this should have been Jesus' fate. An explanation could be that the Sanhedrin had told the Romans that Jesus, as king of all the Jews, had intended to lead the people to seize power.

So Jesus was taken to Golgotha, where he was crucified. Three hours later, two other men, Zealots or robbers, were also taken to the crucifixion area. The Bible says Jesus was six hours on the cross, while the other two men died after three hours. After six hours of crucifixion, Jesus entered a state of near death with a fully conscious mind, his concentration focused on adjusting his breathing and heartbeat to the condition of his tormented body.

Joseph of Arimathea, who was wealthy, knew Pilatus well and made a secret agreement with him. Both men wanted to save Jesus, and Pilatus is said to have been corrupt. One of the soldiers was given an order to push a spear into Jesus' side, just beneath the third rib from the bottom. This action was intended to relieve the pressure of blood and water to prevent suffocation in order to keep him alive. Today, surgeons know that blood and water will not flow from a body if the person is already dead. Thus the spear enabled Jesus to breathe and survive at that time.

It has now become known that at crucifixion sites, the upright posts were normally left in position and the crossbar was carried across the shoulders by the victim. It is also known, from some skeletons, that crucifixion was sometimes carried out with the victim in a crossed-knee position with the two heel bones nailed together and to the cross. In other cases, the two legs were nailed separately to either side of the cross.

When Jesus fainted, the Romans declared him dead and ordered him taken down from the cross. Joseph of Arimathea helped the Romans, carefully removing the nails so no further damage would be done to Jesus' limbs. Also present at his removal from the cross were his mother, Mary, John the Apostle, Mary Simeon, Mary Magdalene, and the mother of Jacob. Immediately, oil and a certain powder were placed on the wounds to prevent any show of bleeding, which would have indicated to the Romans that Jesus was not dead. Jesus was then taken to Joseph of Arimathea's new, empty tomb.

Jesus had suffered the agony of crucifixion, but had transformed his low body energy into a different, high-energy state. The radiation and heat he was emitting are held by some scientists to have been the origin of the image on the Shroud of Turin. For a certain period, while he was lying in his tomb and for some time after, his high-energy body over-shadowed his physical body, which had become very faint and almost transparent. This was why his disciples often did not recognize him, as mentioned in several places in the Bible. His high-energy body was capable of penetrating solid matter, or performing "miracles" (as Jesus had done before his crucifixion). This explains his mysterious appear-ances to his followers and also supports the Christian doctrine of his ascension. By and by, as his physical body became stronger and healed, the high-energy body withdrew. Yet there was still a great deal of energy around and with Jesus.

He went to a place of the Essenes in Damascus (Damas, the Damas-cus of the Dead Sea Scrolls), where he stayed for three years, healing and teaching, part of the time in hiding. Here he met Saul/Paul and asked him why he was persecuting Jesus and his followers. Paul had to say later that he had never met Jesus, but in fact he did, so he used the story of his vision on the road to Damascus. During this period, the Romans and the Sanhedrin were disturbed about the empty tomb and the great power of Jesus' teaching. They set out to capture all followers, friends, and relatives of Jesus and all Essenes they could find. Many died and the situation became very serious. Because he had succeeded so wonder-fully in his mission, it was decided that Jesus and his family would go to a place of safety in southern France. Only John the Apostle and his mother, Mary, knew this secret. Mary, the mother of Christ, went with John to Ephesus, where John died in AD 92 and was buried.

Thus, Joseph of Arimathea took by his ships Jesus, Mary Magdalene, Mary Salome, three other Marys, Jesus' female child, and other relatives and followers to an Essene community in the diaspora, landing near the site of Les-Saintes-Maries-de-la-Mer on the southern coast of France. This was then a wild, marshy area of the Camargue at the mouth of the great Rhone River and was used only occasionally by Roman ships. It was full of wildlife, birds, and mosquitoes.

The Essenes there decided it was vitally important to create a decoy in order to ensure that any Roman inquiry would be diverted away from

Jesus, his family, and his followers. Therefore, a member of the Essenes went to Persia and then on to Ladakh, beyond Srinagar in Kashmir, freely making it known that he himself was Christ. (His tomb in Ladakh still exists.)

Jesus and his family journeyed secretly to their ultimate hiding place in France, the Cahors area on the river Lot, where several caves can be found in the forest and near the river. Later, they came to live in another place in southern France, and Jesus continued to teach and practice healing, supported by Mary Magdalene and others of the Essene community. Joseph of Arimathea lived there as well, but also continued his journeys by sea to other countries, including Judaea and lands in the north such as England, where he traded in tin.

The daughter and the son of Jesus and Mary Magdalene were educated in the Essene tradition and the teaching of Jesus. The daughter learned the art of spiritual healing from her parents. On several journeys to Spain, at that time home of the Celtiberians under Roman rule, Jesus and his family met worldly and spiritual leaders. The daughter later married a prince from a noble family in Compostela, in northwest Spain. Her daughter from this marriage became the founder of a great dynasty in Asturica Augusta (Astorga), which would become the House of Asturias. The son was brought up to be a priest and a king and married into a dynasty in Gallia (Gaul), as Romans then called France.

In later years, Joseph of Arimathea died, then Jesus himself died, and much later Mary Magdalene died as well. They were buried by the Essenes in total secrecy and this great secret has been kept ever since. Jesus had fulfilled his mission and had suffered the agony of crucifixion. He had resurrected from his tomb to continue on earth for many more years. Thus was his wonderful message given to us for all time.

Christianity is a religion of hope. The influence of evangelist thinking on Jesus' followers was such that no sense of sadness or defeat remained. This influence may have caused the early Church Fathers to seek adjustments to the gospels later, when Jesus' return was no longer considered imminent, thus causing some of the differences between the gospels as we have them now. The early Church Fathers were intensely devout but quite simple men; they could not possibly have imagined the enormous success their Church would enjoy in time. In addition, the new faith had to be made acceptable to the Romans early on.

Isaiah, the prophet of the Hebrew scriptures, said that the Messiah will be wounded and suffer pain, *but will not die.* The belief that Jesus died on the cross was the main reason that the Jews did not accept him as the Messiah. Did the Essenes, then, make a big mistake?

But not only mystics and psychics believe that Jesus didn't die on the cross, and that the Essenes had a hand in the preservation of his life, as the next chapter shows.

6

DID HE SURVIVE?

The first and best-known source for the idea that Jesus did not die on the cross—though, some might argue, not the most historically authoritative source—is the Quran. Islam's holy book clearly states this in the fourth Sura, or Sura of the Women (Surat an-Nisaa), verse 157:

> That they said (in boast), "We killed Christ Jesus the son of Mary, the Messenger of Allah"—but they killed him not, nor crucified him, but only a likeness of that was shown to them, and those who differ therein are full of doubts, with no [certain] knowledge, but only conjecture to follow, for of a surety they killed him not.

The Quran confirms that the intrigues of the corrupt Temple priests resulted in the Roman authorities, who controlled Jerusalem at the time, issuing an arrest warrant for Jesus, but it claims that the gospels contradict each other regarding the sequence of events. It indicates that Jesus had indeed been betrayed by one of his disciples, who led the arrest party to the house in which Jesus had celebrated the Passover with the apostles, and that on hearing the Roman soldiers and the crowd approaching, Jesus retreated farther inside the house, where his disciples were sleeping, and locked the doors securely. But, says the Quran, when God found his servant in danger, he commanded his angels Gabriel and Michael to remove his prophet from this world and place him in the third heaven, in the company of the angels. So the Quran reveals that Jesus did not die on the cross.

The end of Jesus' life is said to have been a miracle, just as his birth was. The Quran clearly repeats that Jesus was not crucified and was removed from this world by the will of God. What transpired is given only a vague description, namely that "only a likeness of the Crucifixion took place." Does this mean that another man was transformed by God into the likeness of Jesus and crucified—perhaps Judas Iscariot himself? Or does it mean that the Crucifixion was itself an illusion, that it did not take place at all? The Quran does not answer these questions, which have become a matter of debate for Muslim theologians just as the earthly fate of Jesus has been a topic of heated debate for Christians. The Orthodox Churches believe that Jesus was crucified, rose from the dead, and ascended to heaven, a formula necessary for the theological doctrine of a blood sacrifice and of Christ's atonement for the sins of humankind. Islam categorically rejects this theological notion. Within Islam, the matter of Jesus' death has been interpreted in various ways.

The Chapter of the Family of Imran (Surat al Imran), verse 47, states God's will as "O Jesus, I will take you to Me and will raise you to Me." Some Islamic scholars propose that after the substitution on the cross or the apparition of the Crucifixion, Jesus lived on earth a long time. He died a natural death and his spirit was then lifted up to God in a manner identical to that of the other prophets, martyrs, and truthful men. Other Islamic scholars propose that after dying on earth, Jesus was removed to heaven, body and soul. The essential element of all these beliefs about the end of the ministry of Jesus on earth is that God foiled the plot of the corrupt who wanted him dead, and that his spirit lives on in order to return to earth for the Final Judgment Day.

OTHER BELIEFS ABOUT JESUS' SURVIVAL

Of course, the empty tomb on Easter morning and Jesus' appearances to his disciples have also provided Christian novelists with an incentive to explore the possibility of his not having died on the cross. In 1929, D. H. Lawrence wrote *The Man Who Died,* in which, after surviving his crucifixion, Jesus ends up in Egypt, where he falls in love with a priestess of Isis. In 1972, Donovan Joyce published the novel *The Jesus Scroll,* in which Jesus was revived by a doctor, assisted by Joseph of Arimathea, in the latter's tomb. In Joyce's rather fanciful reconstruction, Jesus ends up as an eighty-year-old defender of Masada, who apparently died while fighting the Romans at the end of the Jewish revolt in AD 73. In this scrolled autobiography, Jesus is of course married to Mary Magdalene, is a revolutionary zealot at war with the Romans, and retires as a monk at Qumran. There is no end to the possibilities.

Not many know, however, that various independent scholars have also postulated that Jesus survived his crucifixion. A summary of these studies follows here so that open-minded, questioning Christians can better explore the roots of their faith and understand how thoroughly the Church has, over the centuries, ignored, suppressed, and belittled evidence it considers unthinkable, for it could overturn the faith. If evidence were to emerge that he survived his crucifixion, the whole fabric of traditional Christianity would come unraveled. Those who believe in God and who follow Jesus would not be concerned about it, but those who believe in fantastic theologies dependent upon particular historical events would find it pretty unsettling and might well retreat further into a shell of dogma and blind belief.

Underlying these survival hypotheses is the knowledge that death on the cross was designed to be long in coming—up to several days—while Jesus is said to have been taken down, with legs unbroken, relatively early, on the same day his crucifixion began. Further, as many scholars have pointed out, Josephus wrote of an instance in which he recognized three Jewish prisoners who had undergone crucifixion but were not yet dead. He obtained permission from Titus to take them down from their crosses and administer aid, and one of them survived.

Apart from the mention in the Quran, a nonorthodox branch of Islam, the Ahmadiyya, founded in Pakistan in the nineteenth century by Hazrat Mirza Ghulam Ahmad, affirms that Jesus survived his crucifixion. Briefly, it posits that Jesus lapsed into a deep swoon while on the cross, that the spear thrust into his side missed his heart, that he received medical attention while in the tomb, and that his exit from the tomb was aided by Essenes. The Ahmadiyya supposition that Essenes were involved in Jesus' recovery stems from the assumption that the angels in white in John 20:12 and the man in white in Luke 24:4 (or Matthew 28:3 and Mark 16:5) were Essenes. Josephus and others in effect describe the Essenes as wearing white garments.

This assumption turns up in several of these scenarios, together with references to the Essenes' well-known medical skills. Karl Bahrdt, writing in about 1780, postulated that Jesus survived a feigned death, with Luke, the apostle and physician, having administered drugs to him beforehand. Bahrdt supposed Jesus to have been an Essene, as was Joseph of Arimathea, who resuscitated him. On the third day, Jesus came forth, and his appearance scared away the tomb guards. He later lived in seclusion with the Essenes.

Karl Venturini proposed just after 1800 that Jesus had been associated with a secret society that wanted him to become a spiritual Messiah. Though it had not expected him to survive his crucifixion, one of the society's members, dressed in white, heard some groans from inside the tomb. He frightened away the guards and retrieved Jesus, who used up his remaining energy in appearing to his disciples and afterward retired permanently from sight.

Heinrich Paulus suggested in about 1828 that before the earthquake mentioned in Matthew (27:51) as occurring during Jesus' crucifixion, dense fumes caused difficulty in breathing and made it appear that Jesus had prematurely died on the cross. In this version, Jesus somehow survived in the tomb without any help. Like Venturini, Paulus had Jesus use up his remaining energies in the following days and disappear into a cloud after his final meeting with the disciples on the mountain—the Ascension. In the early 1830s, Schleiermacher, the father of modern theology, endorsed a form of this hypothesis.

In 1920, Ernest Brougham Docker proposed that Jesus had lapsed into a state of catalepsy or self-hypnosis on the cross, that the spear may not have been thrust into his side, and that he was aided in the tomb by Joseph of Arimathea and Nicodemus. The gardener of John 20:15 then supplied Jesus with fresh clothing. Docker, a district court judge and a student of the Christian scriptures, offered an interesting discussion of how the bystanders at his crucifixion may have mistakenly thought Jesus dead, while Joseph discovered otherwise. This scenario seems more realistic than the preceding ones, though surely Joseph or Nicodemus could have supplied the clothing.

Robert Graves and Joshua Podro, both well-known scholars, wrote in 1957 of Jesus having collapsed into a coma on the cross because the spear thrust into his side failed to pierce the lungs. The outflow of blood and water mentioned in John 19:34 and Matthew 27:49 indicated to them that Jesus had not died, a point made also by the Ahmadiyya. In this theory, one of the guards at the tomb is supposed to have entered it to steal the valuable ointment smeared on the shroud in which Jesus had been wrapped. Finding Jesus alive, he informed his officer, who let Jesus go. That evening Jesus showed himself to the disciples, but from then on became a wanderer, living in hiding.

The Talmud of Jmmanuel was allegedly discovered in 1963, translated from Aramaic into German in 1974, and destroyed soon afterward for what Christianity and Judaism considered heresies. In this mysterious document largely unknown to scholars, Jmmanuel (Jesus) is said to have lapsed into a very deep trance on the cross, and after the spear thrust, only Joseph of Arimathea noticed that he was not dead. Upon enshrouding Jesus and carrying him to his tomb, Joseph quickly sought out his Essene friends for help because of their skill with medicines and herbs. The Essenes used a second entrance to the tomb known only to Joseph so as not to arouse the suspicions of the guards who were posted. After three days, Jmmanuel was helped out of the tomb very early in the morning via the secret entrance and continued to recover rapidly. During his subsequent meetings with his disciples, he warned them not to disclose his survival to others. This may actually be history, but for those who insist that the Talmud of Jmmanuel is a literary hoax, it is the hypothesis of an unknown perpetrator.

Hugh Schonfield, an authoritative Scottish scholar of first-century languages and scripts, published a volume in 1965 entitled *The Passover Plot*. According to his reconstruction, "The Essenes contrived for Jesus to be arrested the night before Passover, fully aware that he would be nailed to the cross the following day but taken down before the onset of the Sabbath, in accordance with Jewish law. He would have to survive the agony of but three hours on the cross."

According to Schonfield, by using to full advantage their political clout as one of the major religious sects and Jesus' connection to an established noble family (that of David), the Essenes planned a daring redemption play: Jesus would only seem to die, but instead would be rescued, resuscitated, and made to reappear on the third day, in classic messianic form, to certain witnesses who would spread the Good News. In doing this, Jesus, the Davidic claimant, would not only have confirmed his worthiness as a descendant of the Judaean kings, but also would established his right to reign in the divine order of the messianic kingdom.

In any case, in my opinion, even if this plan were successfully executed, Jesus would still not have been able to return to public life after his "resurrection" for fear of exposing the ruse to the Romans and risking an inescapable death the second time. His whereabouts would have to be kept secret until the time was right. Unfortunately, the failure of the Jewish revolt and the ultimate literal death of the claimant Jesus ended any immediate hope of his return as king. This would explain—though this is not Schonfield's reasoning, but my own—why the tone of the Christian scriptures turned from immediate fervent expectation of Jesus' return to a resigned waiting until the End Times. The gospel of Paul and that of Peter differ substantially, but both were derived from an earlier messianic tradition and neither depended any longer on the immediate restoration of the Davidic kingdom.

According to Schonfield, to ensure Jesus' safe removal from the cross, Joseph and another Jew concocted a plan in which Jesus would be given "not the traditional vinegar, but a drug that would render him unconscious and make him appear dead. He would then be cut down from the cross in a deathlike trance and removed by accomplices to the tomb, where he would be nursed back to health and 'resurrected.' " Schonfield's new interpretation of the life and death of Jesus captured the imagination of the world. Scholars, newspapers, and even ministers lauded it as perhaps the most important book in that decade. *Time* magazine wrote, "Schonfield does not discredit Christ. Instead, he argues that Christ was indeed the Messiah—the Son of Man, as he thought of himself, but not the Son of God, as others declared him—the Messiah who had been foretold by the Jewish prophets of old, and that this is glory enough."

In 1982, J. D. M. Derrett also surmised that Jesus had lapsed into unconsciousness or a self-induced trance during the crucifixion, being taken for dead by bystanders and the Roman soldier who stabbed him in the side. Derrett chose the likelihood that Jesus' heart and lungs had not been pierced and he assumed that Jesus subsequently revived himself in the tomb. Derrett inferred that the young man of Mark 16:5 (and possibly of Mark 14:51) was a self-appointed guard and that some noise inside the tomb caused him to check the tomb, where he found Jesus in poor shape but alive. Jesus muttered a few things to this guard to relay to the disciples, and died not long afterward from his injuries. His disciples cremated his body because they considered him the Paschal Lamb who was meant to be sacrificed. We can note that Derrett seems to be more interested in denying resurrection than in affirming survival of the crucifixion.

Finally and most recently, Barbara Thiering, an Australian scholar, pictures Jesus as having been given snake poison on the cross, which rendered him unconscious. He recovered from this, was helped to escape from the tomb by friends, and ultimately settled in Rome. This author imagines the entire ministry of Jesus as actually having occurred in the Dead Sea area rather than near the Sea of Galilee. She regards nearly everything in the gospels as a coded version of what actually occurred, a puzzle to be deciphered by the pesher method of Dead Sea Scroll fame.

Up until 1835, the resuscitation hypotheses were roundly rejected by German theologian Professor David Friedrich Strauss, and this put a damper on such musings for nearly a century. His criticism was largely in the form of ridicule over the idea of a "half dead" being creeping out from the grave, weak and ill, yet managing to instill in his disciples "the impression that he was a conqueror over death and the grave." Strauss assumed Jesus had not received any medical attention while in the tomb. Several of the survival hypotheses, however, do postulate such medical assistance, and are therefore immune to Strauss's objection, yet his rejection is often referred to by scholars even today as if it were germane.

Strauss was the first scholar to emphasize the possibility that after the Crucifixion the disciples so longed for their Lord that they invented his appearances. By doing this, he could simply dismiss all testimony that Jesus had risen from the grave and physically appeared to his disciples. He pointed out inconsistencies in the various accounts, but didn't explore the reasons why such inconsistencies would be expected. We have very little solid information about what the disciples saw, but can increasingly find evidence that they, or at least some of them, were not simply deceived by appearances.

Despite all this supposition from researchers over the years, why do virtually all scholars agree that Jesus died on the cross? Many of these have no desire to prop up orthodox Christianity—for example, members of the so-called Jesus Seminar certainly don't—yet they agree that the evidence for the crucifixion death of Jesus is overwhelming. One of the main goals of any historian's reconstruction of Jesus' life is to explain the Resurrection stories and their huge impact. In fact, scholars like Schonfield and Eisenman maintain that it was the Resurrection accounts that eventually gave rise to these types of miracle stories in the early Church. Yet in spite of this, hardly anyone, even among those who insist that the miracles didn't happen, has supported the idea that Jesus didn't actually die on the cross, that he revived in the tomb, that he talked to his disciples before he actually died, and, finally, that others misunderstood or distorted what these witnesses said of their experiences and decided to apply the term *resurrection* to their misunderstanding. We know how theologically loaded that term was in first-century Jewish society: *Resurrection* was not a term that was tossed around lightly. It had very specific meanings for Jews of that day and different meanings depending on whether you were a Pharisee, a Sadducee, an Essene, or something else again. For all of them, however, the meaning was definitely *not* that someone survived death by the skin of his teeth and then stumbled around for a little while.

The only people I am aware of who dared to apply common sense to their theories were Schonfield and D. H. Lawrence, and even Schonfield claimed that the ordeal of scourging and crucifixion was too much for Jesus and that he died before he could be revived in the tomb. We know, however, that a person may appear dead and not actually be dead. Some people have suffered unusual cardiac conditions and were actually diagnosed as dead until they then revived. Surely after suffering the kinds of injuries Jesus suffered, a person might well go into a coma and remain motionless and unresponsive for quite some time. Then again, if we suppose that Jesus went into a coma from the shock of the suffering he endured and remained motionless as if dead, are we prepared to believe that once revived from such a fate, this individual would inspire his followers to conclude that he had risen from the dead?

WHAT IF HE DID NOT DIE?

As I've said, we cannot know exactly what the witnesses saw or what the disciples believed. What we have is the record of the victors in a struggle in the early Church between factions that believed quite different things about the message of Jesus and his nature. The only record we have of disciples who believed that Jesus didn't die on the cross is in the Nag Hammadi Codices, where Jesus in the Apocalypse of Peter says: "They crucified another one." But then, that record had to be buried to survive, didn't it? To me it appears increasingly likely—and in the future will quite possibly be provable—that Jesus did survive his crucifixion. This is a powerful miracle in itself that in no way lessens his fulfilment of the prophecies regarding the Messiah, but it does put a huge hole in the complex theology conceived by Paul that developed, a few centuries later, into Christian dogma.

History is written by the winners (military, political, or ideological), and the Christian scriptures are no exception. Nevertheless, historical accounts often contain concessions to the losers, especially when they still represent a significant voice both among the people and in the conscience of the winners. It is from these concessions that often, but only through masterful detective work, a more accurate picture of history can later be reconstructed.

A prominent medical-theological treatment of the Crucifixion recently concluded that if Jesus did not die on the cross, he must surely have died from the spear thrust in his side. This conclusion was based most notably on pre-1980s analyses of the Shroud of Turin, and therefore is based on the assumption that the Shroud is genuine. The Ahmadiyya also use the Shroud of Turin as evidence, but to support the opposing conclusion, for they point to the outflow of blood and water from the spear thrust as indicating that Jesus had *not* died from asphyxiation prior to that action.

I'll have more to say about the Shroud later, but here I will mention that in 1988 carbon dating seemed to indicate that the Shroud is a medieval fake. It has been pointed out that the carbon dating was organized by the Catholic Church, specifically by Turin archbishop Cardinal Ballestrero. Skeptics add that it was clearly in the Church's interest that the Shroud be declared a fake for the simple reason that dead men don't bleed! In fact, a fascinating esoteric tradition holds that the real reason for including the spear wound episode in the gospels at all is that it was a message to the initiated that Jesus had not been killed.

I would point out a different paradox: Although the authors of the attempted debunking were Christian clerics and must therefore have believed in the reality of Jesus' miraculous cures of lepers, the lame, the blind, the deaf, and other afflicted people, they seem never to have questioned whether his healing powers could have extended to his own body. None of the theories above really explains how Jesus was able to recover so quickly, and we are indeed left wondering if his miraculous healing powers could be applied not just to others, but to himself as well.

Miracles aside, the likeliest explanation, as most scholars realized, is that someone was on hand to administer to the badly wounded Jesus. As we shall see, it is no coincidence that most scholars who consider this likely also postulate that the helpers were members of the Essene sect. This is not just because of the sect members' reputation as knowledgeable healers (remember their Greek name Therapeutae), or because of the white garments some of them wore. Rather, it is because of the strong circumstantial evidence that Jesus' teaching was not all that different from Essene teaching, that his mentor, John the Baptist, was actually a member of the sect, and that Jesus himself was one.

Therefore, we had better take a closer look at these heretical Jewish Sons of the Light.

7

THE ESSENES

First, as we did for Jesus, let us consider the evidence for what we might call the historical Essenes. To understand who the Essenes were, we must first take a big step backward. After Alexander the Great conquered what was then the known world, the Jews were greatly influenced by Hellenism. Alexander divided his empire among three generals of his army: Ptolemy took Egypt, Seleucus ruled Asia, and Lysimachus controlled Greece. In the second century BC, Palestine became part of the Seleucid empire and Greek paganism thus infiltrated Jewish thinking and daily life, which provoked a Jewish puritan reform movement as an answer to apostasy and all kinds of perceived wickedness. The Chasidim (Pious) as well as the militant nationalist group the Maccabees evolved in this period.

The Dead Sea Scrolls tell of a "wicked priest" who misled Israel. This was in all likelihood a symbolic name for a corrupt high priest of Israel. Forgetting their spiritual tasks and driven by desire for prestige and power, the high priests of the time became involved in bribery, sacrilege, robbery of Temple treasures, and even murder. In order to end all fighting and uproar in the country, Antiochus IV stormed Jerusalem, killing as many as eighty thousand and taking the same amount of captives into slavery. Two years later he converted the Temple of Jerusalem into a temple to Zeus and tried to force the Jews to stop circumcising their sons, to make offerings to Zeus, and to eat pork—in short, to abandon their religion.

Of course, this led to resistance among the population and a period of heroic struggle and martyrdom described in Maccabees I and II of the Hebrew scriptures (although because they were written in Greek, these two books never made it into the Jewish canon as defined immediately before the revolt against Rome in the early sixties of the millennium). Mattathias, father of the Maccabees, led the faithful ones into the wilderness, where they would be able to live in the way of the Jewish faith. His sons, called the Maccabees (hammers), continued the fight against the Seleucids. In 156 BC, Jewish rebels under Maccabee leadership were able to recover, cleanse, and rededicate the Temple in Jerusalem. Jonathan Maccabee became high priest, as did his successors of the House of Maccabee, also known as the Hasmoneans.

In the third generation, the Hasmoneans took over the kingship and moral decay commenced. The priesthood was not pleased at all with the warrior-king, Alexander Janneus (Jonathan), and offered sacrifices at the Temple both because he had been made impure by all the killing in numerous battles and, perhaps more important, because he was of impure descent. Events escalated, the agitated people screamed at Janneus, and in the end his troops massacred thousands of his own people.

The Qumran Scrolls also speak of the "true teacher" or the "Teacher of Righteousness," who was the opponent of the "wicked priest." It was probably he who at this time gathered together some of the faithful priests and fled into Qumran exile. His real name was never revealed, though he seems to have been immensely revered by his Essene followers. There are all kinds of theories as to who he might have been, but still there is no evidence.

Alexander Janneus's successor was Aristibulos, who, having encountered problems because of his usurpation of the throne, appealed to the Romans. The new lords of the world did not show much gratitude and replaced him after some time with his brother Hyrcanus, who was only allowed to be high priest. Effectively, the kingship was taken from the Hasmonean house. In 63 BC, the Roman general Pompey marched his army into Jerusalem and found serious resistance only at the Temple. About twenty-three years later the Romans accorded to the Jews the pretense of self-government by providing a puppet king, Herod the Great.

As a result of this long period of unrest, at the time of Jesus we find a large variety of Jewish fundamentalist groups and sects in Judaea. Sadducees, Pharisees, Zealots—Essene roots appear to be present in all of them. The name Sadducee in all likelihood derives from Zadok, high priest of Solomon, which means that this party claimed to continue the Zadokite line and his spiritual heritage. They seem to have been pro-Hellenic and diplomatic and they accused the Pharisees of teaching things not written down in the Law of Moses.

The Pharisees were eager to keep themselves apart from the "heathens" and to strictly observe the Law. They believed in the immortality of the soul and an afterlife in hell or heaven, resurrection of the dead at the end of time, and the kingdom of the Messiah. The Zealots were a radical branch of the Pharisees who broke away because independence from Rome was more important to them than strict observance of the Law. Like the Maccabees, they tended toward violence and rebellion against Roman rule. Some scholars think that Jesus himself, at least at the beginning of his mission, may have been a Zealot. Certainly some of his disciples were Zealots.

The discovery of the Dead Sea Scrolls gave us access to writings of the Essenes themselves for the first time after almost two thousand years. Although Israeli archaeologist Yigael Yadin said there is only an assumed identification of the Qumran sect with the Essenes, the resemblance of the Qumrans' creed and conduct—as *they* write of them—to the description of the Essenes written by ancient historians such as Josephus and Pliny the Elder would seem to justify a more definitive identification.

Coin finds indicate that an isolated community (now generally accepted to be Essenes) lived at Kirbet Qumran from early in the second century BC until it was destroyed by Roman legions under Vespasian in AD 68. Archaeological work has shown that their main building there had two floors and included a strong stone tower. They also maintained a water-storage facility, a mill, a forge, and a writing area, and there was a cemetery with about twelve hundred graves.

The Dead Sea Scrolls were discovered in several caves near Qumran between 1947 and 1956. In 1947, a young Bedouin came upon the first scrolls in a cave near the main Qumran ruin. It is said that he threw a stone to retrieve his goat but heard the sound of the stone striking ceramic pottery. Many fragments of manuscripts were later found by archaeologists in the same cave.

The scrolls were written on papyrus, parchment, leather, and copper. Carbon dating, which is still not completely accurate, dates the scroll wrappings to between the first half of the second century BC and the first half of the third century AD. Most documents proved to be in their library, hidden during the Roman destruction between AD 67 and 73. The majority are supposed to have been written during the first century BC and first century AD, but some damaged documents were hidden in one cave by Samaritans massacred by soldiers of Alexander the Great way back in 331 BC. Others were hidden by fleeing fugitives of the defeated army of Bar Kokhba in their last suicide revolt against Rome in AD 132–135.

From 1951 to 1956, more documents were discovered in other caves, some scrolls but mostly fragments and pieces that had suffered immense damage from illegal excavations and amateurish tampering. There were forty to fifty jars in the caves, each one containing several scrolls. The famous Copper Scroll, found in 1953 in the third cave and opened in England in 1955–56, became the focus of much speculation because it contains an inventory of the hidden treasury of the Essene community (or perhaps of the Temple in Jerusalem) and lists its various locations.

I have been permitted to enter many of the caves at Qumran, and from the presence of concealed and blocked entrances, I gained the impression that there are more finds to be made. In 1947 seven manuscripts were removed from the first cave:

1. The longest is the so-called St. Mark's Isaiah Scroll (because it was kept for a while in St. Mark's Monastery). It is made of

leather and contains the complete book of Isaiah in Hebrew. The text differs slightly from our Bible text.

2. Another scroll is known as the Hebrew University Isaiah Scroll. Here, some parts of Isaiah are missing, but the text is closer to the Bible version.

3. The Commentary on the Book of Habakkuk explains the Book of Habakkuk, with the prophet using a special technique called pesher, which means commentary or interpretation and involves taking special words as symbols for something else. Its references to the Teacher of Righteousness make this manuscript one of the most interesting among the scrolls.

4. The Manual of Discipline, a manuscript in two sections, contains among other things the rules and conduct of the community.

5. The War of the Sons of Light with the Sons of Darkness is an apocalyptic book on the conflict between the righteous and the evil ones.

6. A collection of many pieces forms the twenty Thanksgiving Psalms, which are very similar to the Psalms of the Hebrew scriptures.

7. The Apocryphal Genesis is called Lamech by scholars because of their failed hope to find in it the lost apocalypse of Lamech. It is in fact an elaboration on Genesis, but is written in Aramaic, not in the Hebrew of the other scrolls. Therefore, it is also called the Aramaic Scroll.

The main sources for our knowledge of the Qumran community itself are the Manual of Discipline and the Damascus Document. Damascus was the name the sect gave to its place of exile, almost certainly a symbolic name and not identical with the Damascus we know today. A copy of this document had already been discovered in the famous Cairo *genizah* in the late nineteenth century, but only when the Qumran Scrolls were found, among which were fragments of a copy of the same document, was it clear that it dated from the Qumran period. Its similarity to the Manual leads to the belief that they come from the same source.

Both documents give a much more detailed description of the community than we learn from Flavius Josephus.

It must be said that neither the name Essenes (meaning Holy Ones) nor any other is used in these documents. The members of the order call themselves the Covenant, the Congregation, the Party or Council or Community. In his study *Beyond the Essene Hypothesis,* early Jewish and rabbinic scholar Gabriele Boccaccini implies that a convincing etymology for the name Essene has not been found, but that it almost certainly applied to a larger group within Palestine—and perhaps beyond it—that also included the Qumran community.

The main idea of those in this community was to share everything, not only material things but also spiritual things. Every member had to hand over all his belongings to the common fund, from where individuals would receive everything necessary for life. Members worked, prayed, and ate together, though there existed a kind of hierarchy in the order, and they were seated in their assemblies, called the Many, according to their rank. In any group of ten there had to be one priest. Voting and speaking were permitted to any member, regardless of his rank. Sessions of the community were held under strict rules that governed such matters as who was to sit first and who was to speak to the Many. A young man could not marry before he was twenty, which was the age he was expected to have fully matured to take responsibility.

The discovery of female skeletons in the cemetery proves the presence of women in the community, and some argue that women and children were admitted to the group. A special council of twelve men and three priests formed the executive board, and there were overseers to supervise work, keep the accounts, and examine applications for membership. The judges consisted of four priests and six members who were knowledgeable in the Law, and judgments were made following a penal code. Even minor offenses such as interrupting somebody's speech or sleeping during a session were fined with temporary excommunication from full membership, similar to a probation.

Any novice had to pass three stages of initiation: After he had been admitted by the Inspector, he had to become acquainted with the conduct

and spirit of the order. Then, after an unspecified period, the Many examined his case and either admitted him to the next stage or rejected him forever. If admitted, he proceeded to stage two, becoming a member of the
community although not being admitted to the Many. After one year and
with the consent of the Many, he passed to the third stage for a further
year, when he submitted all his belongings to the overseer but not to the
common fund and joined the Many. Only after completion of this stage
would he be admitted to the Messianic banquet, take part in all decisions
of the community, and share the possessions of the order. This final initiation was celebrated with a special ceremony of blessings, recitations from
scriptures, and confirmation of the Covenant with God.

It was the strong belief of the Essene community that they were the
chosen ones who had entered a new Covenant with God because the Jews
had became corrupt and unobservant of the Law and had therefore broken the old Covenant. They also believed that God would soon send the
Anointed One (the Christos, in Greek) or the Messiah (the Meshiach, in
Hebrew). Different from other Jewish expectations of the Messiah, the
Manual announces the appearance of *two* such men: a priest from the
House of Aaron and a king from the House of David. Did the Qumran
sect believe the Teacher of Righteousness to be the priestly Messiah? Or
was he perhaps the prophet who had to come first to prepare the way for
the Anointed One? Attempts to interpret John the Baptist as this prophet
or James the Just as the Teacher of Righteousness have been dismissed
because they contradict the now generally accepted dating of the scrolls
to at least a hundred years earlier.

In Essene teaching there is a dualist concept of light and darkness
and a belief that both influence us during life. Those who returned to
righteousness would be saved by the Messiah. The following is from the
Manual of Discipline:

And he assigned to Man two spirits in which he should walk until
the time of His visitation. They are the spirits of Truth and Perversity: Truth born out of the spring of Light, Perversity from the well
of Darkness. The dominion of all the children of righteousness is

in the hands of the prince of Light so that they walk in the ways of Light, whereas the government of the children of Perversity is in the hands of the Angel of Darkness, to walk in the ways of Darkness.

Much has been written about the unusual dualistic and markedly gnostic outlook of this Jewish sect. The dualistic elements in the scroll the War of the Sons of Light against the Sons of Darkness were taken by some as evidence of Persian Zoroastrian thinking penetrating into Judaea. Professor and Rabbi Ben Zion Wachholder once wrote that the first Essene had been the prophet Ezekiel, who lived in Babylonia during the exile of 586–516 BC, while my friend Robert Feather, on a markedly different trail, suggests in his books that Essene tradition was the surviving remnant of an Egyptian monotheism of the heretical pharaoh Amenhotep IV, better known as Akhenaten.

HISTORIANS WHO MENTION THE ESSENES IN THEIR WRITINGS

The remarkable Jewish (and later Roman) historian Flavius Josephus left us vital histories in his two works, the *Antiquities* and *The Jewish Wars*. He names the beliefs of the Pharisees, Sadducees, and Essenes as the three important schools of thought that arose in about the middle of the second century BC and describes the Essenes as severely disciplined, rejecting pleasure-seeking and passions.

The members of one Essene order, he writes, did not marry and adopted children with the intention of bringing them up in the Essene doctrine. Another order permitted marriage to devoted Essene women after a three-year trial. As stated earlier, the Essenes had no private ownership; their earnings were given to a common fund, which in turn was used to serve the needs of the community. Traveling members found in every city a place that would supply them with food and garments; thus, they never carried any baggage on their travels. (We can compare this with Jesus' words in Mark 6:7–8 as he sent off his disciples in twos: "Take a staff only, no bread, no wallet, no money.") To help the poor, whether or not they belonged to their order, was an Essene duty. To cleanse and purify their bodies, they used not oil but only water, and they always dressed in white garments. Josephus wrote that they did not speak of worldly things before sunrise, but instead "offer to Him some traditional prayers as if beseeching Him to appear" (a strangely Egyptian-sounding ritual). After this prayer, everybody went to work until an hour before noon, at which time they came together again and washed all over with cold water, entered the refectory building, and sat down in silence. Their sustenance, a loaf of bread and a plate of one kind of food, was set before each member. It was forbidden to taste the food before the priest had said grace, and after the meal and a second prayer of thanks to the Giver of Life, they returned to their work till evening, when they ate another meal in the same manner.

Although the Essenes depended in every activity on orders from the group's supervisors, they could, of their own initiative, help any person in need or give food to the poor. They controlled their tempers; no shouting was ever heard among them. Every word they spoke was more binding than an oath. They cherished the work of ancient writers, especially those who wrote on curing soul and body. They learned all they could about medicinal roots and the properties of stones. (This, of all the traits Josephus mentions, is the most relevant to our investigation.) They answered major offenses by exclusion from the community, a punishment that often led to a miserable end for the outcast because he could not go back to the world from which he came. Driven by pity, the order thus took back many offenders at the last moment. The verdict in trials was given by a jury of not fewer than a hundred.

After the described three-year period probationary period before becoming a member of the group, one who aspired to membership had to swear

> . . . terrible oaths, first that he will revere the Godhead, and second,
> that he will deal justly with men, will injure no one either of his own
> accord or on another's bidding, will always hate the wicked and
> cooperate with the good, and will keep faith at all times and with

all men—especially with rulers, since all power is conferred by God. If he himself receives power, he will never abuse his authority and never by dress or additional ornament outshine those under him; he will always love truth and seek to convict liars, will keep his hands from stealing and his soul innocent of unholy gain, and will never hide anything from members of the sect or reveal any of their secrets to others, even if brought by violence to the point of death. He further swears to impart their teaching to no man otherwise than as he himself received it, to take no part in armed robbery, and to preserve the books of the sect and in the same way the names of the angels.

After God, the Essenes most revered the Lawgiver (which may have meant either Moses or the Teacher of Righteousness). Members had to be obedient to older men and to the majority, and the Sabbath was observed more strictly than by other Jews. Four grades existed in the order, assigned according to the stage of a person's preparation. The simplicity of their daily life made the members live a long time, often more than a century. They could overcome pain by sheer will, and an honorable death was welcome.

The Essenes believed in the immortality of souls, who, according to their way in life, would find either reward in Paradise or eternal punishment in Sheol. Josephus compares this belief to the Greek myths of the afterlife. He also mentions the Essenes' ability to tell the future, which required a lifelong study of both sacred literature and the utterings of prophets, as well as different kinds of purification. Their predictions, writes Josephus, were nearly always right.

In his writing *That Every Good Man Is Free* (about AD 20), Philo of Alexandria describes the Essenes as living in Syria or Palestine, with their number being about four thousand. At first they lived in villages, but later they also lived in cities. They did not sacrifice animals but instead regarded a reverent mind as the only true sacrifice. As a consequence of this belief, they were excluded from Temple worship by the Orthodox. The Essenes worked as artisans and in agriculture and were strictly opposed to slavery. They did not waste time on questions of philosophy, but were engaged more in moral teaching. They observed the Sabbath, meeting in their synagogues and listening to readings of the scriptures and explanations of the text by means of symbols. Love of God, virtue, and man was their main concern. They were known for their kindness, their idea of equality, and their low regard for money and worldly pleasures. The Essenes, writes Philo, lived in colonies equipped with a common storehouse, common clothing, and a common treasury to which every member contributed all his belongings and from which all expenditures were paid. Brethren from other settlements were warmly welcomed and shared a community's meals and religious duties.

Pliny the Elder describes the "Hessenes" in his *Historia Naturalis* (Natural History, written about AD 70) as living without women on the west shore of the Dead Sea. They eschewed money, and although they had no children, their numbers were maintained by daily newcomers who wanted to join their life in the wilderness. This description of a settlement on the Dead Sea very probably refers to Qumran. In his *Refutation of All Heresies,* Hippolytus (AD 160–235) gives a detailed description of the Essenes, among whom he even counts the Zealots and Sicarii (Assassins). Finally, Eusebius, quoting Philo (in about AD 300), says that Essenes inhabited many cities and villages of Judaea, that they did not marry, and that there were no children in their communities.

JESUS AND THE ESSENES

Having looked at the historical evidence, let us now consider some unproven scenarios.

Some Christians think that Jesus came down to earth completely equipped with his message from heaven. Certainly this was not so. He was born in a rather troublesome corner of the Roman Empire where underground movements preached insurgency and Messiahs often emerged, promising to lead the people out of slavery. Jesus lived at a time of great change. For the two hundred years before his birth, the Jewish people had been exposed to much suffering at the hands of foreign rulers. There was an ever-growing expectation for the prophesied

Messiah who would come to free them. All this must be considered when we try to understand why Jesus thought and taught the things he did. Jesus was educated in the spiritual teachings of his time, which are those of the holy scriptures of the Jews and of the mysterious Essenes. In fact, there is much reason to believe that he and his parents were Essenes.

Scholars who have now been studying the Qumran scrolls for half a century have found many similarities between the Essene doctrine and the life and teaching of Jesus. According to some scholars, these similarities explain the tight control exercised over research of the contents of the scrolls by the secretive (some would say manipulative) École Biblique of Jerusalem, an organism controlled by the Dominican order. To put it another way, there is the instinctive fear of theologians in the Vatican that too much early Christian language would be found in the Essene documents, which was why the writings were released to nonclerical scholars only after unusually strong international pressure. This is actually an intriguing and quite recent story, which transpired as follows.

All Qumran manuscripts were placed under the control of a committee of scholars. Many of the longer, complete ones were published soon after the discovery, but dozens of scrolls, though they consisted of tiny, brittle fragments, were published at a rate considered by many as needlessly slow. In 1991, the Hebrew Union College of Cincinnati announced in Jerusalem with much scandal and indignation that using computer concordance techniques, it had reconstructed a previously unpublished text. Not long after that, the Huntington Library announced it would allow full access to its complete set of photographs of the scrolls. Maverick professor Robert Eisenman, who—as we saw in the story of the attempted dig under the church of Mary Magdalene in Rennes-le-Château—is always at the forefront of the academic offensive against the official version of Christian beginnings, was involved in every stage of this rebellion against what amounted to a Church monopoly on the study of the scrolls. Once the monopoly had been broken, the École Biblique (and a complacent Israeli Antiquities Authority) removed their restrictions on access to the scrolls.

Since then, Hebrew University in Jerusalem undertook the continuous publication of the manuscripts. In 1997, Geza Vermes's *The Complete Dead Sea Scrolls in English* appeared in London. In June 2000, I attended a conference of the world's most distinguished Dead Sea Scrolls scholars at Hereford. Work on translating the scrolls is now virtually complete, and it can be stated with little doubt that much of what Jesus taught took form from that desert community.

The Jewish roots of Christianity no longer constitute a problem for Catholic theologians as they did, say, a century ago. In 1986, in a speech on the historic occasion of his visit to the Great Synagogue in Rome, Pope John Paul II referred to the Jews as "our elder brothers." Yet if the Church was reluctant to concede the presence of Christian concepts and language in Jewish writings officially dated to more than a century before Jesus, it was because the revelatory nature of Jesus' teaching—the fact that it came directly from his father in heaven—might be compromised. It wouldn't do, after all, to have Christian revelation actually born in the minds of a band of fundamentalist, heavily gnostic desert misfits.

So much for the way theologians look at the Essenes. Yet I happen to think that the Essenes were both the heirs of an ancient spiritual tradition and the initiators of a new desert lifestyle so closely entwined with early Christianity that we today know it as monasticism. As I mentioned in the introduction, to the people of that time the desert was both a place of temptation and devils and the only place where direct communion with God could be reached. Jesus claimed that the kingdom of his father was both in every man's heart and all around us. In this, as in many other cases, only the monastic choice of removal from the distractions of the material world enables understanding of what Jesus meant.

In fact, there are many similarities between Essene tradition and the life and teaching of Jesus:

• Jesus clearly understood himself to be the expected Messiah, although his Kingdom of God was quite different from that expected by the Jews. It referred to an enlightened consciousness of being one with the heavenly father.

- In John 18:36, Jesus says, "My kingdom is not of this world." Even more tied to Essene tradition in the words of the gnostic Gospel of Thomas recovered in Nag Hammadi, Jesus says, "Rather, the kingdom is inside of you, and it is outside of you. When you come to know yourselves, then you will become known, and you will realize that it is you who are the sons of the living father."

- Jesus taught the ritual of the sacred meal, which he had learned from the Essenes. There seems to have been a connection between the sacred meal and the promise of the coming Messiah, which would explain the importance to Jesus of the Last Supper. As a fragment of a scroll says: "The Messiah of Israel shall stretch forth his hand on the bread; and after giving a blessing, all the community shall partake, each according to his rank."

- Baptism as a ritual of entering the Christian community was influenced by the daily baptism of the Essenes, although the Christian belief was that one single baptism was enough for the rest of one's life.

- The early Christian communities such as the Essenes practiced the principle of having all things in common. In the Manual of Discipline, fraud against the wealth of the community was punished severely. The early Christians seem to have been even stricter about this, as told in the story of Ananias and Saphira in Acts 5:1–11. The couple sold their possessions to surrender their money to the Christian community, but kept a part for themselves and lied about the amount they had kept. Having discovered the fraud, Peter condemned them both and told Ananias that he had lied not to men, but to God. Both Ananias and his wife died within a few hours from the shock.

- As recounted in Matthew 5:22, Jesus said, "Whosoever is angry with his brother without a cause shall be in danger of the judgment: and whosoever shall say to his brother: Raca [vanity, worthlessness] shall be in danger of the council." These words have an exact match in the Essene Manual of Discipline, with "brother" here referring to the Essene brother and "judgment" and "council" referring to the Essene Judgment and Council.

• When Jesus praised the poor and the meek, he probably meant the Essene community, for these were the very words they used to identify themselves.

In short, what seems most likely is that Jesus was brought up in the Essene order but later in his mission developed a more moderate, tolerant, and loving approach.

Our inquiry into the Essene movement had taken off from the frequently cited notion that if Jesus survived his crucifixion, it was probably thanks to the medical assistance he received in Joseph's tomb, and that the white-clad figure seen by Mary Magdalene at the tomb on Sunday morning after the Crucifixion might have been a member of the desert sect, who were well known both for wearing white linen and for their medical skills. But where can we find further evidence that the Essenes—assuming that Jesus was a member of their community and that they therefore had a motive for wanting to save him—were capable of reviving someone who had undergone the unimaginable ordeal of crucifixion, if only for three hours?

This is the point at which we examine the powerful link between Jesus and his family and the nearby, very ancient culture of Egypt. It is known that there are marked similarities between the Essenes and the Therapeutae of Egypt (who are sometimes called the Alexandrian Essenes). It seems that there were several forms of such protomonastic communities, all called Essenes by ancient historians, that were Jewish in origin but slightly different in rules and thinking. Some of these communities, such as the Therapeutae, were found as far away as Egypt, where they may have existed much earlier as esoteric Egyptian-Jewish enclaves. The name Therapeutae clearly points to the group's practice of medicine and its members' reputation as healers. Let us then peel another layer from the onion, so to speak, and briefly examine medicine and healing in antiquity.

8

SCETIS AND THE THERAPEUTAE: HEALING IN ANCIENT TIMES

Who were the Therapeutae? Were they Greek, Jewish, or Essene? Not much is known about this sect whose name derives from the Greek word *therapeutai* (healers). The only source of knowledge about them is the writing *On the Contemplative Life* by the Jewish-Greek historian Philo of Alexandria (c. 20 BC–AD 40). According to his account, they were a Jewish sect spread out over the world but located mainly in the Alexandria region. Their main center was on the shores of Lake Maryût (or Marea), southwest of Alexandria. Like the Essenes, they were ascetics devoted to prayer and study. Some scholars believe that the Therapeutae were indeed a branch of the Essenes. Both male and female members prayed twice every day, at dawn and at sunset, and, as was their custom, ate only bread, salt, and hyssop and only after sunset. They spent the rest of the day in spiritual exercises with the aim of curing the soul from lusts, pains, and fears and practicing in solitude the mysteries of the higher life.

Members of the community lived near one another in separate houses. Each house contained a chamber, or sanctuary, consecrated to study and prayer. They read the holy scriptures, guided by the belief that the words of the literal text were symbols of something hidden. In addition to the Hebrew scriptures, they had books written by the founders of the sect on allegorical methods of interpreting scripture. Philo also refers to their "new psalms" to God, composed in various meters and melodies. For six days a week, members lived apart, seeking wisdom in solitude. On the Sabbath they met in the common sanctuary for a festival, which was opened by a prayer. Then all men and women ate a meal of coarse bread and water while their leader gave a discourse on some topic of their scriptures based on allegory. After this, they sang a hymn and the "most holy bread," symbol of the holy bread in the Temple at Jerusalem, was brought in. The festival was concluded with ritual dances and songs in memory of the crossing of the Red Sea.

Wisdom, Philo says, was the main objective of the Therapeutae, which distinguishes them from the Essenes, who were quite anti-intellectual. Like the Essenes, they had a dualistic view of body and soul. As Philo beautifully puts it, "[T]hey appease the mistresses which Nature has set over mankind, Hunger and Thirst, but do not pamper them."

Various views have been held about these ascetics. This description of the Therapeutae by Philo—their daily life, their assemblies at the end of the week, and the nature of their food—strongly recalls the account of early Christian monks (as well as reminding us of the lifestyle practiced in the south of Italy five hundred years earlier by the disciples of Pythagoras, but more on that later). Eusebius goes so far as to assume that they were a kind of primitive Christians, a result of the many conversions caused by St. Mark's preaching in Alexandria. He points out that the leaders of the Therapeutae resembled the ecclesiastical canons of his own time and that the community's way of life was nearly identical to that of the Christian ascetics of the fourth century (in which he lived). He tries to explain the fact that they observed many Jewish rites and customs by postulating that they were of Jewish origin and did not abandon their practices after becoming Christians. According to Philo's description, however, the Therapeutae had many Jewish traits but not a single Christian characteristic: They had no sacraments, nor did they observe the first day of the week as a Sabbath.

Some modern critics regard Philo's description of the Therapeutae as a Utopian picture, like Plato's ideal state, for there is no geographical account of the alleged settlement on Lake Maryût or of the lesser communities, which, according to Philo, were scattered throughout Egypt and the world. The problem with this view is that the settlement described by Philo may not have been large and could easily have been overlooked by travelers, who would simply have regarded such a settlement as a small Jewish place without any importance. According to Hugh Evelyn-White, author of *The Monasteries of the Wadi' Natrun,* the precise picture drawn by Philo proves in itself that he had seen the settlement on Lake Maryut with his own eyes. White writes:

> If we accept the account of the Therapeutae as genuine, and recognize them as Jewish, may they not have contributed something towards the establishment of Christian monasticism? There is nothing to show for how long the Therapeutae continued to flourish, but their system must have vanished long before the period of Eusebius; for had it still existed, the historian's theory concerning it would have led to investigations which could not have failed to leave some record in literature. It is therefore certain that Saint Antony and his fellow founders of monasticism can have had no contemporary Therapeutic community before their eyes to serve as a model. It is practically as certain that they neither read Philo's tract, nor knew of any tradition concerning these Jewish ascetics . . . while in Palestine . . . the semi-monastic system of the Essenes was in front of the eyes of the early Christians.

We also know that the Therapeutae practiced medicine—but what kind of medicine was it? Here we make a brief detour into the world of first-century healing.

HEALING IN THE FIRST CENTURY

The process of change from magic to medicine lasted for many centuries. When the Greeks assumed the cultural leadership of the Western world, they had already left the dark mystery areas of magical imagination. To them, the clear-thinking mind and its logic were more important. In fact, great Greek thinkers laid the foundation of science. Clearly, however, Greek knowledge gained much from Babylon and Egypt and India and ancient China. Asclepius lived about 1200 BC and is believed to have performed many miracles of healing. He was later regarded as the Greek god of medicine and was worshipped in hundreds of temples throughout Greece. Some of these remains may still be seen at Cos, Athens, and Epidaurus.

In 460 BC, Hippocrates, whose thinking produced great advances in medicine, was born at Cos, where ancient writers say that he taught and practiced and eventually died, apparently at a great age. He preferred treatment by direct methods rather than by drugs, and his greatest legacy was the ethical code (the Hippocratic Oath) that has guided physicians ever since.

In the fourth century BC, Aristotle's work in the fields of anatomy and biology produced substantial advances in these areas. Soon after his time, the center of Greek culture moved to Alexandria, where a famous medical school was established. Later, Greek doctors even moved to Rome, with one example being Galen, who achieved much progress there in about AD 160. The main sites of Hellenistic healing were Epidaurus, Cos, Delphi, the temple of Apollo at Didyma, Smyrna, Pergamon, and Alexandria.

Hippocratic principles were directly opposed to magic and ritual. Yet the continued success throughout antiquity of the cult of Asclepius shows very clearly that medicine was never fully divorced from its religious connections. Beginning in the sixth century BC, health resorts, or sanctuaries, known as *asclepia*—that is, presided over by the god of healing, Asclepius—sprang up all over the Mediterranean. The cult of Asclepius was both a religion and a system of therapeutics, and his sanctuaries were built outside of towns on particularly healthy sites, and in temples and spas.

Epidaurus, a still wonderful but much damaged complex of buildings in the finest Greek style and the grandest of all the ancient healing places, was built on the eastern coast of the Argolid in the northeast of the Peloponnese. It is most famous for its fourth-century-BC temple of Asclepius and the combined temples of Asclepius and Artemis. Still to be seen there is a hospital and an *abaton,* the area where patients slept while under treatment. Inscriptions describe divine medical cures (no failures or deaths are recorded). Epidaurus was originally Ionic, then became Doric under the influence of Argos, to which it owed religious allegiance while remaining politically independent.

Delphi, situated on the slope of Mount Parnassus and overlooking the Gulf of Corinth, was the most sacred place from the earliest days of ancient Greece due to the presence there of the unique oracle. Originally part of the earth mother cult of Gaea and her serpent child Python, hence the name Pythia of the oracle Sybilla, the place later came to be dedicated to Apollo. The ancient Greeks believed Delphi to be the middle point of the world, and to demonstrate this, a stone called the Omphalos, the navel of the world, was erected there. Sensitives can still feel a strong energy emanating from this stone, which is perhaps much older than Greek civilization. An amphitheater and a temple to Apollo still exist at Delphi, though only the foundations and some steps and columns are preserved. There is evidence of medical treatment at this place, too.

The island of Cos, the world-famous sanctuary of Asclepius, was the first medical school in Greece and also a health resort that became famous for the work of Hypocrates. In about 333 BC the island was occupied by Alexander the Great, probably because of its medical importance. Later, Cos passed under the control of the Egyptian Ptolemies, who used its schools intensely. It was then annexed to the Roman province of Asia but in AD 53 was declared a free city, again because of its medical importance. The sacred buildings of Cos are remarkably intact, save for the loss of columns.

At Titane, west of Corinth, there are some of the oldest traces of the cult of Hygeia, the goddess of healing. She was worshipped together with Asclepius, initially as his daughter and later as his wife. The cult reached Rome from Epidaurus as early as 293 BC and became known as Salus. Hygeia and Asclepius gradually became protecting deities.

Finally, there are several important sites of Greek healing centers that are now in Turkey: Priene, Miletus, Aphrodisias, Side, Pergamon, and Didyma. The most impressive is the temple of Apollo at Didyma, which has never been robbed of its stones. One day, the huge fallen columns could be erected again. The oracle's cave and healing place are nearly intact.

Knowledge of what happened at the healing places of Greece is still available. In the asclepia, special rites were observed: After purification preparation, baths, fasting, and sacrifices, the patient would spend the night in the god's precinct or temple, a process known as "sleeping in" (*enkoimesis* in Greek, *incubatius incubatus* in Latin). The fashion of incubation (dream therapy) seems not to have really caught on until the fourth century, when the great healing centers such as Cos and Epidauros were established. Thus, we have rational and thaumaturgic medicine developing together through the Hellenistic period. During the night, as the patient slept, Asclepius would appear to him or her in a dream and give advice. In the morning, the priests would interpret the dream and explain the god's precepts. Patients would thank Asclepius by tossing gold into the sacred fountain and by hanging ex-votos on the walls of the temple.

It is said that groups of pilgrims and patients approached the healing place along the road toward the reception, where priests and priestesses awaited them. The hopeless infirm cases were taken to buildings of rest nearby, where immediate treatment and comfort were given. Few, if any, were turned away, though if anyone wasn't accepted, he or she was given money and food. The main party was asked to divide into three groups: men, women, and women with children. The groups were taken to a series of buildings intended for each. Here they washed, were fed, and rested for some time. Teachers then explained at length the process of healing and how the patients themselves could help. Each patient was told to wait until the time in sleep when he or she was gifted by a direct vision of the healing god Asclepius.

At the medical school at Smyrna there are several such buildings still in existence. Visitors can see a number of tubular clay pipes about six inches in diameter that pierce each roof in many places so that aromatic, medicinal, and opium fumes could be forced into the rooms of the sleepers during the night. After a number of days of diagnosis, teaching, and simple treatment, each patient was taken in turn and alone to a small area and then surrounded by priests. Within each area there was an empty rectangular, marble-lined tank or pool. The patient entered by a rear stairway and descended and was then required to kneel and join the priests in lengthy prayers to Asclepius. After this, all awaited a sign that the patient was to be cured, if he was to be so blessed. Springwater then flowed into the pool. A small pool like this can still be seen at the ancient medical school at Smyrna, and it can be seen how a priest controlled the water flow into the pool.

Certainly, this modest healing routine would have been used only in cases requiring simple treatment. We have no real knowledge of the methods used in complex cases. It seems probable that in those times already widespread was the belief in mental self-healing powers and their value to recovery. I have seen such treatment emphasis in India, Nepal, Tibet, and even some places in Europe, where remarkable diagnostic skills still seem to exist.

Physicians in modern Western societies are generally seen as well educated in anatomy and physiology. They might be seen as analogous to craftsmen who use specific tools to fix physical problems. It is important to recognize, however, that this is a feature not of medicine in general, but only of medicine as practiced in modern society. Hellenistic Egyptian medicine from the second century BC to the second century AD, for example, differed in that the current image of the body is mechanistic in nature. Today, when illness occurs, the patient knows that something is wrong and seeks a physical explanation. A physician is expected to fix the physical problem, much in the way that a plumber is expected to fix a leaking pipe.

In ancient Egypt, more so before the spread of Greek and Roman medicine but even as late as the time of the Therapeutae, the body was seen as a sacred vessel that was intimately tied to the soul. Any imbalance in one would be reflected by an imbalance in the other. When physicians approached a disease, therefore, their treatment of the body was dependent on their belief of its relation to the soul; the two had a relationship of eternal interdependence. Medicine was not viewed in strictly physical terms, but instead was intimately connected with magic and religion. Those who were functioning as physicians often invoked the power of the gods to cure a patient. Because of this, one individual often combined the functions of priest, physician, magician, interpreter of dreams, and even, at times, kingship.

Under the rule of Ptolemy, Alexandria became the chief school of anatomy and medicine in the world. The Ptolemaic rulers gave lavish financial support to the library and museum there, which consequently attracted researchers in fields such as philosophy, mathematics, history, and poetry as well as medicine. Medical research in the Alexandrian museum became world renowned, with two of its most influential investigators being Herophilus of Chalcedon (circa 280 BC) and Erasistratus of Iulis (circa 250 BC). Most of our knowledge of these two scientists of antiquity is derived from later commentators such as Celsus and Galen in the Roman period.

Erasistratus and Herophilus gained particular favor with Ptolemy and purportedly were even granted the right to practice vivisection on criminals who had been given a death sentence. Through these elaborate anatomical studies, the two learned a great deal, and while some of their theories regarding movement of blood and digestive processes and the like were later proved wrong, they did describe in great detail organs that had been largely ignored in previous epochs. Erasistratus recognized that veins, arteries, and nerves traveled through all bodily tissues. Herophilus described the various features of the brain and especially the eyes. The direct experience of these men led to great improvements in medical understanding.

Herophilus's most important contribution to clinical medicine was his theory of the diagnostic value of the pulse, of which he developed a far-reaching doctrine. According to Herophilus, the essential phenomenon in the pulse, as in music, is rhythm. To understand the pulse, then, we must study the theory of music. Erasistratus, Herophilus's rival at Alexandria, also made remarkable progress in anatomy. He described the brain more accurately than Herophilos, distinguishing the cerebrum from the cerebellum and determining that the brain was the originating point for all nerves. He distinguished sensory nerves from motor nerves and was the first to dispel the notion that nerves are hollow and filled with *pneuma* (air), proving instead that they are solid and consist of a kind of spinal marrow. Further, in his account of the heart and its function, he distinguished between pulmonary and systemic circulation.

It is interesting to note that although the popular practice of mummification offered much opportunity to Egyptian physicians to explore the inner world of the body, this opportunity was not utilized. The widely held view of the body as a sacred vessel precluded any inquiry into internal physical states. In light of this, it is notable that the first example of human dissection was, in fact, in Egypt in the third century BC. In Alexandria, the dissection of corpses became a regular practice, whereas before it had been condemned and outlawed on religious principle. The changed attitude to dissection among learned men was due to the philosophical teachings of Aristotle. Plato had taught that the soul was an independent and immortal being that, during earthly life, carried the body as a mere envelope and instrument to be discarded at death. Aristotle, Plato's pupil, declared that the soul, though not separable and immortal, constituted a higher value than the whole organism, implying that after death there remained no more than a physical frame, without feelings or rights. From this position, it was no great leap to claim that the dead body could justly be used for dissection and anatomical study. In the centuries following the lives of these two researchers, in the Hellenistic period, the greatest medical discoveries of antiquity were made in Alexandria.

JESUS IN EGYPT

We can recall that the Akashic record of the life of Jesus claimed that "Jesus was in Egypt as a child for eleven and a half years, until about age twelve, in a settlement of Essenes, known there by their Greek name Therapeutae. The place seems almost certainly to have been Scetis (Wadi Natrun)." I am convinced of the importance of the Scetis area both in the life of Jesus and in Mark's itinerant preaching in Egypt, which enlightened so many Alexandrians to Essene Judeo-Christianity, but I must point out that this thinking remains unproved by archaeology at this time. It is alleged in The Martyrdom of Apa Kradjôn that during Diocletian's persecution, some Christians fled to "the desert of Shiêt" (Scetis), but the only other reference earlier than the fourth century is the bare allusion to the place and district in the geographical work of Ptolemy.

Still, there is a wonderful piece of philological research by the scholar Shlomo Pines (1908–1990) that unwittingly provides evidence for this version of Jesus' youth. Pines was studying a piece of Muslim anti-Christian polemic by a well-known Mu'tazilite theologian of the ninth century, 'Abd al-Jabbar. After noticing in folio after folio the sort of language that a Muslim simply would never have used, he eventually realized that al-Jabbar had adapted a previous text (also an attack on Christians, so it served his purpose) written by a Jewish-Christian author.*

The original text, in Pines's view, was probably produced by a member of the Elkasai Jewish Christian sect. Once separated from the interpolations of the Muslim author, it is a truly exciting source for quotations from apocryphal gospels and for all manner of attacks on Paul and the divinity of Jesus. The text also gives, from the Jewish-Christian point of view, an outline of the events leading to the flight of the original Christian community from Jerusalem and the abandonment and betrayal of what its author regards as true Christianity and its replacement by Greek notions and ways. This accusation of Jesus' betrayal leveled at those followers who had accepted Roman lures makes the text extremely credible, at least in my view, so you can imagine my amazement when I found Pines writing: "In the expression *sa`ala li-Maryam* (94b), the use of the preposition *li* is modeled upon the Syriac. This expression occurs in an account of the childhood of Jesus, which differs

---

*Reported in "The Jewish Christians of the Early Centuries of Christianity according to a New Source," *Proceedings of the Israel Academy of Sciences and Humanities* 2, no. 13, Jerusalem, 1966.

from those of the canonical gospels. For instance, Jesus, his mother, and Joseph are said to have stayed in Egypt for twelve years."

As mentioned, there is little in the gospels on the early years of the life of Jesus. One of the first events is the flight to Egypt to escape Herod's wrath—the story of the slaughter of the innocents. Although history left no record of the murder, which wiped out a generation of male descendants of David in Bethlehem, it was certainly within the character of Herod the Great to have pronounced such an edict. It is of great interest to us that the family of Joseph fled to Egypt, where there existed the large community of Essenes called Therapeutae. This is the only time the gospel records take Jesus out of Palestine.

Evidence has arisen in the last couple of centuries to support the idea that Jesus traveled and studied the world's religions. In the 1880s, the Russian explorer Nicolas Notovitch uncovered a scroll in Tibet pertaining to the life of Issa, whom the Tibetans considered to be an incarnation of the divine Buddha, who was born in Palestine and later traveled to India. Notovitch discovered this to be a story of the early life of Jesus. He made a copy to bring to the world, but it was not received with open arms.

In the controversial Gospel of the Holy Twelve, the training of Jesus is described as follows:

And Jesus, after he had finished his study of the Law, went down again into Egypt that he might learn the wisdom of the Egyptians, even as Moses did. Going into the desert, he meditated and fasted and prayed, and obtained the power of the Holy Name, by which he wrought many miracles. And for seven years he conversed with God face to face, and he learned the language of birds and of beasts, and the healing power of trees, and of herbs, and of flowers, and the hidden secrets of precious stones, and he learned the motions of the Sun and Moon and Stars, and the powers of letters, and the mysteries of the Square and the Circle and the Transmutation of things, and of forms, and of numbers, and of signs.

This sounds like a well-rounded Essene education!

Other legends have Jesus traveling all over the Mediterranean in the company of his uncle, Joseph of Arimathea, who was a wealthy tin merchant with holdings throughout the known world. The debate about the travels of Jesus cannot be solved conclusively with the information available to us at present—but of course it is not necessary for Jesus to have traveled the world. The Essenes could have provided him with any necessary training. I suspect that by the beginning of the first century, the Essenes of Palestine had evolved enough to know that the basis of the Truth transcends cultures and religions. Whether they had adopted Zoroastrian and Pythagorean elements, as Martin Larson suggests, or Zoroaster and Pythagoras drew on the tablets of Enoch, as suggested by Richard Laurence, a translator of the Book of Enoch, the result is the same: Over the period from 200 BC to AD 70, the Essenes had become a storehouse of sacred learning. We can consider it a fact that they had advanced knowledge of healing, agriculture, astrology, philosophy, and spirituality. They had grown over the centuries, absorbing the Truth wherever they found it as well as developing the mysteries passed down to them for generations.

In the final analysis, it would seem that the bulk of Jesus' learning came from the Essenes.

THE IMPORTANCE OF SCETIS

So these were the men who saved Jesus' life in the tomb after he was taken down from the cross. They probably came from Qumran, unless, as Schonfield believed, the plan to stage a death-and-resurrection Messiah play was so important and intentional that doctors were summoned from Jesus' childhood home (perhaps his first teacher among them). If so, they came from the Egyptian community that had hosted Joseph, Mary, and the infant Jesus decades earlier. We might ask: If Jesus' brief mission—three years of preaching and healing, as the gospels would have it—had such incredibly far-reaching notoriety, with accounts and witnesses filling the Mediterranean world in a couple of generations, how could it be that there is no historical trace of the place where he spent his youth—wherever it may have been—a place where he must have met and made friends with dozens of people?

I have no doubts where that place was. They stayed in Scetis, in the Wadi Natrun valley, in the desert, but not thirty miles from Alexandria. Coptic history claims the monasteries at Scetis were founded in AD 330 by the Egyptian Macarius, but recent evidence seems to show the place was inhabited long before, at a time when, according to early writings, there was little or no sand and there was good water, possibly a small lake. Certainly, the site was sufficiently remote from populated areas to ensure that the mystic healing of the Therapeutae could be carried out in seclusion.

From early documents, a few things are known of the history of the four monasteries there that survived repeated destruction and of those that did not. It seems that nearby Alexandria was not too tightly controlled by the Romans and retained much of its Greek character. In fact, it was a center of intense religious and philosophical debate among Greek, Roman, Jewish, Mithraic, dualist, Zoroastrian, and even Indian thinking. Discussion reached high levels of intellect and quality, so it is no surprise that much of the best early Christian theology derived from the Greek thinking of Alexandrian leaders such as Athanasius, Origen, and Clement.

It is almost certain that Scetis retained its Christian importance due to the Coptic belief that this was the place where Jesus spent his early years. For this reason, the earliest monks chose the area, so intimately tied to Christian origins, and referred to it in their writings as the Street of the Angels. We also know that the earliest monks there made baskets to exchange for food given by pilgrims.

If a friendly group of Essenes had already been there, Mary and Joseph could have chosen Scetis for the main part of their Egyptian stay of possibly up to twelve years. Existing writings dating back to the first monasteries indicate that the earlier history of Scetis may have been recorded by the monks who lived there. If so, their work may well be traced in the archaeological digs expected to take place in the next few years.

Hugh Evelyn-White, the distinguished archaeological architect, produced in full detail a remarkable study of the monasteries of the Wadi Natrun. His work was carried out on behalf of the Metropolitan Musem of Art in New York, and the museum kindly offered to us (the Wadi Natrun excavation team) full access to his notes. He records that according to the Arab Synaxarium, we know that Scetis was of importance to the Holy Family during their sojourn in Egypt because the Virgin gave her blessing to Scetis. Under the Coptic date Bashans 24, it is stated that the wanderers, after leaving Samannoud and Bikha Iyesus, "came to the River of the West"—that is, the Rosetta branch of the Nile Delta—and beheld Gebel en Natrûn (synonymous with the Desert of Scetis). As Zacharias, an eighth-century bishop of Sakhâ, writes in *On the Flight into Egypt:*

The Lord blessed its four corners and said: "In this Gebel there shall be a monastery and church, populous with monks and all that desire to serve the Lord, and there shall be there a people pleasing unto me, and there shall come men from all distances to be blessed there: there I will not suffer any beasts to dwell; but it shall be blessed, and a place for my holiness forever; and it shall be called Wadi Habib or Balance of Hearts."

9

THE HOLY FAMILY IN EGYPT: THE STORY OF THE COPTS

When Israel was a child, then I loved him and
called my son out of Egypt.

This line (Hosea 11:1) refers to the people of Israel—the prophet is clearly speaking of the Exodus—but it has often been interpreted by Christian exegetes as a prediction of the journey of the Holy Family to Egypt and of their return to Palestine when the angel announced to Joseph that Herod was dead and the child Jesus was no longer in danger. The traditional story that follows is accepted by the Copts, although historians would point out that there is no real documentary proof for any of it. Shrines exist today at all of the main sites mentioned in the account, and I have followed this entire route myself.

The Holy Family journeyed on the traditional coastal route from Bethlehem to Gaza and thence to El-Zaraniq (also known as Floussiat), some twenty-three miles west of El-Arish (see plate 8). They continued westward along the northern Sinai until they reached Farma (ancient Pelusium, the border town of Egypt), midway between El-Arish and present-day Port Said. From there they went to Tel Basta, or Basta, close to Zagazig (sixty-two miles northeast of Cairo). Here the baby Jesus prompted a water spring to well up from the ground. They reached the nearby village of Mostorod, or Al-Mahamma, which means "bathing place" because the Virgin Mary bathed the child there and washed his clothes. From Mostorod they made their way to Belbeis (ancient Philippos), about thirty-four miles from Cairo.

They then traveled in a northwesterly direction to Meniet Samannoud (also Meniet Genah) and crossed the Nile to Samannoud (or Jemnoty) in the delta, and toward the northwest to Sakha in the lake district of Burullus. The Coptic name Pekha Issous means "foot of Jesus," for the holy child's footprint was marked here on a rock. From Sakha they crossed to the west bank of the Nile to the Western Desert and Wadi Natrun, which was then called Al Asqeet or Scetis. This is recorded in the documentation of a vision of Patriarch Theophilus (housed in the monastery of Al-Moharraq) and attested to by Coptic tradition and liturgy. In the first decades of Christianity, Wadi Natrun became the site of an anchorite settlement. Later, many monasteries were established there in spiritual commemoration of the Holy Family's passage to the valley, and four remain today.

The family stayed here for quite some time and later went on to Al Matariyah and Ein Shams (ancient Heliopolis, the old city of On) on the eastern bank of the Nile. At the time, the large Jewish community living in Ein Shams had already erected a temple, the synagogue of Unias. To this day, a tree stands there called Mary's Tree. Moving northward, the family rested for a while in Zeitoun, then walked on through what are now crowded quarters of Cairo. Their path is still marked with old Coptic churches all through what would become, nine centuries later, the great city of Cairo.

They eventually came to Babylon, a Roman fortress still visible today south of Cairo. Their cave there forms part of the very early church of St. Sergius. From Babylon they moved to Maadi, which, in pharaonic times, was an outlying district of Memphis, today another suburb of Cairo. Oral and written tradition says that after four days, due to danger at Babylon, the family left by boat from Maadi to Bahnasa, in Upper Egypt. This event is in fact recorded on a recently discovered papyrus.

Maadi is marked by the historic church of Al-Adaweya—that is, "the Virgin's church of the ferry." (Maadi derives from the Arabic word for "crossing point.") The boat docked at Al-Garnous, from whence the family went to Abai Issous, the "home of Jesus" (today Sandafa), east of Al-Bahnasa.

In their seemingly interminable trek, they crossed to the east bank to Gebel El-Tair, or Gabal El-Kaf (Palm Mountain), near Samalout. It is interesting to note that Queen Helena, mother of Constantine, built a church here about AD 320, which tells us that the tradition of the family's travels there was already well established at that time. Crossing the Nile to its west bank again, they traveled southward to El Ashmunein, or Hermopolis Magna. The ruins of this town may still be seen today, including the remains of a large Christian basilica with many columns. From here they went to Mallawi and Phyls, where the monastery of Dyrout (Dairout Al-Sharif or, in Greek, Philes), about twelve miles south of Ashmunein, marks their presence to this day. Tradition again holds that the family was harassed at Qussia (now Qusqam), so they went on to Meir, or Meira, where they found a warm welcome.

Finally, they set out for the nearby mountain Gabal Qussqam, 147 miles south of Cairo, where the famous monastery of Al-Moharraq was built in the fourth century. The original Church of the Virgin is unchanged. St. Pachomius (AD 290–346), most famous for his monastery at Nag Hammadi (where excavations have revealed important early Christian documents now known as the gnostic gospels), first built the monastery that surrounds the original church. A nearby castle was then built in AD 491 by Emperor Xenon to protect the monastery from the Bedouins, for his daughter Illaria was a nun in the convent.

Al-Moharraq, a very large monastery, interestingly records its claim to have sent monks to the early Church in Ireland. (In the coming chapters we shall investigate further the links between Egypt and the so-called Celtic Church.) In the nearby Church of the Virgin the altar stands in the very cave where the Holy Family lived for six months. There still exists there an important document written by the twenty-third patriarch, Theophilus (AD 346–412), in which he describes his vision of Mary, who related to him the story of her family's journey. In corroboration of this document, in AD 1441 the important Muslim historian Al-Makrisi wrote that the Christians' belief about the area was fully justified.

All historical and religious sources declare that this monastery was the last place in Upper Egypt reached by the Holy Family and that it was here that in a dream the angel told Joseph of Herod's death, saying that he should take the Holy Family back to Judaea at once.

For this reconstruction of the journey I am indebted to Dr. Raouf Habib for allowing me to draw upon his writings on behalf of the Coptic authorities. The Egyptian government published this story in every language for every visitor in the year 2000 to mark the millennium. I have related the Coptic tradition of the Holy Family's time in Egypt because I have come to the conclusion that Jesus not only was raised among the Therapeutae at Wadi Natrun, but also went back there after his alleged resurrection, more or less at the time of what the Catholic version of events calls his ascension to his father in heaven. After all, Egypt was where all Jewish "troublemakers" fled when the Romans got uncomfortably close to arresting them. It was where a condemned and fugitive leader would seek refuge even if he didn't have previous connections to the place, as Jesus had.

We shall discuss the hypothetical—but highly plausible—scenario of Jesus' flight to France aboard one of the many ships leaving Alexandria, but first let us examine both the figure of St. Mark the Evangelist, founder of the Coptic Orthodox Church, and the early history of the Coptic Church itself. Apart from being a truly wonderful story, it is necessary background to help readers properly judge the claim I made at the end of chapter 4 regarding Jewish-Christian and Gentile gnostics moving to France in the footsteps of their Master.

THE ORIGINS OF CHRISTIANITY IN EGYPT

For some years now I have carried out extensive historical research on the development of Christianity in Egypt and on the early monasteries founded by the Coptic Church in Egypt's Western Desert. The term *copt* is an Arab corruption of the way Egyptians referred to themselves after Greek became the official language under Ptolemy I Soter (367–282 BC). Centuries earlier, *aegyptos* had hardened in the Greek mouth into *kiptos*. Later, the Greek-speaking population decided they wanted to phoneticize their indigenous Egyptian language, which at that time was written in demotic. This new language was Coptic, and it was quite well established long before the arrival of Christianity.

St. Mark the Evangelist introduced Christianity into Egypt, arriving in the country in about AD 40. He was martyred in Alexandria and was followed by his first convert, Annianus, in about AD 65. Mark's achievement in spreading the knowledge of Jesus in Egypt was nothing short of miraculous, and the speed with which his teaching resulted in the birth of new Christian communities is all the more remarkable when we consider the entrenchment there of other established religions. It is clear that his mission concentrated upon the region of Alexandria. He may well have reached Scetis from there, but there is no proof of this.

In Alexandria, St. Mark's relics were venerated up to and beyond the Muslim conquest. Two hundred years later, in about AD 825, they were stolen by two Venetian pilgrims (St. Mark having already become their patron saint) and were taken to the growing town in the lagoon that was not yet called Venice, but rather Rialto. The remains later became the most precious relic in the saint's basilica there, built in the twelfth century. The Copts have naturally always wanted the body of their founding father returned to them, but so far only the head was given by the Vatican to the Coptic cathedral in central Cairo. (This gesture was made by Pope Paul VI in 1968, but his promise to give back the rest of the body has so far not been kept.)

Following is a brief hagiography of St. Mark, following the Catholic tradition.

St. Mark the Evangelist, from the tribe of Levi, was baptized by St. Peter and instructed by him in the Christian faith, after which he followed Peter to Rome and preached the gospel with him there. The faithful asked St. Mark to write the life of our Lord according to the accounts of St. Peter, which the Evangelist did. After examining Mark's work, Peter testified that it was exact and approved it to be read by all the faithful. Later, St. Peter sent St. Mark to Alexandria, where he was the first to preach the word of God. St. Peter consecrated him bishop of Alexandria, and, according to Simon, an old Jew who witnessed the labors of Mark in that city, an enormous multitude converted there as a consequence of the apostolate of St. Mark. St. Peter Damian wrote that God gave St. Mark a special grace by which all the people he converted in Alexandria took up monastic customs. He inspired them to this by his miracles and the example of his virtues.

Nevertheless, in this city the zeal of St. Mark attracted the hatred of the pagan priests. On Easter day in AD 65, they seized him while he was saying Mass and tied a rope around his neck. Then they dragged him through the city like an animal to slaughter. His body was lacerated by the rough, rocky ground and his blood stained the roads. In the prison where they threw him, he was consoled by an angel, after which the Lord himself visited him and told him: "Peace be with you, Mark, my disciple and my evangelist. Fear nothing because I am near you."

The next day, the pagan priests again placed a rope around Mark's neck and dragged him through the streets of the city, but this time his strength gave out and he died, saying: "Into thy hands I commend my spirit." The air in Alexandria suddenly became turbulent and lightning and thunder broke through the sky. His assailants, who had planned to burn his body, instead fled. Thus Mark's disciples were able to collect and piously bury his remains.

As to the veracity of all points in this story, very few scholars today believe that St. Peter was ever in Rome. What actually happened was that Roman bishops in the second century needed to prove that the bishop of Rome had greater authority than that of, say, Antioch or Caesarea or Alexandria, so they fabricated what is known as the apostolic line— that is, they claimed that their church had been founded by Peter and Paul, who, they said, had both been martyred in Rome. This gave them unquestionable authority over the leaders of other Christian communities, for Jesus had entrusted the care of all believers to Peter, the Rock. Biblical scholars give rather more credit to the long diatribe between Paul and Peter on the conversion of Gentiles (and their need to be circumcised before they could join the church) and are, on the whole, skeptical of the claim (in Luke's Acts) that Peter eventually relented to the point of joining Paul on his journey to the capital of the Roman Empire.

We also know from textual analyses that Mark's was very likely the earliest of the four canonical gospels, so it stands to reason that official Church history should seek to give it maximum authority by having it endorsed by no less a figure than St. Peter. It is fairly clear, then, that both the story of Mark writing his gospel in Rome and the circumstances of his arrival in Egypt are the result of theological and political necessities rather than realistic accounts.

On the other hand, that people flocked to the desert monasteries upon hearing him preach the good news is, in my opinion, closer to the truth, however hard it is to explain. Given that Jesus may have been an Essene and a gnostic teacher, the first explanation that springs to mind is the high receptivity in Alexandria to a mixture of gnostic ideas and Egyptian religion. Yes, the rapid spread of Christianity was linked to the many elements the new faith had in common with the language of ancient Egyptians, who were therefore ready to embrace the new Christian creed. More and more historians and biblical scholars are coming around to the view that the parallels between Isis and Mary, Horus and Jesus, Jesus' resurrection and the pharaoh's eternal life, and many other similarities are more than mere coincidences. After all, the formula of salvation through water baptism and faith in the resurrected god Osiris was present in the popular cult of Serapis in the centuries immediately preceding the Christian era.

From the monotheism of Akhenaten, a long process of philosophical and theological evolution had taken place. After the conquest of Egypt by Alexander the Great, the appeal of immortality through this simple faith became dominant in Egypt. It was actively exported, too, beginning with Ptolemy I Soter, and was readily adopted throughout the Greek world. By the early times of Roman rule in Egypt, the result of this development had materialized as the cult of Serapis more than a century before being identified as gnostic Christianity. Its vision made it possible for ordinary people to hope for eternal spiritual life without the need for mummification. All they had to do, in this final stage as preached by St. Mark, was to confess to the resurrection of Jesus and go through a ritual that still included baptism by water.

The cult of Serapis was quite prevalent during Roman times in the first century BC, but began to lose official favor in Rome proper beginning with the demise of Mark Antony and Cleopatra. (Fifty years later, Caligula's love affair with Egyptian religion would cost the young emperor his life.) It was actually a logical refinement on the part of St. Paul to substitute faith in a resurrected Jesus for faith in the resurrected Osiris in the Serapis cult. Most historians will confirm that in writings of the late first century, Egypt, Christianity, and the Serapis religion were in fact considered nearly equivalent.

In his study *Christianity: An Ancient Egyptian Religion,* the Egyptian scholar Ahmed Osman contends that though the Romans fabricated their own version of Christianity, the roots of Christian belief spring not from Judaea, but from Egypt. He suggests that the major tenets of Christian belief—the belief in one God, the Trinity, the hierarchy of heaven, life after death, the Virgin Birth—are all Egyptian in origin. With the help of modern archaeological findings, Osman shows that Christianity survived as an Egyptian mystery cult until the fourth century, when the Romans embarked on a mission of suppression and persecution. In AD 391, the Roman-appointed bishop Theophilus led a mob into the Serapeum quarter of Alexandria and burned the Alexandrian library, destroying all records of the true Egyptian roots of Christianity. The Romans' version of Christianity, manufactured to maintain political power, claimed that Christianity originated in Judaea, but in his book Osman restores Egypt to its rightful place in the history of the new belief system.

Here, then, is one fairly obvious explanation of St. Mark's rapid success in Alexandria. It is, however, an explanation that would hold for the intellectuals, for the city dwellers familiar with philosophy and amenable to sophisticated syncretism. But what about the ordinary Egyptian, the man in the street, as we say today? For him, there is another explanation.

First-century Alexandria was famous not only for its culture, wealth, and political weight, but also for the pomp and luxury of its inhabitants. Its fabulous richness made it shine before the world. Such a city should have been the most difficult place for St. Mark to win conversions. We can easily imagine the contrast between this dignified, chaste, and austere man and the extravagant way of life of the local social elite. Soon after he arrived, however, many people in Alexandria changed their lives and took up monastic habits. Why?

We should remember that after the Romans conquered countries around the Mediterranean, people everywhere adopted Roman customs (much as today they read, eat, wear, and watch all things American). The Roman elite held evening banquets in palaces with garden courtyards. As the breeze came in from the sea, the doors of the palaces were opened and the parties lasted all night and ended at dawn. At these bacchanals, people reclined and ate and drank while music, poetry, songs, sometimes even gladiator fights were performed for their amusement.

Slaves were numerous, for almost every free man of the elite set had more than one slave. These men and women often were not treated as human beings. Considered the objects of their owners, they had no right to marry. The child of a slave belonged to its parents' owner like a fruit belongs to the owner of the tree. Even if an owner killed a slave, it was not considered a crime.

This was the Alexandria to which St. Mark came to preach. We can imagine him walking through its streets: A Jew, with his beard and stately bearing, approaches a group of people, finds them open to him, and begins to preach. Some of the wayfarers laugh at him, others are indifferent, but one here, another there, joins the small group listening to him. In a short time he has a circle of people around him. He finishes, bids farewell to his audience, and goes off to a modest inn. People start to talk about what they heard, about Jesus and his cross, about the urgent need to embrace austerity, chastity, and sanctity. Perhaps for the first time, people contemplate a completely different life. Here a wife abandoned by her husband, there a young man whose eyes begin to open to the immorality of his society, farther along a drunk who stops to see what's going on. St. Mark's words offer a new perspective on eternal life; he speaks of a spirit that is not material, of the resurrection of the body, of heaven and eternal happiness, and also of hell. He explains there is a God who is good and just, who is wisdom itself, and to whom we should pray and ask for help. In men accustomed to life in Alexandria, these words spark contradictory reactions. Some feel an irresistible attraction, others a complete repulsion.

It was precisely because his rejection of current values was so total that Mark had such an impact, and probably more so on younger Egyptians, as is always the case. We can compare the revolutionary effect of his preaching to the way American consumer culture is being challenged in our own day by a confused return to religious values. Thus we can see how the words of St. Mark could have converted many people in a short time and even convince them to give up their hedonistic lifestyle for a harsh, contemplative one. By grace or circumstances, it happened. Arab historians claim that when the Muslim armies invaded the area in about AD 640 under the command of Amr ibn al As, who had been made a general by Muhammad himself, no fewer than forty thousand monks greeted them, happy to be rid of the Byzantine emperor, to whom they were all heretics. If correct, this is an astonishing figure, representing almost one in every twenty Egyptians living there at the time.

Remoteness and solitude were the main objectives of these numerous monks. Scetis, Kellia, Nitria, and some smaller enclaves became their main areas of settlement. What took them to these locations? As we have seen, there are indications that the Holy Family spent not one but twelve years in Egypt, especially in Scetis, before returning to Judaea. Early Christians would have known this and it would have quickly become clear that Scetis would remain a holy site for all time.

Sometimes it seems that the mysticism of the ancient Egyptians has been inherited by their descendants, the Coptic people of Egypt, among whom sensitivity and clairvoyance are almost a rule. They are easily distinguished from the Arab population of Egypt in both outward appearance and behavior. After staying in Egypt for some time, a visitor is usually able to recognize them at once. In addition, Western people with mystic inclination are somehow drawn to Egypt, as in the case of my late friend Omm Sety, a woman of English origin who devoted her life to Egypt and its ancient heritage.

Because Egypt has been a Muslim country for so long, most people do not realize that it was once a cornerstone of Christianity. Many even seem unaware that Christianity never died out in Egypt. Nearly six million Egyptians consider themselves the true descendants of the ancient Egyptians, and they owe spiritual allegiance to their own pope, the 117th successor of St. Mark, who today is His Holiness Pope Shenoudah III. The Coptic splendid and lengthy title of the Coptic pope speaks to the history of this faith: the most Holy Pope and Patriarch of the Great City of Alexandria, all the lands of Egypt, Jerusalem the Holy City, of Nubia, Abyssinia and Pentapolis and all of the teachings of St. Mark, of whom he is the successor.

To understand what went wrong for the Coptic Church after the fourth century, it is important to understand that Egypt was ruled from Constantinople by a Greek minority. This was nothing new in itself, for it followed occupation by the Greeks from the time of Alexander. Egyptians have always had to put up with foreign masters, and Alexandria became the center of Greek influence in Egypt. Not many people are aware that practically all of the ancient Egyptians became Christian in the first two centuries of the millennium—the Arabs now in Egypt arrived six centuries later and found an entirely Christian country. The Copts are the true descendants of the Egyptian people from before the Arab invasion, all of who remained Christian until gradually forced into Islam.

But for nearly two centuries before the Arab invasion—that is, from the Council of Chalcedon in AD 451—these Coptic Christians had been declared heretics because of their Monophysite beliefs. Monophysism (meaning, in Greek, "one nature") holds that Christ was not at all human but entirely divine and that his earthly life was therefore only an apparition. The Council of Chalcedon had instead decided that Christ had two natures, both human and divine, and from that moment the national church controlled by the Copts separated from the rest of Christianity and went its own way. The native population of Egypt believed in Monophysism if only because it had been condemned by the Byzantine emperor, whom they hated.

When the Monophysite patriarch of Alexandria was deposed as a heretic, Egypt descended into riot and bloodshed that lasted for two centuries as patriarchs representing the opposing Egyptian or Greek creeds succeeded each other. Riotous monks, mostly ignorant peasants, broke into Alexandria, burning and killing and then returning to the desert. In view of this difficult situation, the Egyptian Monophysite Church was content to break away from the rest of Christianity and follow its heresy. It was only natural that the Egyptians should no longer want to use Greek in their churches. The liturgy and gospels were thus translated into Coptic. For this reason the Egyptian Coptic Church today still celebrates the Korbân, or Mass, in the language of ancient Egypt, or rather in the debased form of this language that was spoken in the fifth century. Perhaps only 30 percent of the Coptic vocabulary is made up of Greek words, which came into it during the days of Greek domination. Unfortunately, this ancient language, still the language of the liturgy, is now dead. Today few priests understand it.

In the seventh century, the Arabs crashed into this situation. The Byzantine garrisons were driven out and Muslim invaders occupied the country, receiving no opposition from the Egyptians, who seemed to welcome the change of masters. At first the Arabs treated their Christian subjects almost with affection. The Copts were useful to the Arabs, just as Christian Greeks were useful to the Turks when they captured Constantinople eight centuries later. The Arabs had the good sense to let the Copts run the country for them, build their mosques, keep their books, and make their jewelry.

It was not long, however, before religion crept into the relationship. The situation gradually grew worse and Copts were severely persecuted and often tortured. With great resilience, they would recover for a period only to be destroyed again. Large numbers were forced to become Muslim, but many were ready to die for their faith. In fact, the Copts can be said to be forgotten Christians. Their persecution in Egypt continues today, and it is strange that so little has been written in English about them. They have been hidden away in their troubles since the Arab conquest, with their one object being to preserve their way of life and ancient customs. To this day they observe customs once common to the universal Church but that have died out everywhere except in Egypt. Theirs is a primitive Christianity. They have more martyrs than any other community in Christian history. Their whole energy for centuries has been spent on an intensive effort to survive, and the ancient churches of old Cairo (St. Sergius, St. Bacchus, Abu Sargaa) remain much as they were in early times.

Until recently, the Coptic pope had to be chosen from among the monks of the desert monasteries. This was a sound idea when the monasteries were centers of learning, but in recent centuries it has often resulted in the appointment of a reluctant recluse. In 1928, however, the rule changed and bishops have now become eligible for the position of patriarch. Other rules of election include that the head of the Coptic Church must be over fifty, must never have married, and must always have abstained from meat and fish. As for the pope's job, he ordains bishops and consecrates the holy chrism, or sacred oil. There are seventeen bishops in all, and they are celibate. Coptic priests, on the other hand, often drawn from the working class and sometimes uneducated, must be married before their ordination.

The Eucharistic bread of the Coptic Church, leavened bread that is about three inches in diameter and one inch thick, must be baked fresh on church premises on the morning of the Mass. Each church has its own bakehouse, where, on Sunday mornings, the bread is prepared from the finest flour and stamped with a cross. The Eucharist is called Korbân, meaning "sacrifice" or "offering" in Hebrew, and it is the word that Copts also use for the Mass itself. Normally, Coptic churches have three altars in line at the east end of the structure. As for other rituals and practices, the Coptic baptism is still total immersion, and it is Coptic practice to prepare bundles of the bones of their saints and martyrs sewn into leather bags. Most churches have several such bundles. No statues are allowed in the churches, but Copts revere icons. For the Coptic posture in prayer, it is customary to face east, standing upright with feet together, hands held outward with palms upward and elbows close to the body.

THE FOUR COPTIC MONASTERIES IN THE WADI NATRUN

There are four surviving Coptic monasteries in the Wadi Natrun: Bishoi, Suryan, Macarius, and Baramus, all built in the fourth century. Their history is a tale of persecution, attack, robbery, slaughter, and destruction by Arabs, Berbers, and desert tribes.

The first sack, in 407–408, led to the flight of John the Short (Anba Yehnis Colobos), followed by his death in Clysma in 409. A period of recovery lasted until the second sack, in 434. The Towers of Refuge, still a part of the monastery buildings, were built after this event. The third sack took place in 444 and the fourth in 570. The Heraclian persecution of 631–641 forced the monks of Scetis to seek refuge at Nahya. The fifth and final sack was in 817.

Bishoi Monastery

The monastery of St. Anba Bishoi is the largest of the four surviving monasteries in the Wadi Natrun. Legend has it that an angel instructed Anba Bishoi to separate from John the Short, who would not move from the place where he had planted the tree of obedience. Bishoi spent three years in a cave, possibly the one in Suryan Monastery, where many people, attracted by his spirituality and miracles, visited him and became his disciples. According to Butler and Evelyn-White, he built a church in AD 384. The existence of four churches in the Wadi Natrun is recorded in AD 385. Anba Bishoi and Al Suryan Monastery were built on a rock to avoid underground water. Bishoi soon became very big. The Muslim historian Al-Makrisi writes: "Bushai [Bishoi] is a great monastery for the Copts because Bushai [Anba Bishoi] was a great monk like Makarios and Yehnis the Short."

The area of the monastery is fenced in by a high wall erected in the ninth century. The only gate, still used today, is very low and narrow.

Since the fifth century, after Berbers repeatedly attacked the monasteries, keeps or *kasrs* (refuge towers) were built to provide safety for the monks. The kasr of Anba Bishoi is the largest and strongest. Its walls are six and a half feet thick and constructed of hard stone.

The building called the Old Castle was actually built in the twentieth century, for the purpose of receiving guests of the monastery. For some reason is was subsequently destroyed. During the removal of the ruins, the Well of Martyrs was discovered underneath. The present pope rebuilt the castle as a four-floor building with a minaret and a water tank. The historical Well of Martyrs dates from the days of Anba Bishoi himself. Legend has it that in it the Berbers washed their swords of the blood of the martyrs whom they had killed in the monasteries. It is now situated in a garden and is surrounded with fresh green plants.

There are several other churches in the Bishoi compound, a remarkable library, and a refectory. The monastery of Anba Bishoi is also the residence of the current leader of the Coptic Church, Pope Shenoudah III, who has taken great care to restore the old buildings and save them from decay. Because many visitors come to see the pope, a special complex to accommodate them has been built along an alley lined with high eucalyptus trees, which are home to many birds such as wild pigeons and the *hoopuh* depicted in old Egyptian papyruses. Here pilgrims enjoy an atmosphere of peace, harmony, and the friendly hospitality of the monks.

A group of semi-wild cats lives on the compound, feeding on mice and other rodents and the leftovers from the monastery kitchen. They are a kindly lot, some shy, others bold in approaching strangers who may have a friendly word or a cuddle for them. When I visited the monastery, I made friends with a little ginger cat who used to come to my quarters and accompany me to the dining room and back to my room.

The monks in the monastery are delightful, having a wonderful sincerity and an obvious fulfillment in their faith and way of life. They have a keen sense of humor as well, though their daily life is quite hard and sadly their time on earth is rather short. One day I was told by one of my monk friends that another monk well known to me was very ill and that it was no longer opportune to see him. "He is very old," my friend said. "He is thirty-eight." A man of forty years of age is considered by the monks to be "well over the hill of life." I used to answer their questions about my age with "Two hundred," which made them roar with laughter.

10

WADI NATRUN: THE DISCOVERY THAT NEVER WAS

About twenty years ago I decided to develop my knowledge of early Christian sites in Egypt because these tended to have been ignored by the leading archaeologists of the world due to the greater attraction of pharaonic sites in that country. At that time even the British Museum did not have a qualified academic Copticist. Since then, French, German, and Dutch archaeologists have carried out great work at Nag Hammadi, Abu Minah, and other Coptic sites in southern and northern Egypt, but I am sorry to say that until relatively recently, the remains of early Coptic churches in Egypt were regarded by some archaeologists as inconsequential or, worse, as so much rubbish to be cleared away as rapidly as possible.

I found it very rewarding to study this neglected part of Egyptian archaeology and the intriguing questions connected to it. We might ask, for instance, why Wadi Natrun was such an important place for early Christianity and monasticism. As we have seen, an early form of pre-Christian monasticism, the Therapeutae, lived nearby in the region of Alexandria and may well have lived there, too. The Copts have their own record of the flight of the Holy Family to Egypt and their stay in Scetis (Wadi Natrun). Could they have gone specifically to this place because brethren in spirit lived there? Could there be a bridge between ancient Egyptian mysticism and the great spiritual movement of the Therapeutae and Essene period, a link between Egypt and Judaism leading to gnosticism and early Christian thinking?

MY ARCHAEOLOGICAL EXPERIENCE IN WADI NATRUN

Before delving into these questions in later chapters, I must here briefly relate my experience in this crucial but neglected area of Egypt. For ten years, from 1984 to 1994, I took part in archaeological surface searches in the area of Wadi Natrun. I decided to search areas of the Western Desert a few miles south of the road between Cairo and A00lexandria and gradually move westward in the direction of the Libyan border.

Here shard finds (pottery fragments) became more and more frequent. I was able to examine the remarkable work of the American archaeological architect Evelyn-White, who produced superb architectural studies of the four early church monasteries still remaining in Wadi Natrun.

Some miles to the west of these monasteries I traced, just below the surface, more than one hundred mud-brick buildings. I later found out that these were Manshoubia—that is, fortified group dwellings of the early monks who, in the fourth and fifth centuries, were attacked and killed so frequently by Bedouins. Always, however, they returned to continue their worship. These, together with about eight much larger buildings, were carefully photographed and recorded. I later found many other mud-brick walls of buildings just below the surface of the desert sand. It seemed probable that in early Christian times, the sand had not yet encroached from the desert. I had to take photographs of these by lying down on the surface of the sand, and the results showed these outlines fairly clearly only at certain times of the day, when the light and shadow were favorable.

During my travels in the area, I visited three of the four early monasteries that had survived most of history's catastrophes, and was welcomed by the monks of Baramous, Suryan, and Bishoi. These men, notably Father Shadrach, now Coptic metropolitan bishop of Jerusalem, joined me in my search. We discussed at length the willful damage being done by the water drilling and bulldozers of those attempting to create their own settlement over this vital area. If nothing else, my survey work at Scetis secured for the monks government approval and protection—in perpetuity, it is hoped—of land so important to them.

In time, I found that the buildings now accepted to be the monastery of John the Short had never been entirely lost, although they were forgotten. At first no one would believe me, but Evelyn-White himself had noted that some "lost" monasteries were not in fact lost at all, though he never found time to make a thorough study. I also found that Prince Omar Tusson, about eighty to one hundred years before Evelyn-White, had recorded his discovery of four large buildings and had erected four concrete markers to prevent their destruction. In later years, these had been protected by a small number of marker signs erected by the Egyptian Antiqities Organization (EAO), although they did not pursue any work at that time. Eventually, all had been removed or destroyed.

I approached my archaeologist friend Professor Bastian Van Elderen, an American then teaching at Vrije University in Amsterdam. We had first met seven years earlier at Nag Hammadi in south Egypt, not far from Luxor. The next season we made a careful reexamination of all the areas near the monasteries and agreed to submit together an application to the EAO for an excavation permit. Pope Shenoudah III showed great interest in an early discussion with us at his Coptic cathedral in Cairo. In fact, he gave us a three-hour audience and later agreed to make accommodation and limited funds available for us at the Bishoi monastery. For some reason, our first application did not reach the correct level at the EAO, but our second attempt succeeded, giving us authority to make a full-scale surface survey (which did not include excavation).

Due to the first Gulf War, Cairo had become rather dangerous for Americans, although the English seemed to be accepted. I was therefore obliged to carry out the archaeological survey alone, with the help of only one Arab surveyor and his equipment. The monks helped us to take satisfactory photographs by bring out to the desert area some high ladders so that we could photograph our surface clearing work from above. It was Christmastime. To reach the excavation site, after a jeep had driven us most of the way, our party and some monks had to walk through desert sand. Each time we made the trip, we passed by a farm building guarded by a fiercely barking dog. No attempts to quiet him succeeded. Finally I shouted at him "Happy Christmas!" To everyone's amusement, he became silent at once. The dog is called Happy Christmas to this day.

The EAO permitted us to excavate one test trench within the site of what we believed to be the destroyed monastery of John the Short. Our friends Bishop Samuel of Suryan Monastery and Fathers Angelos and Sourial of Bishoi joined Van Elderen and me and we identified a section on the west side (but facing east) that we hoped would reveal itself as part of the main church. To our great surprise and pleasure, we found the side wall of the church itself in that area, and it consisting of well-preserved, solid stonework.

Delays occurred in obtaining approval, but we made a new application for further investigation. To my pleasure, Van Elderen established a close relationship with a rich American benefactor who had started a new institute for research and ancient document study in the United States. He kindly agreed to provide us with funds for a first season of work. This commenced under the codirectorship of Professor Van Elderen and myself. We were joined by a director of administration, who was an American with knowledge of ancient history (though not of archaeology).

The First Season of Work, 1994–95

Professor Van Elderen and I found the location of the church during survey work conducted in 1991 and 1992. Ten years after the original field research work, the EAO finally granted permission for excavation, in January 1995.

From the start, a heavy burden of six to ten feet of windblown sand and stone debris together with frequent wind and some heavy rain caused problems at the site. Shard and other dating proved difficult due to the continuous use of almost identical ribbed Byzantine pottery throughout the monastery period. Some shards of the Mameluk period were also found. The Tower of Refuge site was selected for my work with the help of Ingrid Riedel, and we expected it would follow the same white stone and burned brick construction of Suryan, Baramus, and Bishoi monastery towers, which still exist.

There are in fact three possible sites for the tower. Of these, the southeast corner was considered most probable. Few real floor levels could be established, although many occupation levels were traced with numerous intervals of site desertion for long periods. We excavated four sixteen-foot squares. No doors or entry points were found in the principal rooms throughout the entire depth of five meters. The monks seem to have existed under poor conditions. One area for water-storage pots was examined, but no well or latrines were found. Four of the sixteen-foot squares were left undisturbed for work in later years so that we could concentrate on probing center squares to a deeper level to trace the ground floor wall of the original construction. We succeeded in finding heavy white stone walling at the base, about sixteen feet down. We could go no farther, however, without proper timber shoring, ladders, and more workers, which Van Elderen could not secure for me.

There were indications that the original vaulted roofing below has survived. It became apparent that the original top floor had collapsed and disappeared, probably during the century that followed the plague and famine series of disasters of 1350. Most of the mud-brick walls that collapsed in the ensuing years fortunately fell inward, encapsulating the whole complex. Certainly there was no sign of disturbance or excavation of this complete mud seal. Unexpectedly, we found that all floors were built entirely of mud brick, with little or no stone reinforcement.

We found no precise proof that this location is in fact the main Tower of Refuge. If it is not, however, it is difficult to see why the monks would have created this series of dwelling places that had no real value as a refuge. We therefore believe that the original four-story tower was stone built and that all but the ground floor was destroyed and the stone removed after the sackings in 410–450. It is possible that this stone material was used to repair other monastery buildings nearby. After this, the reconstruction must have been entirely of mud brick, and building must have occurred without regard to the exact position of the original walls and layout. The new construction was built largely without even removing the windblown sand that had built up at frequent intervals when the site was deserted from time to time.

Following the early total destruction of the monastery, perhaps as early as AD 410 or soon after, the surviving monks may have decided, in view of limited manpower and resources, to build a new tower more capable of defense in the northeast corner of the outer wall surrounding the site.

Finds at the site included about a dozen ceramic pots; incense burners and lamps; two larger ceramic pots; a small, undamaged bronze Christian cross; and a stone-carved monk's visiting card believed to date from the tenth century. This card showed the visiting monk's monastery near Giza and had been carved into the flat face of a hand-sized stone. Sadly, the all-important date was not included—but maybe we shall find another. Substantial progress was made by Van Elderen in clearing the church during the first season. A variety of buttresses and external walls were found, together with a pedestal for a column. The extent of clearing required a major part of our resources.

The Second Season of Work: January–March 1996

To my great chagrin, I could not be present during the second season of work at the monasteries, but Van Elderen gave me this account of his accomplishments:

> The excavation in the two-month period of mid-January to mid-March 1996 defined the north, east, and south walls of the church and part of its western elevation. In the apse, the altar was excavated and was fairly intact. In the northeast corner of the north wall there was an intact doorway giving access to a room on the north side of the apse. The room, which appears to have its ceiling intact, was not excavated (left for next season).

The opening in the floor, detected in 1995, was investigated. This was an underground chamber about thirteen feet square, with a domed firebrick ceiling and plastered walls. Through a break to the west in the floor of the church, the west wall of this room was exposed, which was plastered and had frescoes and inscriptions. The chamber and adjacent rooms appear to be the earliest chapel in the monastery, and one room was preserved as a place of veneration when the later (possibly late fifth or sixth century) church was built over the area. In the debris about twenty inches above the church floor in the nave there was found a small clay jar containing gold Islamic coins dating from the late tenth and early eleventh centuries. This gives a date for the abandonment of the site. Thus, the earliest date is the fourth century in the lower chamber complex and the latest is the eleventh or twelfth century in the destruction debris in the church floor. More rooms in the kom nearby were also uncovered, with more frescoes and inscriptions.

The Third Season of Work: January 15 to the End of February 1999

Resources were very limited. Our team this time was confined to Van Elderen, Dr. Tim Vivian, and me. Professor Peter Grossmann, a distinguished archaeologist, known for his work on Christian sites in the area of Alexandria, worked with us for several weeks. His special skill is the result of his architectural knowledge.

With only a small number of workers, we concentrated on the remaining clearance of the church building. The two chambers discovered beneath the nave were reexamined at the end of our work period, when little time remained. It seems this either was part of an earlier building or was the dwelling place or cell of a holy person.

Intentions for the 2001–2002 Work Season

We had great expectations for our work in September and October 2001, especially hoping to find out more about the mysterious rooms under the church. Perhaps the idea that there could have been a settlement there even earlier than that of the Christian monks could become further substantiated.

But the disaster of September 11, 2001, in New York caused another deferral. Sadly, our American benefactor died. His wife and heir offered to allow us funds for one more season, but although promised, these funds never materialized. Mainly, they would have been used to pay the Christian workers on-site.

An important conference of scholars with knowledge of the Wadi Natrun monasteries, under the patronage of Pope Shenoudah III, was attended by many bishops and Professor Van Elderen's party, which presented lectures and slides. I am sorry to say that although Van Elderen, Peter Grossmann, and I offered to create a committee to continue study at the monastery, so far no other funds have been found. Although I have always paid my own flight and personal expenses, I think it is unlikely that the monks at Wadi Natrun can provide additional excavation funds beyond their normal generosity of accommodation and food.

I still have great hope that in time the work will continue. I remain convinced that our excavation site is, in fact, Scetis for these three main reasons:

1. The writings of the Greek and Jewish historian Philo
2. The defined and certain presence of Essenes on the shores of a nearby lake
3. The firm conviction of the Coptic community at the four monasteries and throughout the Coptic Church in Egypt and worldwide that Wadi Natrun is the place where Joseph, Mary, and Jesus stayed during their time in Egypt

The only find to hint at the veracity of our belief is a small bronze cross, but this of course can in no way be regarded as proof. My search so far would appear to have been a frustrating, fifteen-year bout of shadow chasing. To me, however, it simply means that the time has not yet come.

I I

INTO EGYPT HAVE I
CALLED MY SON

I f Jesus was called out of Egypt, then I must have been called into Egypt—and not just physically. If, as we have seen, Jesus being called out of Egypt is a metaphor for the real roots of Christianity being in Egypt, then being called into Egypt might be said to be a metaphor for heeding a call to explore, understand, and reveal those roots.

No other ancient civilization we know of cultivated thinking about life, death, and afterlife as intensely as the Egyptians, and these ideas are beautifully expressed in the myth of Isis and Osiris. Variations of this love story can be found in other religions, for it was changed and retold in many nations as a fairy tale. The original tale tells that Osiris is killed by his evil brother Seth. His grieving sister and wife Isis searches for his body, but Seth has cunningly cut it into many pieces and spread them all over the land. Isis collects these pieces and, with the help of Anubis, restores her beloved husband to life.

At the famous site of Byblos in Lebanon, I found small ancient steps leading down to an active spring of water with a moss-covered flat stone carrying deeply cut hieroglyphs. The carving appears to be authentic and identifies the area as an original spring of Isis, where she found one part of Osiris's body. There have been many interpretations of this myth, including that it tells of the origin of death or the fight between light and darkness. I like best the idea that Osiris represents everything that has been born and lives on earth. Like the grain that dies in the earth in order to live again as a plant bearing many grains, Osiris dies and is reborn. He is the symbol of resurrection and rebirth, but because he had to pass through the underworld before he came back to life, he is also lord of the realm of the dead. As a representative of man, the pharaoh has to join him on his barque, follow the sun when it sinks down in the west, pass through the underworld on the river flowing there, and resurrect with the sun.

The ancient Egyptians believed that man consisted of the body, the Ba, and the Ka. The nearest explanation for Ba in our terms is *soul*. The Ba is often depicted as a bird and its hieroglyph is a foot—perhaps to indicate that only a small part of the eternal soul was incarnated in the flesh. The Ba was that part that was reunited with the body in eternal life. To allow for this, the body had to be preserved, and as a result, more and more sophisticated mummification techniques were developed so that the Ba could find its body again. The Ka is the eternal life energy, the ever-living spirit double of a person, so we might say that the Ba is peculiar to the individual, while the Ka is the divine spark common to all humans.

Various texts on papyri, pyramid texts, and inscriptions on coffins later became collectively known as the Egyptian Book of the Dead, which provided all the knowledge, prayers, and formulas needed to go safely through the twelve regions and twelve gates of the underworld, which was full of snakes and other evil beings. The magnificent paintings of deities in the burial shafts and chambers of the pharaohs at Luxor concentrate on complex magic and incantations to ensure the pharaoh's safe passage through the underworld toward rebirth. Most fascinating are the pictures of this passage in the tombs in the Valley of the Kings, especially the tombs of Amenophis II, Thutmosis III, and Horemheb.

The beautiful pictures of the Papyrus of Ani show the Last Judgment: In the presence of forty-two gods, the Ka of the dead is brought before Maat (the Truth, the Law), Anubis (the jackal), and Thoth (the scribe). While the deceased repeats the magic incantations of the negative confession ("I have done no evil"), his heart is weighed against a feather. If it is heavier, it is devoured by a monster with the head of a crocodile. If it is lighter, the deceased passes on to Osiris to become like him and live forever. It is hard to deny the striking resemblance between old Egyptian thinking and the Christian teaching of hell or Purgatory (the underworld), Last Judgment, and resurrection.

According to Egyptian belief, for the body to enjoy eternal life, there would be the need for food, a pleasant place to stay, and workers *(ushabti)* to do everything necessary so that the deceased did not have to take an active part in this work. Therefore, painted vines richly laden with grapes hang down from the ceiling of the tomb chamber, musicians play their instruments, and beautiful girls dance for the delight of those in further life. There is an abundance of food and drink. Fragrance and flowers embellish the rooms. Meanwhile, the ushabti, small clay figures made to represent the helpers, assist in fieldwork, look after cattle, make pots, spin, weave, bake, and cook to maintain this life. Many today wrongly believe that the ancient Egyptians were obsessed with death but this is not true. They simply loved life so much that they wanted to make sure they would live forever.

Mummification was a complex procedure. Relatives were offered four possible techniques at different charges. Normally, all the hair and the intestines were removed and the brain was pulled out through the nostrils by iron hooks. The body was cleaned and soaked in a bath of natron (a mixture of sodium bicarbonate and sodium carbonate) for thirty days. Vital organs (viscera), except for the heart, were kept in four separate canopic jars guarded by both human deities and jackal-, falcon-, and other animal-headed deities. Those relatives who could afford the highest grade of mummification arranged for the application of oils and spices to the corpse. All bodily apertures were closed and a series of scarab amulets (the dung beetle, symbol of rebirth) and flowers were placed on these openings. Clearly the mummification process had secrets we no longer possess today. We have only the writings of Herodotus, the early Greek traveler and historian who visited Egypt in about 450 BC.

Of course, a great amount of natron was needed for mummification, and this was found in a lake at Wadi Natrun, in the Western Desert. In fact the name Scetis, or Shiêt, means, as we've learned, "balance of hearts," an expression that still hints at the weighing of the heart against a feather in the ceremony of the Last Judgment. It would seem, then, that Jesus, who was to bring eternal life without the need for mummification, grew up at the place where previous generations over many centuries had gathered the natron that had provided a semblance of immortality.

Admittedly, much biblical scholarship of the last few decades (especially since the Second Vatican Council absolved the Jews from the nineteen-centuries-old charge of deicide) has rediscovered the "Jewishness" of Jesus. In this context, those who search for the historical Jesus have interpreted his self-sacrifice mostly in terms of Jewish Messianism. But if Jesus grew up among Egyptian Essenes and his teaching is much more a gnostic initiatory message than the sacrificial absolution rite that St. Paul imagined, then the Crucifixion can be interpreted as the ultimate gnostic rebirth ritual performed for those who would understand it, a death and resurrection play just like the one Schonfield supposed to have been the Essenes' intentions in rescuing Jesus from the cross.

In the second part of this book, we shall further explore the spirituality of Egypt and its connection to early Christianity in part through the telling of my own experience and of how my search eventually brought me to southern France, just as, I believe, Alexandria's gnostic came to these hills in the footsteps of their Master.

✝

Part 2

EGYPT AND
FRANCE

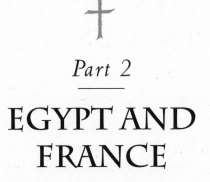

12

•◆•

HOW IT ALL BEGAN:
MY EGYPTIAN
ENCOUNTERS

I seem to have always had a flair for finding things with my hands. This has proved a great good fortune, but I've never known how it really happens.

My father died when I was about twelve and an uncle and aunt were generous in hosting me for holidays at their home in Norwich in Norfolk, England. The castle museum there then had an Egyptian section of some size, and the curator soon noticed a small boy with his nose quite often pressed to the display glass. One day, he took me in and let me examine some artifacts with him. This hands-on experience proved to be premonitory. I never ever lost the thrill of Egypt, which in time developed into a great appetite for reading about her history.

One day, I jumped on my bicycle and cycled to Caister St. Edmond, a village about twelve miles west of Norwich. I do not remember if the museum curator told me about it or if I found out for myself, but though I didn't know this at the time, the place was and still is an untouched Roman site. I saw a two-meter-high ancient redbrick wall surrounding a five- or six-acre area, square in shape. A ditch with a protection bank surrounded the area and is still visible today. By good fortune, it had been plowed and then subjected to heavy rain and a dry wind. As a result, I could clearly see the outline of the walls of houses and connecting streets of a Roman military encampment. What's more, I was able to wander over the surface, finding inscribed brick and minor artifacts of no intrinsic value, but that provided great excitement for me. I still have my childhood box of these small items.

Had I grown up in America, I would now write something like "I was the kind of kid who liked going to dumps and rummaging through trash, and archaeology is basically rummaging through very old trash." But I grew up in England and feel very European, and thus every little item I recovered over the years was to me an intense experience tied to history, memory, identity, *genus loci,* and other similarly weighty ideas.

And so it began—searching for fossilized shark's teeth with my history teacher and friends at the foot of Reculver near Herne Bay, south of the Thames, or looking for Roman pottery on the sandbank in the middle of the Thames estuary at Southend (still shown on charts as Pudding Pan Sands), where a Roman ship carrying ceramic dishes from Belgium sank in the first century AD.

Later, during the war, my duties in the Far East provided me with the opportunity to visit a number of sites in order to keep them clear of jungle and wilderness encroachment: Lumbini in India (the place where Buddha spent his childhood) and several sites in Ceylon (now Sri Lanka) such as Anuradhapura, Sigiriya, Polunarua, and the Temple of the Tooth at Kandy.

In 1948–50, with a few friends I set up the South Buckinghamshire Archaeological Society at Slough. With the help of early-Saxon specialist Brian Hope Taylor, we traced an important site at Old Windsor through shards brought to the surface by road-digging equipment. Major work followed for three seasons, in which I learned excavation techniques and much more from Taylor.

In the ensuing years I developed something of a dual career—life as a businessman on the one hand and field experience in archaeology, whenever possible, on the other. It is a fact that much work in archaeology is carried out by knowledgeable amateurs who are trained and experienced in fieldwork and are generally although not academically qualified and generously accepted by those who are. I found many friends who, like me, do the work just because they are passionately interested. Many of the members of the Egypt Exploration Society are such student excavators, and I have been a member for more than thirty years.

KEYS TO WIDER UNDERSTANDING

Early in the war, I was responsible for a Royal Air Force training school in the foothills of the Himalayas. Initially it was located at Solan, near Simla, and later at Murree in Kashmir, at seven thousand feet and near the great mountain range of the Karakorum. There was a continuous flow of Tibetan traders, mystics, holy men, and teachers of many faiths who were willing to explain their beliefs, frequently in good English. I was thus exposed at a relatively early age to the thinking of wise men in the Himalayas and in particular to the principle of reincarnation, which, they said, was the only deficiency in my Christian faith. I never spoke of this because I learned that one basic purpose of life is to seek out truth for oneself. It is no good to transmit your own experience to others: All must find out for themselves and seek their own true understanding of religion.

In the East I had the great privilege of seeing many strange things and being an eyewitness to mysterious happenings I would never have believed had I not seen them. A holy man once asked me in perfect English for permission to live alone in a cave some ways above the area of my training schools at Solan, near Simla. One day this man told me to go to a nearby village of farmworkers the next day, and a close friend and I did so. We were met by the village headman and asked to sit among a wide ring of women of the village. In the middle sat a *fakir* (an itinerant Hindu ascetic) covered in ash and apparently in a trance.

The woman beside me showed me her very young naked child, whose left foot was deformed; the heel was not there and the foot consisted of only tiny, crumpled toes. She also showed the child to all the women in the ring and then knelt in front of the fakir and placed the child in his hands. There was total silence for many minutes. Then he lifted the child above his head, making a loud cry. Nothing seemed to happen for about twenty minutes. Suddenly he repeated his loud cry and the woman rushed toward him and seized her child. I am quite certain of what I saw and so is my friend. There was no chance of deception. She went around the whole circle, eagerly showing the baby to each woman. After a time, she came to my companion and me and we saw that the foot was now utterly normal.

My unit was in the center of a small independent hill state with very little income, ruled by the rajah of Baghat. The rajah was a remarkable person who taught me much of his philosophy, including the Hindu and Buddhist concept of reincarnation. Others there introduced me to their belief in healing with the hands. I saw what is known as *tumo* (a meditative practice that produces tremendous body heat): On a barren section of a flat, sandy rock, a *sadhu* (ascetic holy man) would sit on the deeply frozen ground, naked except for his *dhoti*, or loincloth. He would then go into a deep trance in front of me. Slowly, as I watched, the ground around him would melt completely over a diameter of more than ten feet.

The southern frontier of Tibet is one hundred fifty miles northeast of this mountainous region of northern India. For a while, at about the middle of World War II, entry into Tibet was not permitted as it had been before. It was possible, however, to make brief visits to this upper area of northern India, where a number of small Tibetan monasteries existed. I visited several and was given a kind welcome. There were no tourists or other visitors at that time, and I was allowed to attend and take photographs of many ceremonies, including the driving out of devils, a lengthy ritual in which are used human skulls, goat's blood, and flutes made from human ribs. At one small temple, the lama discussed with me for many hours his faith and convictions about reincarnation, often answering my questions before I asked them. He suggested that I walk to a flat hilltop nearby where I would see an outstanding panorama of this high plateau.

Accompanied by a young monk in his saffron robe, we went to this place and sat and listened to the majestic sound of the ragdong trumpets of the temple. When all became quiet, the young monk moved to sit a few paces behind me. Soon after, I turned and saw that he seemed to be in a trance, eyes closed—and to my astonishment, his body was suspended horizontally about three feet above the ground. Skeptically, I examined his rigid body with my hands, fingers extended, and arms, but there was no support of any kind above or below him. I gently attempted to lift or press down his body, but this proved simply impossible.

I sat down quietly in my original place for perhaps an hour, meditating about what I had been shown. The young monk made no sound or movement. Almost another hour later he sat down beside me, saying nothing before walking back with me to the lamasery. I was both shocked and profoundly impressed. Neither the lama nor the young monk said anything when we returned or when I left at dawn the next morning. I decided not to speak to anyone about this experience, for I felt sure that no one would believe me. I never saw anything like this again.

In another part of India, my duties once required me to spend a week or so in a village to the east of Bombay. One evening I walked alone not long before dusk, when India is at its best—no one was around and there was no sound. I walked slowly toward a huge peepal tree of great age and saw sitting beneath it a sadhu with no clothes on and coated in white wood ash. He was in deep meditation and took no notice of me when I sat on the ground not far away.

After about half an hour, all at once he lifted his arms above his head, making a loud, long cry—"Coo–ee–ee!"—before resuming his posture. Suddenly, a large black crow flew to sit near him, and then another and another. This went on until he was surrounded by a huge flock of crows. They were seated on his shoulders and hands. All was still for more than an hour, by which time it had become dark, though I could still just see. Still seated, he suddenly lifted his arms again and made the same loud cry. Shortly after, the birds began to fly away, one by one, until all was still. The sadhu did not stir. I left without a sound soon after, deeply impressed by what I had seen. I learned much later that this ceremony is extremely rare and seldom seen. It is known as the Calling of the Birds. Clearly, I had been taught something in the realm of a wider understanding—truly a great privilege.

The only other place in which I have encountered such a scene is in biographies of St. Francis of Assisi. In the Catholic hagiographic version, the ritual takes the name of St. Francis Preaching to the Birds, and it is depicted in a famous painting by Giotto. I have always loved Francis, but how typical that a Hindu saint only "calls" birds, while a Catholic saint has to "preach" to them.

MYSTICISM IN EGYPT

Still, as I wrote in part 1, it was Egypt that left its spiritual hook in my soul and it is the spirituality of Egypt whose traces I am still following in this French village at the foot of the Pyrenees. After the end of the war, I made many visits to Egypt, coming to know some of our most important archaeologists there, among them Professor Emery, Professor I. E. S. Edwards, Professor Geoffrey Martin, and Barry Kemp. All were very generous to me, particularly on their sites, and I like to think that some of their expertise rubbed off.

Traveling widely all over the world for my business profession made possible lengthy visits to Turkey, Priene, Didyma, Miletos, Aphrodisias, Side, Goreme, Urgup, and Catalhouyuk, and also to Jerusalem, Jordan, Jerash, Masada, Delphi, Mycene, Marathon, and many other places. On these journeys it was always my hope that if I could gain enough field experience and training, I would one day be able to participate in an Egyptian field excavation of importance, though I knew this would be possible only when my two children grew and became established in their own careers.

As you might expect, on my trips to Egypt I met many fascinating people not only from the world of archaeology and not because I made my early journeys half a century ago, when tourism was a relatively limited phenomenon. Some of my encounters with scientifically unexplainable events occurred there, too, and in my mind these episodes relate to the mysticism that survives in the character and inclination of the original Egyptian people—that is, today's Copts.

This mysticism is intrinsically connected to the stream scholars call gnostic Christianity, whose adepts I believe slowly migrated to France over the first four centuries (especially the fourth century) of the new millennium after Jesus' supposed death. They followed in the footsteps of a spiritual tradition that was later enriched by contact with the Sufis— followers of the Muslim stream of gnosticism—and with the Jewish mystics whose theosophical speculation would later be called kabbalah. Eventually, the very same Egyptian mysticism would compel a great proportion of the population of the medieval Languedoc to embrace the Christian heresy we know as Catharism.

In the interest of this connection, I would like to briefly relate some of my encounters with unusual episodes, for I think they well illustrate the power of Egypt to cast a spell of sorts on truth seekers from anywhere in the world; the insights on life, death, and reincarnation that are the religious legacy of this great civilization; and my own profound metaphysical relationship with the country and its people.

Omm Sety

During my early visits to Sakkhara and Luxor, in 1958, I came to hear of a remarkable mystic called Omm Sety living at the Temple of Abydos, and I decided to visit her. At that time, the only way there was by a dust track on the west bank from Luxor via Dendera, a long and uncomfortable journey on a potholed road. After arriving at Abydos and recovering from dust and fatigue, we paid a visit to the temple. To our surprise, my wife and I discovered that Omm Sety was English, a delightful, happy personality who was intensely clairvoyant but totally unaware of it. She lived in an aura of the ancient past and made almost no attempt to relate to the present, and her world had an atmosphere of happiness, tranquillity, and fulfillment. She became close to my late wife, Winifred, and through our many visits we became perhaps her closest friends at that time. She told me her story in detail and I still treasure my notebook from that period.

Omm Sety, a name she took later, was born Dorothy Louise Eady in 1904 at Blackheath, South London. When she was three, she fell down the stairs and remained unconscious. The family doctor declared her dead and went away to bring a nurse before returning to the Eadys' home. When he came back, he was simply astounded to find the child recovered to full health, though he remained convinced that his original diagnosis had been correct. Omm Sety believed she was reborn at that moment as a reincarnation of an Egyptian priestess who had lived more than three thousand years ago. This conviction shaped her entire life, most of which she spent in the Osiris Temple at Abydos, 350 miles south of Cairo, where she once served as a priestess. Some mystics known to me think that her interpretation of this event was not correct: Since her birth she had always been the reincarnation of the priestess, and the "apparent death" incident had only stirred her memory of the previous life.

After her strange accident, Dorothy kept saying that she wanted to go home, and would not accept her parents' statement that the house where she was living was her home. The identity of her true home was quickly established when her family took her to the Egyptian gallery at the British Museum some time later. There she was utterly certain that she was with her people. Soon after this, she started to hide under the dining room table and weep. She said she knew where home was and very much wanted to go there.

After her museum visit, she had a recurring dream of a large building with columns close to a garden with tall trees. One day she saw a photograph in a magazine of the Temple of Sety I at Abydos, and she ran to her father, saying, "This is my home. But why is it all broken and where is the garden?" Her father was upset and told her that the picture showed a building called a temple in a country called Egypt and that she had never been there. It was broken, he said, because it was several thousand years old and it had no garden because it was in the desert, where nothing ever grew. These words, however, did not discourage her from going on about that garden all her life. Eventually, many years later, the remains of it were found, southwest of the temple.

Dorothy also saw a photograph of the mummy of Pharaoh Sety I and assured her father that she knew him and that he was a nice, kind man. She flew into a rage when her father said that Sety I had been dead for three thousand years and that she could not possibly have seen or known him. Things got worse when she was expelled from her girls school at Dulwich for refusing to sing a hymn calling on God to "curse the Egyptians." She told me she threw the hymnbook at the teacher and ran home.

Her education continued, in a way, at the British Museum. Omm Sety remembered with warmth the curator of the Egyptian department, Dr. Wallis Budge, who noticed her frequent visits and took an interest in her. She yearned to learn how to read hieroglyphs, and he arranged for her to be taught. He was surprised at the progress she made but appeared to accept her explanation that "I used to know the language, a long time ago, but have forgotten it." That is how things seemed to her, as things once familiar but since forgotten. Ancient Egyptian is the only foreign language she has ever been able to learn—after forty years in Egypt, she could neither read nor write Arabic.

In the 1920s, Dorothy worked for a magazine that campaigned for Egyptian independence and met Emam Abdel Meguid. "I had turned down several offers of marriage," she explained, "because from the age of fifteen I have really been in love with King Sety I. But I had come to like and respect Emam and finally accepted him." She was twenty-nine when she sailed to Egypt for her wedding. At the sight of the coastline, she wept with joy. As she recalls it, she "had come home at last."

The marriage, however, was not to last. Emam did not share her interest in ancient Egypt. They had a son, and Dorothy persuaded Emam to call him Sety, after Sety I. It is customary in the Arab world, especially in the villages, to call a married woman "mother of" her eldest child. Thus Dorothy became known as the "mother of Sety"—that is, in Arabic, Omm Sety. When their child was two, Emam, a teacher, was sent to Iraq. With his consent, Omm Sety bought a couple of tents and went to live with the child in the desert, beside the Giza pyramids. There she helped Professor Selim Hassan, an Egyptologist she had met, and learned archaeological excavation methods.

Young Sety and his mother enjoyed their life in the desert for two years, but when Emam returned from Iraq, he married one of his cousins and Sety left his mother and went to live with his father. Omm Sety continued her excavation work at the pyramids with Professor Selim Hassan, and in 1952 she was given a few days of leave to go at last to Abydos to see the tomb of Osiris. Although she could not read the station name, which was written in Arabic, she found it was not necessary. Looking out of the window of the train, she saw a range of limestone hills that were overwhelmingly familiar to her, although she had never seen them before. When the train stopped, she set off down the road to the village of Balyana (Abydos).

She told us that she would never forget her first glimpse of the temple. It was so familiar to her, exactly as if she had returned to a well-known and much loved place. Entering the temple was like entering her own house. The antiquities inspector and others were astonished to find that she knew the exact place of each chapel and the scenes on the walls, both in the temple and in the Osirion, the mysterious building that lies beside and below the temple. To the west of the temple there is a puzzling building built of the massive blocks typical of Old Kingdom and the time before. This building, at a lower level, is now flooded due to changes in subsoil water level. Omm Sety claimed it was a cenotaph, a memorial built by Sety I at the same time as his main temple was constructed on the traditional site of Osiris. This has now been proved by the discovery of cartouches with the name Sety I carved on the underside of the small locking stones.

In 1954, Omm Sety visited Abydos again, this time for two weeks, and on her return to Cairo her heart was so obviously in Abydos that the Department of Antiquities kindly arranged for her participate in on excavation work near the temple with Professor Edward Ghazouli. Thus in 1956, with her cats and books, Omm Sety went back home. Two years later the budget for the work was exhausted and the job came to an end. Omm Sety was urged to leave Abydos and accept a job in the antiquities department, but she refused to go. Having saved thirty pounds, she was determined to own a small part of the sacred land. For fifteen pounds, she bought a small, dilapidated mud house in the middle of the village, made it habitable, and moved in.

A few months later, on the eve of her birthday, she ran out of money. It was January 15, 1959. Her belongings were negligible. She went to the temple and prayed to Osiris, explaining her problem and saying, "If you want me here, find a way for me to live and feed my cats. If you don't want me here, please give me a swift death." Apparently, she says, the response was rapid. Two hours later, the architect in charge of the restoration of the temple came around to tell her of a telephone call from Cairo: She was to be reemployed on restoration work. Though a small woman of slight build, with her energy, enthusiasm, quick sense of humor, and hard work, the temple of Sety I has again, after three thousand three hundred years, become a shrine to the god Osiris and a center of his religion.

She told me that she did have the problem of where to be buried. The villagers objected to a pagan being buried in a Muslim cemetery, so she had prepared for herself a tomb on the grounds of her house, near the temple. Sadly, the local authorities much later refused to permit Omm Sety's wish to be buried in her garden tomb on the sacred land and insisted on her burial in the Coptic Christian section of the nearby Muslim cemetery.

We tried to help her because she had become undernourished, and we managed to persuade her to complete the work she had commenced on a history of the temple and the adjoining Osirion. At that time I did marketing work with the Thomson Organization, which then owned the *Sunday Times*. I was able to recommend articles about Omm Sety in the color supplement to provide income for her. I suggested to my friend Youssef Gafaar, the owner of Eastmar Nile Cruise Ships, to have them moor at Nag Hammadi overnight so Omm Sety could talk to and guide visitors to the Temple.

A Secret Discovery

Omm Sety once described to me a strange experience that occurred in 1958 and which, at that time, she regarded as very secret. She showed the location only to me and took care to emphasize her uncertainty as to whether it really happened. Much later she recorded this story in some detail in her autobiography: She was working in the Hall of the Sacred Boats, fitting together pieces of inscribed stone that had once formed doorways and grilles in the audience hall of the temple. Work to add a roof to the temple was in progress, and although she had the key to all doors, it was easier to get in and out by going upstairs to the roof and walking along on the top of the southern wall to the unroofed portion of the western corridor and then down the scaffolding at the west of the temple.

A flu epidemic had developed at the time and she had caught it. One morning she was feeling unwell, and because aspirin had no effect, she decided to go home. She went upstairs and started walking along the top of the wall, but suddenly she became dizzy and fell, twisting her right ankle and injuring her left shoulder. She remembers hearing a loud grating sound like that of a grindstone at work, and she rolled down a steep slope. She heard the grating sound again and found herself in darkness. When the dizziness passed enough to allow her to stand up and grope for a wall, she touched some smooth limestone blocks and stood there, wondering what to do.

Soon she sensed very faint threads of light filtering down from above through cracks in the roof. She found she was standing in a narrow passage less than four feet wide. A narrow path, twenty inches wide, ran along the base of the wall, but the remainder of the width of the passage appeared to be completely filled with boxes full of offering tables, vases, and bales of linen, and everywhere was the gleam of gold. Feeling her way, she limped along the passage, which seemed endless, while to her left the path was crowded with objects. She fell over and saw the god Horus himself bending over her, his hand raised. From his waist down he was standing upright, but from the waist up his falcon face peered down to her, with his double crown sticking out at right angles.

She sat there, wondering how she should speak to a god in the circumstances. Then she realized the Horus was only a painted wooden statue, life-sized and originally standing upright, with arms bent at the elbows and hands raised. Insects had eaten away part of the front of the body, causing the upper part to lean over. She noticed similar statues of Isis and Osiris leaning undamaged against the far wall. Near her a golden vase, ten inches high, stood in a wooden frame. It had a long neck and an oval body. She could see that a cartouche had been engraved, but it did not look like the cartouche of Sety; possibly it was one of the later kings. She found it heavy, and after first thinking she would take it out as evidence, she finally decided against it. She began to feel ill again but continued to limp along, only half conscious. Suddenly she found herself in open air, blinded by the light. She was standing beside the wall of the second court of the temple.

Two days later, when the chief inspector of antiquities for the area came, she told him about the experience. He was astonished, but neither of them could decide whether it really happened or was instead a dream caused by fever. Speaking to me, she said she still could not know for certain and that all she was sure of was that she fell. She did injure her ankle and shoulder and really was covered in dust and cobwebs. If this really did happen, then there is only one possible explanation: She must have hit a stone with her shoulder, which turned on a pivot and opened into a sloping passage. This would account for the grating sound. But how did she get out again? All that she could suggest was that a deserted hyena's lair in the side of the well might have connected with the treasure passage. The chief inspector became interested and told her to try to find the supposed pivot stone, which she did but without success. There is an important point to note here: The paving stones of the aisles in the Hypostyle Hall are large, single slabs. These could well be roofing over subterranean passages, while in all other places the paving stones are smaller and irregularly shaped. Omm Sety was certain that the Temple still held secrets.

I remember once asking Omm Sety why the stone plinths at the base of the Hypostyle Hall pillars had been cut back sharply from their original round form. She recalled the scene with much amusement, mentioning the anxiety of the priests in full regalia dragging the wooden sledges displaying god replicas and many precious items. The difficulty of getting around the pillars at the entrance of each chapel caused the heavy sledges to wobble dangerously, so the priests had the base of all pillars cut back. The groove markings of the sledges still show in the floor stones. No one had been able to explain the strange features before, but her story offered the simplest and most logical explanation.

In the earlier days of our friendship, Omm Sety had often told us that she remembered full well the attack on her by priests that ended her life. This was due to her personal relationship with Sety himself, which appears to have been grossly improper.

As world knowledge about Omm Sety increased, so the flow of her visitors grew to include many well-known personalities. About this time, the American author Jonathan Cott came to prepare his book *In Search of Omm Sety*, which has since been widely acclaimed for his thorough research. In addition, Julia Cave produced her excellent BBC program about Omm Sety, which was released in May 1981, about one month before Omm Sety's death. Omm Sety's health declined rapidly after she broke her hip. Peter Davalle wrote a commentary on the BBC program *Chronicle* for the *London Times* on May 6, 1981, and this served indirectly as a fine obituary. I saw her for the last time shortly before this. Her spirit was still strong and she even seemed to look forward to her passing.

The Mystic Dhalil Al Khalil

There is one last encounter I'd like to mention here. I worked for some years as an executive in aviation under Sir Miles Wyatt, then chief of Air Holdings, the largest British aerospace conglomerate in those days. Thanks to this position, I was able to make many private visits to Egypt via Beirut. In the winter of 1978, my wife and I stayed in El Minya. From there, many important archaeological sites, including Akhenaten's city, can be reached. At that time there was only one modest hotel at Minya, and on our arrival it was full. Therefore, we stayed at a modest but satisfactory Arab guesthouse.

On the first day in El Minya, my wife had to rest in bed due to a severe cold. I joined my old friend Adly Michael, a Coptic Christian with archaeological knowledge of this rich historical area. We crossed by car to the east bank of the Nile, where we hired donkeys for the long climb to the rock tombs of Beni Hassan. There we found about thirty decorated tombs dating from the Middle Kingdom. On our return, my wife was much improved, but she preferred to stay in her room to recover completely. Downstairs again, I was approached by an Egyptian dressed in a traditional galabya. He suggested in his modest English (not much helped by my equally modest Arabic) that we eat together. While we ate, he asked if he could speak to my wife, whom he knew was upstairs. I told her about this invitation, suggesting that she join us just to listen. She knew that this kind of thing happened often to me.

Dhalil Al Khalil, the name of this man, was a clairvoyant who told me of my Air Force experience and background. He talked of the events ahead of us in the coming weeks. When my wife joined us, he repeated his information about our two children and gave background to gain her confidence. He said that when we returned home, it would be important for her to see her doctor. He stressed that all would be in order and she should not worry, but that she had a small problem on the right side of her stomach. He repeated this many times and made her promise to do as he asked. With some reluctance, she promised, but I could see that she did not regard this advice as important. Then she went upstairs for an early night.

I continued a discussion with Dhalil, not knowing then that he was no tourist-hunting charlatan but rather a wealthy healer and one of the most famous mystics in the Middle East, who was not available even to those prepared to disburse substantial sums. Apparently he had a high reputation in many areas of Egypt.

The next day, my wife and I continued on to Balyana, near the temple of Sety I at Abydos, where we had come to discuss with Omm Sety the possibility of her publishing a book. Here I met Professor Robinson's team working at the Nag Hammadi site, where gnostic documents had been found thirty years before. I also met Professor Van Elderen, later my friend and partner at Wadi Natrun. At that time my wife and I forgot Dhalil's story and advice.

In the summer of 1979, while on a cruise ship holiday in the Mediterranean, my wife had minor digestion problems, and in August 1979 we visited our doctor in Croydon. After hearing of my wife's experience, he sent her to the Mayday Hospital for some tests. The physicians examined her and had X-rays taken, and fortunately I was with her when she was given the results. They had found a tumor in the upper bowel that required immediate removal. Because she had never experienced pain there, however, she had difficulty accepting this at first. Nonetheless, she was operated on and made a complete recovery in a few weeks. I later discovered that the staff of Mayday Hospital and her physician Dr. Wesson had recorded her story of the Egyptian holy man. They could not for the life of them understand how Dhalil had made his prediagnosis, for she had told them about it before she herself had known the results of the X-rays. With the help of her doctors, my wife overcame the cancer and had twelve more years of full health. Sadly, inoperable lung cancer attacked her later and she died in May 1992.

In that first meeting, Dhalil Al Khalil had also said to me: "One day you will work in the desert with priests in black. You will make a great discovery, one of the greatest of all time—not money, just secrets." At that time I had never met the Coptic priests at Wadi Natrun who would become so important to me later. I asked about his great gift: Did he possess vision? What did he see and feel? Pointing at me, he said: "Some people have light—you have blue light." Touching my left shoulder, he said: "If there is trouble in this place, then there is no light here." He said he was used to this sort of experience and had helped others many times. When I asked if he lived locally, he said he lived in the Minya area and that he would see me again. I asked if money was acceptable to him, but he said this was not needed because he was wealthy and gave his gift only when and where he was guided or "told" to do so. He said he had been sent.

Two years later, I was alone in Minya and suddenly remembered that Dhalil had not been told of his success foretelling of my wife's illness and of the important cure that had taken place. After much searching, I found the Arab hotel again, but my enquiries about Dhalil Al Khalil proved fruitless. After several days, I went to the ancient city of Akhetaten with my old friend Adly Michael and I told him about the experience I had had with Dhalil and asked him how I could possibly find him in a city of two million people with no telephone directory. He smiled and said, "He is my friend—we will see him tonight."

We visited Dhalil's son's apartment. Dhalil was in bed, and I could see a catheter. Adly said: "I brought an old friend of yours from England." I sat beside his bed, where I could see that Dhalil had a cataract in each eye. He drew his face close and, to the astonishment of Adly, said: "Ah! Wife cancer . . ."

Dhalil told me he had lost his fortune in cotton futures trading. His illness followed and now he relied entirely on his son in his family's modest apartment. This was a Coptic family, and it was wonderful to see their happiness. We left soon, for the clairvoyant tired quickly. When we returned the next day, Dhalil spoke to me at length of world events ahead and of my future work in archaeology. By this time I was searching alone in the Wadi Natrun Desert and had become known and accepted by the Coptic monks there. Happily, I was able to help Dhalil with money.

The following year I telephoned his son on my arrival in Minya. He asked me to come at once to the apartment, where the whole family was assembled. Although it was clear he was near death, Dhalil wanted to see me. Strangely, he became stimulated and revived by a strange energy as he talked of my wife's good fortune and of others he had helped. I thanked him gratefully once more and left soon after. He died that night. The next day, with the help of his son, I prepared and published a eulogy in the Arab press.

In later years I had many happy visits with his family. During that time there were many attacks by Muslim extremists on the Copts at Minya. Little protection was given to them and I was able to help by reporting to the police what I had seen there. During my work at Wadi Natrun, I had several audiences with Pope Shenoudah III, and once I asked him if he would give approval for me to write this true story, for I knew that for some churches it was not permissible for believers to become involved in such matters of spiritual healing. His Holiness answered, "Certainly, you should tell the story. I have met many with this wonderful gift. All Christians will gain encouragement to learn of this miracle."

Thus my experience with Dhalil Al Khalil was fully recorded and authenticated, and to this day I marvel that my wife and I happened to be in that remote place at that particular moment. And I wonder, too, why Dhalil was there.

13

THE FRENCH
CONNECTION:
PYTHAGORAS

As suggested in chapter 9, if Jesus did survive his crucifixion, the likeliest place to which he would have escaped was Egypt, to Scetis, the Egyptian Essene community where he quite probably had grown to the age of twelve and among whose members he could best be tended to as he recovered from his ordeal on the cross. In addition, given that Alexandria was by far the largest port in the Mediterranean after Rome itself, it would have been easier to smuggle a fugitive aboard a westbound ship there than anywhere else east of the Roman Empire.

But why would Jesus want to board a westbound ship once he had taken refuge with his childhood teachers in Scetis? In Judaea the danger of someone recognizing the crucified pretender to the throne of Israel was real and imminent, so vanishing from there was understandable, but once safely ensconced in a string of oases some fifty miles south of Alexandria, why would Jesus want to keep running? After all, Egypt, though like Judaea under Roman rule, was a relatively pacified province. There were no Roman patrols stopping pilgrims and caravans at every crossroad, as there were in Galilee or in the Judean desert, nor were rebels crucified almost every week for attacking legionaries.

The most likely answer lies in the political agenda of the Essene movement. Robert Eisenman is not the only scholar who thinks that if Qumran was laid waste during the war in AD 68, it was because the ascetics living there were evidently not limiting themselves to fasting and interpreting prophecies. With their constant talk of the imminent final battle between the sons of light and the sons of darkness, they had become what would be known today as the ideological arm of a revolutionary movement.

The Romans were no fools, and above all they possessed what every ruling power has had since the dawn of society: an intelligence apparatus. We should never think of spies as a recent development in the way people wage war on each other. In fact, we find mention of people infiltrating enemy ranks to gain useful information in Sumerian epics such as *Gilgamesh* and through Egyptian history and Bible tales all the way to the Roman Empire's *exploratio,* the Latin term for the ingathering of intelligence from frontier provinces, which was much more developed in the Near East than on the northern borders of the empire.

Flavius Josephus, having been a commander on the Jewish side of the war before defecting to become an adviser of the Roman general Vespasian, was perhaps the most important intelligence asset the Romans had in Judaea, and he undoubtedly briefed Vespasian on the various factions in the country. That the most dangerous and militarized Jewish groups were the Zealots and the Sicarii—both, incidentally, rogue branches of the Essenes—was no secret, but as in all rebellions against an occupying power, the crucial information the Romans sought concerned clandestine supporters, or flankers, people who feigned indifference to the struggle and led apparently apolitical lives but who were in reality the logistical arm of the insurgency, providing assistance of all kinds, from safe houses to weapons, from up-to-date information to victuals.

That the Romans considered Jesus a dangerous subversive is abundantly proved by the fact that they crucified him, which was the standard way of executing rebels. The gospel tale of Judas's treacherous kiss in the garden of Gethsemane was, in this context, a case of espionage. We haven't the space here to go into the many contradictions of the episode, but I would like to underline one of them: the fact that the cohort's officers needed Judas's help to recognize Jesus amid his disciples. But didn't the Sadducee collaborators who paid Judas know all about Jesus' entry into Jerusalem and about the riot he'd caused in the Temple? How credible is it that none of them could recognize him among his friends?

Thus the Essenes' reputation for subversive activities and support for insurgents, coupled with the presence of spies wherever the Romans thought enemies of the empire might be scheming against them, made Scetis a place where Jesus might have felt safe for a short while after arriving in Egypt, but it certainly did not provide a long-term solution. Had he started teaching again (let alone effecting miraculous cures), word of his presence there would have spread and soon the Roman garrison in Alexandria would have heard of a charismatic Jew in Scetis who was rumored to be the resurrected Messiah of Israel. It just wouldn't do to remain there. Sooner or later, he would have to leave the region altogether.

The question for this chapter is where in the West Jesus chose to spend the rest of his days or, more clearly, why it might be that the ship Jesus boarded was headed to the south of France.

Earlier, when discussing Jesus' religious affiliation (though I don't question for a minute that he defined himself as a Jew), I mentioned the importance of the protomonastic communities at Scetis and Qumran, places where men and women practiced ascetic lifestyles, observed a rigorous initiatic hierarchy, ate sparsely and communally, studied prophecy and medicine, dressed in white linen, and stressed purity of body and soul above all else. If we believe that John the Baptist and Jesus were members of such a community, it is reasonable to expect that Jesus, forced into exile after his resurrection, would choose a place where he could continue to live in such a community.

What I have not yet mentioned is that the Essenes were not the first group in history to have practiced such a lifestyle. A strikingly similar community was established in southern Italy more than five hundred years earlier by one of the best-known—and perhaps most misunderstood—thinkers that Greek culture ever produced: Pythagoras of Samos.

THE COMMUNITY OF PYTHAGORAS

In the words of Bertrand Russell in *A History of Western Philosophy,* Pythagoras (c. 570–c. 480 BC) was "intellectually one of the most important men that ever lived." After the age of fifty, fleeing persecution by the narrow-minded despots of his Greek island, Pythagoras founded a philosophical and religious school in Croton (in eastern Calabria, the "toe" of the Italian boot) that quickly attracted many followers.

Initiation into the school took place through seasonal Mystery Plays and other rites he derived from his previous membership in the Orphic sect. Pythagoras himself was the secretive master of the society (he was said to teach from behind a curtain), with an inner circle of followers known as *mathematikoi*. The mathematikoi lived permanently within the society, had no personal possessions, obeyed strict rules, and were vegetarians. Both men and women were permitted to become members of the hierarchical society, and several women later became famous Pythagorean philosophers. Members of the outer circle of the society were known as the *akousmatikoi* (listeners) and lived in their own houses, joining the society only during the day. They were allowed their possessions and were not required to follow dietary rules. (We can note the similarity to the division within the Therapeutae as described by Philo.) Our most reliable primary sources on Pythagoras are:

- Diogenes Laertius (c. AD 200), who wrote *Vitae philosophorum* (Lives of the Philosophers), which in turn references the lost work *Successions of Philosophers,* by Alexander Polyhistor (c. 50 BC)
- Iamblichus (AD 245–325), an important Neoplatonist philosopher, perhaps best known for his compendium on Pythagorean philosophy
- Porphyry, who in about AD 270 wrote *Vita Pythagorae* (Life of Pythagoras)

It would be too ambitious to go into Pythagoras's thought system in any depth here, for despite the fact that not a single page of the master's own writings has survived, hundreds of books have been written that have not yet fully plumbed its depths. In a very concise summation of their principal tenets, however, Pythagoreans held that:

- At its deepest level, reality is mathematical in nature.
- Geometric and arithmetic "harmonies" are present in nature and constitute its secret structure (including the concepts of music of the spheres and microcosm–macrocosm).
- Certain symbols have a mystical significance.
- Philosophy and "clear thinking" (what Asians call meditation) can be used for spiritual purification.
- The soul can rise to union with the divine. (It is no wonder that all later gnostics claimed Pythagoras as one of their original masters.)
- Human souls are reborn into the bodies of animals. (This is akin to the Hindu form of metempsychosis, or reincarnation.)
- All sisters and brothers in the order should observe strict loyalty, diets, and secrecy.

There are myriad stories and legends about Pythagoras and his school in Croton, many of them intriguing and all in some way confirming the gnostic inclination in everything he taught.

Diogenes, for example, writes that Pythagoreans practiced constant baptismal purification to renew and maintain their sanctity, a rite that the Essenes may have adopted from them rather than from the more apparently available Jewish equivalent, the ritual bath, or *mikvah*.

PYTHAGOREAN SCHOOLS IN THE SOUTH OF FRANCE

Now for the next step in my argument: to show that schools like the one in Croton sprang up in the south of France and would later become chapters in an international network of Essene settlements.

At the time of Pythagoras, the Celts, who inhabited most of what the Romans would later call Gaul, came into contact with the Pythagoreans in two ways: The first was through the presence, as mentioned in chapter 1, of Greek colonies on the coast in what is now Marseille and in several locations further west. These colonies entertained lively commercial links with Celtic settlements farther inland, as testified to by numerous Greek (Attic) artifacts of the period found throughout the region, including near Rennes. The second form of contact was through the presence of Celtic mercenaries fighting in Magna Graecia (southern Italy) starting in the fifth century BC. This is borne out by finds of Gallic coins closely modeled on those of the Pythagorean cities of Magna Graecia, especially Taranto.

The Celtic cultural establishment was led by the famous Druids, a priestly caste not unlike the Brahmins of India, who counseled leaders, performed religious and magical rites, and set up schools throughout Celtic lands from Ireland to the Balkans. These schools had strong similarities to Pythagorean ones, such as admitting women to sacred studies, belief in the immortality of the soul, the notion of what we might call magical numbers, and a belief in the importance of music in sacred functions (their preferred instrument being the harp). It is particularly remarkable that Druids, like Pythagoreans, transmitted their lore orally and forbade writing it down.

We don't just surmise that Druidic schools had many traits in common with Pythagorean schools; the links between them are actually mentioned in the writings of several authors—for example, Hippolytus Romanus, who, in the third century AD, writes in *Philosophumena,* part of the wider work *Refutatio Omnium Haeresium:* "The Celts' Druids have assiduously studied the philosophy of Pythagoras, which they hold in the greatest esteem, clinging especially to the doctrine that the human soul is immortal and that, after a precise number of years, every soul comes back to life in another body."

These contacts are not the only reason I believe Pythagorean communities were established in Gaul. To them we must add the record of events in the late fifth century BC, when the original center of Pythagorean thought was destroyed and a Pythagorean diaspora ensued. Despite

Pythagoras's desire to stay out of politics, his society at Croton was not unaffected by events. In 510 BC, Croton attacked and defeated its neighbor Sybaris, and there are suggestions that Pythagoras became involved in the dispute. Then, in about 508, the Pythagorean society was attacked by Cylon, a violent exponent of the local nobility. Pythagoras escaped to Metapontium and many authors say he died there, some claiming that he committed suicide because of the attack on his society. But Iamblichus does not accept this version and argues that the attack by Cylon was a minor affair after which Pythagoras returned to Croton.

It was widely reported that Pythagoras was around one hundred years old at the time of his death, but many sources claim that he taught Empedokles, which implies that he must have lived well after 480 BC. The evidence is unclear as to when and where the death of Pythagoras occurred.

Certainly the Pythagorean society thrived for many years after his death and expanded rapidly after 500 BC, spreading from Croton to many other Italian cities. It soon became political in nature and split into a number of factions. In about 460 BC, the society was violently suppressed and its meetinghouses everywhere were sacked and burned. Mention is made in particular of the house of Milo in Croton, where fifty or sixty Pythagoreans were surprised and slain. Those who survived took refuge in Thebes and other places, including, very likely, the schools in southern Gaul.

What we have so far, then, is strong circumstantial evidence of the presence in what would later become the Languedoc of the same sort of protomonastic communities that existed in Scetis and Qumran. As we shall see, these two were part of a neo-Pythagorean revival at the time of Jesus.

JESUS THE KABBALIST

Now we must pursue what seems to be a totally different trail: the assorted clues and circumstantial evidence—much like the evidence for the presence of Pythagorean communities in the south of France—pointing to the notion of Jesus as kabbalist. For this very Jewish insight concerning the true nature of the historical Jesus I am much indebted to my friend, editor, and agent, Tuvia Fogel, an Ashkenazi Jew of Transylvanian origins who now lives in Italy.

What is kabbalah? The word comes from the verb "to receive," and modern Hebrew uses it for the receipt one gets after making a payment, but the concept is, like Pythagorean teaching, that of knowledge transmitted orally from master to disciple without ever being written down. The knowledge of kabbalah concerns the hidden meanings in the Torah, or the Five Books of Moses. Jewish tradition holds that innumerable secrets about these meanings were transmitted by Moses to the elders and by them down through the sages of every generation.

Christian contact with kabbalistic tradition in the early Renaissance has made us familiar with some of the techniques kabbalists use to arrive at this knowledge, such as Gematria (numerology), Temurah (permutation of letters), and Notariqon (the use of acrostics). Another kabbalistic concept many people are now familiar with is that of the Tree of Life, the geometrical arrangement of God's ten attributes, the Sephirot, which, as would later emerge in the treatises by medieval kabbalists, act in the visible world in an almost identical way to the emanations of Neoplatonic thought. So extreme are some of these theosophical secrets that kabbalah has long been in danger of being denounced as a heresy—a gnostic heresy, to be exact—by the leading lights of Judaism.

The great scholar Gershom Scholem wrote many books to show that kabbalah is the gnostic stream in Jewish tradition, just as Catharism and Rosicrucianism are forms of Christian gnosticism and Sufism is Muslim gnosticism. It had been fashionable for a long time to consider gnosticism a Christian heresy arising in first-century Alexandria from the meeting of Mark's messianic preaching and the Greek and mystery-religion culture of that great city, but Scholem knew this wasn't so. He wrote, "Gnostic ideas, though taken over by Christian heretics, were originally Jewish—a fact that has often, oddly enough, been denied or disregarded."

Recently, more and more scholars have come around to the view that gnosticism was originally a Jewish heresy, something Jews had picked up in their Babylonian and Persian sojourns and that manifested mainly as a dualist cosmology derived from Zoroastrianism. In other words, it was a vision of the world as an eternal struggle between a principle of good and a principle of evil. In effect, Jewish debate in the first century (to which Jesus was no mean contributor) includes condemnations of "those who claim that there are two powers in heaven," as the Talmud puts it (as concise a way of defining a dualist as we might find anywhere).

Kabbalah, then, is a gnostic and dualistic tradition probably originating in Babylon (although Talmudic legends attribute the first knowledge of kabbalah to Abraham and sometimes to Adam himself) and is therefore much older than gnosticism itself. In his *Histoire du Gnosticisme,* Jacques Matter writes that Jewish scholars fully understand that the secret oral traditions of kabbalah preceded any Christian gnosticism: "The kabbalah is anterior to the gnosis, an opinion which Christian writers little understand, but which the erudites of Judaism profess with legitimate assurance."

Now we can come back to Jesus. We know that he was no ordinary rabbi. At twelve years of age (still short of his bar mitzvah) his teaching enthralled the sages in the Temple courtyard and later he often taught in local synagogues. We also know that not everyone understood his often cryptic lessons and parables—in fact, we are told they were meant for those "who had ears to hear." These are perhaps the traits of a rabbi whose teaching is founded on kabbalistic notions, and any knowledgeable Jew who studies Jesus' teachings closely can soon see this.

Jesus told a tale of five wise virgins and five foolish virgins (Matthew 25), the difference between the two being that the former could "light" their lamps when the "bridegroom" came (for they had brought oil with them) and the latter could not. To a student of kabbalah, these are two very clear references to the kabbalistic Partzufim (pairs of Sephirot in the Tree of Life) that divide the ten Sephirot into two groups of five and to the Bridegroom, Zauir Anpin, a group of six Sephirot in the Tree of Life whose image is that of a son and a king. It is no wonder, then, that Jesus made it clear that he was the bridegroom in the parable.

It doesn't take a scholar to realize that the Pater Noster is a kabbalistic prayer. The last part of it, known as the doxology, reads, "For Thine is the Kingdom, and the Power, and the Glory," very clearly a reference to the seventh, eighth, and tenth Sephirot of the Tree of Life: Kingdom is Malkhut, Power is Netzach, and Glory is Hod. Here we are at the very heart of the kabbalah. Whoever constructed this prayer was a consummate kabbalist—and the one who constructed it was Jesus.

There are more instances that point to Jesus being a rabbi of the kabbalistic school, a notion perfectly compatible with his being a gnostic and an Essene, but for now we must move on to Ezekiel.

THE PROPHET EZEKIEL

Pythagoras is described by all his biographers as an almost maniacal traveler—from Syria to India, from Phoenicia to Gaul, from Persia to the Black Sea, he methodically visited all places where ancient wisdom was said to be found. In about 535 BC, Pythagoras went to Egypt, a few years after the tyrant Polycrates seized control of the city of Samos. Polycrates established an alliance with Egypt, and links between Samos and Egypt at this time were strong. The accounts of Pythagoras's period in Egypt suggest that he visited many of the temples and took part in many discussions with priests there, though according to Porphyry, Pythagoras was refused admission to all the temples except the one at Diospolis, where he was accepted into the priesthood after completing the rites necessary for admission. It is not difficult to relate many of Pythagoras's beliefs, the ones he would later impose on the community he set up in Italy, to the customs he came across in Egypt. The secrecy of the Egyptian priests, their refusal to eat beans, their refusal to wear cloth made from animal skins, and their striving for purity were all traits that Pythagoras later adopted.

In 525 BC, Cambyses II, king of Persia, invaded Egypt, and Polycrates betrayed his alliance with Egypt to send forty ships to join the Persian fleet. After Cambyses won the Battle of Pelusium in the Nile Delta and captured Heliopolis and Memphis, Egyptian resistance collapsed. In the ensuing chaos, Pythagoras was taken prisoner and deported to Babylon.

Iamblichus writes that Pythagoras "was transported by the followers of Cambyses as a prisoner of war. While he was there, he gladly associated with the Magoi . . . and was instructed in their sacred rites and learned about a very mystical worship of the gods. He also reached the acme of perfection in arithmetic and music and other mathematical sciences taught by the Babylonians."

And here is the nugget: The Talmud claims that Pythagoras visited Babylonia during the exile of the Israelites there . . . and became a student of the prophet Ezekiel!

Incredibly enough, the dates tally. Ezekiel would have been an old man by the time Pythagoras met him, for his twenty years of prophesizing had occurred at the beginning of the exile "by the rivers of Babylon," roughly between 585 and 565 BC, when he was a young priest who had been deported from Jerusalem as a child.

But there's more. In his *Stromateis,* Clement quotes Alexander Polyhistor, writing in about 50 BC: "In his 'De Pythagoricis Symbolis', Alexander Polyhistor claims that Pythagoras was a student of 'Nazarate the Assyrian.'" Who was this Nazarate? Could it have been Ezekiel? Finally, we can refer to an apparently outrageous statement from Ben Zion Wacholder, a partially blind professor at Hebrew Union College in Cincinnati who has the ability to see through the tangled undergrowth of intertwined scrolls and is a much respected father figure among his peers. In the celebratory fiftieth-anniversary conference of the finding of the first Dead Sea Scrolls, held in Jerusalem, he created a major sensation by going against his colleagues in claiming Ezekiel as the first Essene! Wacholder set out his arguments in the article "Ezekiel and Ezekielianism as Progenitors of Essenism" (*The Dead Sea Scrolls: Forty Years of Research,* E. J. Brill, 1992), which neatly closes the circle.

So what do we have? Following is a summary of the circumstantial evidence presented in this chapter.

1. There were Pythagorean communities in the south of France from early in the fifth century BC, both in the Greek colonies

and among the Celts, whose Druids were heavily influenced by Pythagorean thought.

2. It seems possible that Ezekiel transmitted his esoteric knowledge—Zoroastrian and Chaldean secrets that, within Judaism, would later develop into the gnostic tradition known as kabbalah—to Pythagoras, who transformed it into his mystical numerological system.

4. Philo Judaeus, the Therapeutae, and other first-century gnostics in Egypt were referred to by almost all later writers as neo-Pythagoreans—that is, revivers of a tradition born in the sixth century in the south of Italy that had survived in—among other places—the south of France.

5. Jesus was very probably an early kabbalist—that is, a follower of a gnostic tradition dating back to Ezekiel and preserved by the Essenes. He was therefore himself a neo-Pythagorean.

All of this together explains why, when Jesus had to choose a remote hideaway where a gnostic, neo-Pythagorean kabbalist could feel at home, he most likely would have boarded a ship heading for the south of France.

14

THE EARLY DOCUMENTS: THE BEGINNING OF THE LIE

What import does everything I've written so far have on the search for the real origins of Christianity? If I suggest, as I have dared to do, that the gnostic communities of Egypt earlier and France later transmitted the true meaning of Jesus' teaching, then what is the Christianity we are taught today and from where does it come?

Obviously, Jesus' teaching must have been changed (corrupted?) by people and events in early times, but can we ever find out how, when, and by whom? Text criticism, philological research, and archaeology can all throw a degree of light on these questions, and without turning this book into a treatise that only biblical scholars would want to read, we can explore just one example of the corruption of historical truth by both well-meaning and thoroughly devious manipulators. This is the story of one word in the Christian scriptures: Nazareth.

THE ORIGIN OF NAZARETH

An intriguing statement appears in Acts 24:5. Paul is accused of being a ringleader of the "Nazarene" sect. The label Nazarene or Nazorean is considered by most scholars to refer to members of the earliest Christian community in Jerusalem, who were not initially designated Christians.

Schonfield and others attest that early Christians in Judaea were designated as Nazarenes (or Nazoreans). On the surface, it would appear that the term refers to a person from Nazareth, the village in the Galilee where Jesus is said to have been raised as a child. A closer look, however, shows that Nazarene could not have derived from the word Nazareth. German theologian Holger Kersten, author of *The Greek-German Dictionary of New Testament Writings and Other Early Christian Literature,* openly admits that a connection between the name Nazarene and the place Nazareth is not possible because no archaeological dig in Nazareth has ever yielded a first-century stratum. What's more, Nazareth, a Galilean village, is not mentioned by Josephus in his detailed list of Galilean settlements. It was only in the third century that an insignificant village, En-Nazira, was designated as Nazareth and officially chosen as the village in which Jesus was raised.

How, then, do we account for the term Nazareth in the gospels? Simply put, Nazareth is a mistranslation. In all cases where it occurs, the correct translation should be "Jesus the Nazarene," not "Jesus of Nazareth." In the Gospel of Mark, considered the oldest canonical gospel, 1:9 should instead read, "And it came to pass that in those days Jesus came from the Nazarenes of Galilee and was baptized by John in the Jordan."

Schonfield reports:

> The name borne by the earliest followers of Jesus was not Christians. They were called Nazoreans (or Nazarenes), and Jesus himself was known as the Nazarene. It is now widely agreed that this is a sectarian term, of which the Hebrew is *Notsrim* (or *Nozrim*), and is not connected with a place called Nazareth. The name relates to a community whose members regarded themselves as the "maintainers" or "preservers" of the true faith of Israel . . . The same may be said of a pre-Christian sect of Nazarenes (Aramaic: *Natsaraya*) described by Church Father Epiphanius.

But if Jesus and the earliest Christians were in fact associated with the sect of the Nazarenes, which predated Jesus' own birth, then we may well ask where the Nazoreans originated and what their teachings were. Other questions are still more interesting: If the village of Nazareth didn't yet exist, why did copyists consistently translate "Nazarene" as "from Nazareth"? What kind of faith were the Nazarenes trying to preserve? Could Jesus' association with the Nazarenes have become a source of embarrassment to the Church Fathers?

Theologian Holger Kersten brings more light to the issue: The word Nazarene derives from the Aramaic word *nazar,* which means "to keep watch," "to observe," or "to own." In a figurative sense, the word also means "to vow" or "to bind oneself to serve God." Used as a noun, it refers to a diadem, the symbol for an anointed head. Thus a Nazarene was a keeper or celebrant of the sacred rites. If Jesus was a keeper of the sacred rites or mysteries, he must have been a threat to the Temple leadership in Jerusalem, which considered itself orthodox. Most important for us, the Nazarenes were a branch of the Essenes, as were the Ebionites. The Essenes were considered a heretical sect by the Sadducees and the high priests. No doubt Nazarenes were also considered to be heretics. That Jesus might have been a member of or associated with a cult practicing unorthodox rites or mysteries was too much for the architects of established Christianity to bear. This association had to be camouflaged. From here, most probably, came the necessity of mistranslation and the birth of Nazareth.

But is there any evidence that Jesus did, in fact, practice secret rites? The discovery by Professor Morton Smith in 1958 of a portion of the so-called secret Gospel of Mark does show Jesus as a practicing hierophant of the mysteries. I cite a portion of the gospel, preserved in a letter of Clement of Alexandria, following a scene in which Jesus raises an unnamed youth (Lazarus?) from the dead: "And after six days Jesus told him [the youth] what to do and in the evening the youth came to him wearing a linen cloth over his naked body. And he remained with him that night, for Jesus taught him the mystery of the Kingdom of God. And thence, arising, he returned to the other side of the Jordan."

According to this text, Jesus practiced nocturnal initiations, imparting the mystery to the initiate. The scene demonstrates vividly that Jesus' religion (if that is the proper name for it) did not depend on and most certainly was not a part of Orthodox Judaism. Jesus and his followers were sectarians practicing their own rites, which they knew to be the true faith of Israel.

Are there any records of the teaching of pre-Christian Nazarenes? In his 1843 book *Kabbalah,* Adolph Franck quotes from a Codex Nazareus: "It is in Nazara that the ancient Nazoria or Nazireates held their Mysteries of Life or Assemblies . . . which were but the secret mysteries of initiation . . . The oldest Nazarenes . . . were the descendants of the Scripture's *nazars* . . . whose last prominent leader was John the Baptist." Jesus, as we know, was baptized by John the Baptist.

It is quite possible, then, that true, original, primitive Christianity as it was preached by Jesus can be found only in these so-called Syrian heresies. These Nazarenes apparently were baptized in the Jordan and could not be baptized elsewhere, and they were circumcised and had to fast before and after their baptism. We can recall that Jesus also fasted for forty days following his baptism. The Nazarenes were known for their long hair, as was Samson, the Nazarite—and the Shroud of Turin, reputed by some to be the burial cloth of Jesus, shows him with long hair.

The Nazarenes were numbered among the gnostic sects and believed Jesus to be a divinely overshadowed prophet sent for the salvation of nations in order to recall them to the path of righteousness. Furthermore, the Talmud refers to the Nazarenes as a sect of physicians and wandering exorcists. Jesus, of course, is described in the gospels as an exorcist who casts out demons at will—some of which, he states, respond only to prayer and fasting.

GOSPEL ERRORS AND "LOST" GOSPELS

As you can see, a totally new, and some would say unbelievable, portrait of Jesus has emerged from analyzing the corruption of just one word in the gospels and taking the results of that analysis to their extreme consequences. Scholars—especially Germans—have been certain for some time that important discrepancies among the gospels stem from translation errors probably caused by working from an Aramaic original. It is important, then, to be sure that what we read has been through the reworking of as few hands as possible; contains the least possible number of interpolations by later writers, copyists, and censors; and is not only old—the older the better—but either has been preserved by intellectually honest keepers or, better still, has lain hidden for centuries and has only recently come to light. There are many important documents that do fulfill these conditions, but for some reason, most Christians do not even know they exist.

It is important to realize that almost all of these so-called missing gospels were not lost but were deliberately excluded by the early Church Fathers. We now know that some of the missing fragments that have come to light were suppressed on the order of Clement, bishop of Alexandria. Many works omitted from the Canon have since proved to be historically accurate. In AD 367, Bishop Athanasius compiled a list of works for inclusion in the Christian scriptures, and this list was ratified by the Council of Hippo in 393 and by the Council of Carthage in 397. The process was selective and in no way definitive. Most important, text criticism clearly shows that much editing took place.

Some of the documents that were excluded later turned up in the so-called Apocrypha (from the Greek word for "hidden"), written as late as the sixth century. Others that were in use in the second century can claim to contain much truth. The Gospel of Peter, found in 1886, was mentioned by a bishop of Antioch in AD 180. It states, among other things, that Joseph of Arimathea was a close and wealthy friend of Pilate. There is also an Apocryphal work called the Gospel of the Infancy of Jesus Christ, which is dated to before the third century.

The remainder of this chapter provides an outline of the primary sources for the early Christian period, complemented by brief accounts, where available, of my personal experiences of them. The intent is to give readers a more accurate perception of how much literature on Jesus was circulating from the end of the first century outside of the four gospels by the Evangelists that would later be officially "approved" as canonical.

THE SINAITICUS AND SYRIACUS CODICES

One of life's great experiences is to visit the Greek Orthodox monastery of St. Catherine in the Sinai. Many times I have had the good fortune to visit the monastery, where I was received with great kindness by the monks, in particular by Father Michael, with whom I have spent many hours in what is arguably the greatest library of ancient documents in the world. Its collection of icons dates from as early as the tenth century.

The Sinai is reached by bus from Cairo: After crossing the Suez Canal, you head for the tip of the peninsula and arrive at the foot of St. Catherine before nightfall. From there, a walk up a long trail brings you to the gate. St. Catherine looks like a small piece of Greece, with its green trees and Greek-style buildings. Only a small mosque and the Arab workers are reminders that it is still Egypt. The place has an atmosphere of timelessness, desert wisdom, and great faith.

The Hebrew scriptures tell us that this is the place where God came to earth to speak to Moses through the burning bush. It is also where Moses later received the Ten Commandments, on top of nearby Mount Sinai, reached by ancient though now broken steps. Within the monastery is the legendary Well of Moses, the only water within many miles of desert.

The Arabs invaded Sinai in 639, and a time of great terror for the monastery ensued. It was decided to send a deputation to appeal to Caliph Omar himself, asking that the monastery be spared destruction, for both Muslim and Christian faiths believe in Sinai as the holy place of the prophet Moses. Omar granted their appeal and the monks still possess a copy of his document (the original is now in Mecca) with the imprint of the palm of Omar's left hand. Kept with the document is a sketch of the monastery building at that time.

In about 1850, a young German specialist in ancient languages, Constantin von Tischendorf, who had been frustrated in his efforts to work on the Vatican's fourth-century Codex Vaticanus and hoping to find other, even older documents, set off to visit and search early monasteries. On his first visit to St. Catherine, Tischendorf secured only four minor documents, perhaps because he showed too much interest in them. Much later, armed with credentials provided by Alexander II, czar of Russia, he was allowed to take away several documents of the very greatest value, among them what we now call the Codex Sinaiticus.

It is now accepted that the Codex Vaticanus and the Codex Sinaiticus, both dated to about AD 350, still remain the earliest Christian scriptures in existence, together with probably almost identical copies made at the same time, though perhaps in different places. In superb condition, the Codex Sinaiticus is written on vellum that required the skins of between three hundred and four hundred sheep or goats, paid for at great cost by some important unknown benefactor. This work was carried out within twenty-five years of the Edict of Tolerance (AD 313), so vital to Christianity in that it granted freedom for all religions.

The monks are absolutely certain that Tischendorf stole the documents. I have also been shown by Father Michael a receipt signed by Tischendorf for the loan of the document. Tischendorf declared he used money provided by the czar to purchase the document, not to secure its loan. In 1933 the Soviet government, desperate for Western currency, sold the codex to the British government for the enormous sum of one hundred thousand pounds. It remains on view at the British Museum. The monks have since found six more pages, which the museum does not yet have.

Today, the monks feel bereft and still bitter about the exchanges. They do not have a good copy of the document, only a poor one provided by the Russians and written in Russian, which is of no value to them. I am still attempting to find a benefactor willing to provide them with a first-rate copy, which the British Museum might well permit to be made.

There does still exist in the monastery another document, one I am tempted to define as mysterious. The monks have in fact shown me this most precious document owned by the monastery. Called the Codex Syriacus, it was in superb condition, written on loose ten-inch by ten-inch sheets of thick vellum and wrapped in strong white flaxen cloth tied loosely with soft string. It is carefully stored in the small, air-conditioned section of their library. Each leaf of the script appeared perfect. They said it was the oldest existing document of the Christian scriptures, dated to before AD 200.

After my return to London, I searched all possible publications to find reference to this document, but I was able to trace nothing. I find it difficult to believe that such a treasure could exist and not be known to the world.

THE FIND AT NAG HAMMADI

Most people have heard of the Essenes and the Dead Sea Scrolls, found at Qumran, written by them. But though of enormous importance, these documents have been more interesting to scholars of Judaism and make no direct reference to Jesus and his teaching.

In 1945, however, some peasants made the greatest discovery of ancient documents of all time. A group of seven illiterate Muslim field workers, led by Muhammed Ali el Samman, were digging for *sebakh,* a fertilizer found at the foot of the great precipice of Jabal el Tarif, a fearsome place where many anchorites (or early hermits) had found refuge in caves in the face of the rock, often high up, some distance from the Nile and water. Here they lived a life of prayer and devotion in great privation, wearing animal hair and coarse clothing, living on the most frugal diet of rock-hard bread probably baked only twice a year with salt and water. Gradually they banded together for protection, and later formed the nucleus of the great place of teaching and learning founded by Saint Pachomius, which heralded the beginning of organized monastery life.

One hundred miles north of Luxor, this remote area where the Nile makes a huge bend and where early Christian settlements developed in safety is known as Nag el Hammadi. My late wife and I were present there during part of the work at about Christmastime in 1978 and 1979, when James Robinson, in collaboration with the Institute for Antiquity and Christianity in Claremont, California, headed a UNESCO delegation involved in search and excavation work.

Professor Bastian Van Elderen and I spent much time in the Nag el

Hammadi area over the last ten years. We tracked down and met the original finder, Muhammed Ali, and believe we have located the still hidden area of what may be the second not-yet-discovered half of this remarkable library. Muhammed Ali, a murderer deeply involved in local blood feuds, is still alive today but has no worthwhile memory of where he made his find. He now says he found a large intact ceramic pot that was completely buried. He smashed it hoping for gold, but the contents were papyrus documents. These were extracted, divided up, and carried on seven camels to his mother's house nearby at Chenoboskia. Some were put on her fire and were thereby lost. It took more than thirty years, until the late 1970s, and several million pounds and dollars in secret transactions with shady dealers and others, for the documents to reach scholars, whose work continues today.

Uncertainties remain about the site of the find. Professor Van Elderen and others, using magnetometers and other equipment, carried out extensive searches to locate the original site and find other possible ones. About 150 caves and early tombs were examined, some with early Christian writings of psalms on the walls. No doubt there are many concealed caves not yet located.

One cave, more than a hundred feet up the precipice face and seemingly inaccessible from both above and below, was strangely filled with the bones of camels, horses, oxen, and sheep. We may well wonder why the carcasses or the bones of animals would have been dragged to such a place.

Muhammed Ali told me that he had also found the body of a very tall man with huge hands, buried facedown, which is the sign of a heretical burial. Ali now says he was afraid of ghosts, djinns, and evil spirits, which prevented him from making this known earlier. The body was covered by a black layer of the dust of decayed material, probably the remainder of the rush matting placed over the body at the time of the burial. We know that at about that time a plague swept through the area, wiping out most of Pachomius's followers and himself.

The monastery was on a piece of land slightly higher than the surrounding area, so at Nile flood times it became an island. Amazingly, we have an account describing the discipline and daily life of the monks there at the time. But why should documents of such great importance have been hidden in pottery above the Nile flood level? After studying the area for many weeks, Van Elderen and I constructed what appeared to be a plausible scenario.

St. Pachomius must have returned from discussions in northern Egypt, perhaps in Alexandria, or even outside the country in Antioch. There was much debate at that time over dissenting religious groups and unorthodox thinkers in the early evolution of the Christian faith. In all probability, St. Pachomius found a group of perhaps six or seven monks within his fold who were Arian or gnostic in their belief. He may have ordered them out, asking them to take their writings with them. We surmise that they located themselves in several caves two or three miles away, near Jabal el Tarif, still in sight of the monastery. Pottery shards there have allowed fairly precise dating.

In the early 1980s, Van Elderen excavated the first, second, and Roman levels of the site, including the area of the original basilica of St. Pachomius, which was flooded in later years during changes in the Nile flood level. Fortunately, the flooding was confined to that area and did not extend to the place where the documents were hidden, at a higher level about a mile away. At Dishna, an open field some three miles to the east, close to the mountains, another set of documents was found by peasants and these works have recently come into the possession of scholars. Sadly, we do not know the exact find site and there is little possibility of it being discovered. These documents almost certainly came from the St. Pachomius monastery as well, but because there are no signs of other Christian sites nearby, we don't know the reason for their burial. The documents themselves are largely Orthodox Christian (a very small part are gnostic) and are of great importance.

As for the Nag Hammadi gospels, how did someone carry and bury (so fortunately for us) the most remarkable collection of early Christian documents ever found? Maybe we shall never know what really happened. There are indications that only half the important library of gnostic material removed from the monastery at that time has been found, and we have real hope that we have located the site of a burial area and of the remaining find. At the time of this writing, Van Elderen and I hope to apply for further excavation permits at Nag Hammadi.

Regarding the texts themselves, the whole collection was copied early in the fourth century from documents originally written early in the second century to about AD 200 and was subsequently buried about AD 350. Scholars today are divided in their interpretation of this library. Fifty-three tractates have been found. The level of the original writers' scholarship and thinking is very high, well beyond that of many Renaissance scholars, who wrote so many centuries later. The Gospels of Philip and Thomas have attracted much attention and controversy. The Apocalypse of Peter, the Apocalypse of Paul, the Letter of Peter to Philip, the Secret Book of James, and many more project a ray of light onto this vital period in the evolution of Christianity.

The gnostic authors clearly believed they had secret knowledge of Jesus and his writings. The Gospel of Thomas contains about 120 sayings of Jesus not known to us before. The words on the first sheet are in Coptic and can be translated as: "These are the secret sayings of the Living Jesus as written by Didymos Judas Thomas." We now know that the Gospel of Thomas is the complete version, in Coptic, of the Greek papyrus fragments found by Grenfell and Hunt in the nineteenth century. The original must therefore have dated from no later than AD 200. There are no references to the Crucifixion or Resurrection, only sayings of Jesus, each preceded by the words "Jesus said." The mysterious Kingdom of God, only briefly referred to in the canonical gospels, is here described in some detail. Whereas Jesus' parables in the known gospels are relatively easy to understand, those in the Gospel of Thomas are understandable only to the initiated mystic.

Religious leaders and churches continue to study this material but, like scholars, are divided in their interpretation. For the most part, all are rejected completely as being gnostic, but about half of the texts are in fact Orthodox (including those from Dishna). Of course, some documents do appear to derive from early forms of Christianity such as gnosticism, Arianism, Nestorianism, and other belief systems that were eventually crushed. For this reason, the judgment of some religious authorities has so far been to regard this material as heretical.

In the early days of interpretation, great faith was attached to "gospel truth," but recently scholars have discovered wide discrepancies in these gospels as well as among the four canonical texts. There is nevertheless remarkable conformity in the texts between what we have always had and the early documents now coming to light. Much early material is still being found. How vital it would be for Christianity, for example, if we could find the Aramaic "master document" of Matthew's gospel, described as the Sayings of Christ. Discrepancies among the four gospels could then be resolved once and for all and Christian doctrine could be greatly strengthened. Let us consider that there are about 270 vellum manuscripts relative to the Codex Sinaiticus alone, all dating to between the fourth and eleventh centuries, and as many as ninety papyrus fragments datable from between the second and fourth centuries, as well as other remarkable manuscripts. I, like many others, believe that in the next twenty to thirty years, much new vital material will come before us that will result in a great increase in our understanding of all the gospels.

VARIOUS OTHER FINDS

The great archaeologist Flinders Petrie became aware of papyrus scraps found in rubbish heaps at the site where he once was working. Some years later, the Egypt Exploration Society, acting on his advice, appointed Bernard Grenfell, a young graduate who had dug with Petrie, to search for papyrus scraps in rubbish heaps on other sites. Grenfell asked Arthur Hunt, a college friend, to join him in what proved to be, as work progressed, one of the most successful excavations ever undertaken.

In the first season, in the Fayoum area, results were negligible, but in the next season they chose to search the Greek settlement of Oxyrhynchus, where many early Christian monasteries and churches had existed. Nothing had ever been found in this area and it had been abandoned for centuries, but with remarkable perception, the two men chose to dig in large rubbish heaps some distance from the main ruins. The dust and heat made working conditions extremely difficult, but the results grew rapidly in both value and quantity. As papyrus finds increased, Hunt concentrated upon the work of sorting. Many scraps related to private letters, contracts, and various official documents. These were of great interest in illustrating everyday life at the time they were written, but there were also many fragments showing the handwriting styles of early Christian writers.

In a six-inch square, Hunt recognized the words "then you will clearly see to cast the mote from your brother's eye," which he of course immediately compared with the extract well known to him from the Christian scriptures (Matthew 7:3–5 and Luke 6:41): "And why beholdest thou the mote that is in thy brother's eye but considerest not the beam that is in thy own eye?" Hunt found six or seven other sayings, each proceeded by the word, "Says Jesus." Several were unfamiliar and yet appeared genuine. The style of the writer, probably a copyist, showed clearly that the document had been written in about AD 200. Later in the excavation period, a number of other fragments from the same unknown gospel were recognized by Grenfell and Hunt. Thus was the antiquity of the Codex Sinaiticus surpassed by material written only some one hundred fifty years after Jesus lived. This was a discovery of the greatest importance.

Another important find of papyrus scraps, bearing verses 37 and 38 from chapter 18 of the Gospel of John, was found by Grenfell in 1925. In 1934, Oxford graduate Colin Roberts paleographically dated it to between AD 100 and 125, making it the earliest piece of Christian papyrus yet found.

In 1935, English millionaire Alfred Beatty declared his purchase on the Egyptian black market of papyrus fragments similar to those from Oxyrhynchus, and the calligraphy of these indicated they were from the same date, approximately AD 200. This time the invaluable acquisition comprised parts of the Gospels of Matthew and John, pieces of the Gospels of Luke and Mark, substantial parts of the Acts of the Apostles and Revelation, and more than eighty of the original 110 pages of the letters of St. Paul. These are now at the University of Dublin, Princeton University, and the University of Michigan and in the Austrian National Museum.

In 1941, Dr. Morton Smith, professor of ancient history at Columbia University, stayed for a short time with the Greek Orthodox monks at the Mar Saba Monastery near Jerusalem and in 1958 he was invited to catalog and study their manuscript collection. In the process, Professor Smith came across an extraordinary find of tiny handwriting on the back of a seventeenth-century edition of letters by St. Ignatius of Antioch. It turned out to be a letter copied from an original dating from the end of the second century and written by an early bishop of great fame whose remains were the most venerated of all the early Church Fathers: Clement of Alexandria.

In 1950, the famous collector and Swiss diplomat Martin Bodmer bought on the Egyptian black market large parts of a codex of the Gospels of Luke and John, again dated to about AD 200. In the Egerton Papyrus Number Two, dated by its handwriting to before AD 150, there is proof of the existence of yet another gospel not known to us containing an account of Jesus escaping stoning and healing a leper. And that's not all. In 1:1–2 of his gospel, Luke writes that even in his time there were "many other gospels in existence." Scholars are now certain of the existence of a fifth gospel addressed to the Hebrews, now lost but mentioned by both Jerome and Origen. A gospel of the Egyptians was noted by Origen and Clement of Alexandria, and a gospel of the Ebionites, whose contents seem virulently opposed to the writings of the apostle Paul, is also being studied by scholars.

UNDERSTANDING THE NEW DOCUMENTS AND WHAT THEY REVEAL

It is not generally realized today that the four gospels bearing the names of Matthew, Mark, Luke, and John were not written by these people at all. These names are in fact only attributions—or, technically speaking, the texts are pseudepigraphic—a rather common practice in late antiquity. Additionally, few people are aware that each gospel was originally written for and used by a particular community or locality. They were not expected to be placed one beside the other, as we find them today.

Some readers may have difficulty accepting this because the account given in Catholic tradition has become embedded in our way of thinking. For example, in about AD 175 Irenaeus, the bishop of Lyon and a famous fighter against heresies, wrote:

> Matthew composed his gospel among the Hebrews in their own language, while Peter and Paul proclaimed the gospel in Rome and founded the community. After their death, Mark, the disciple and interpreter of Peter, transmitted his teaching to us in written form and Luke, who was Paul's follower, set down in a book the gospel which he preached. Then John, the Lord's disciple who had reclined on his breast, himself produced a gospel when he was staying at Ephesus.

This version of events, however, has turned out to be wishful thinking at best, propaganda at worst. Contradictions, inconsistencies, conflations, phrases lifted from one text and inserted into another, interpolations by one hand in the middle of a period clearly written by another hand, knowledge of things that had not yet occurred—all are in the text and cannot be explained away. This critical view developed during the nineteenth century, as a scientific approach to the scriptures took hold among theologians, especially in Germany. No attempt will be made here to review this work, but it is important to review the many excellent works produced through the last century in this area of study. Wilhelm Wrede, Albert Schweitzer, Rudolf Bultmann, Karl Schmitt, Werner Kümmel, Dennis Nineham, Helmut Koester, and many others produced far-reaching thought in theology in the first half of the twentieth century and John A. T. Robinson's excellent reviews *Redating the New Testament* and *Honest to God* are also enlightening reading.

There are many discrepancies in the presentations of certain acts by Jesus among the four gospels. A comparison technique called *parallel research,* developed particularly in Germany, proved to be quite valuable. It involved examining each incident in juxtaposition in the two or more gospels in which it appeared. It was through this technique that

The remains of the monastery in the famous Wadi Feiran (Faran), the largest oasis in the Sinai, a place that once had the privilege of being the Holy See of the first bishopric of the Sinai Peninsula.

The two Marys in their boat—Church of Les-Saintes-Maries-de-la-Mer, Camargue. (Note the jar in one of the women's hands, marking her as Mary Magdalene.)

Aerial view of Rennes-le-Château. (Photograph by the author's son, John Simmans.)

Receipt for Abbé Saunière's coffin showing the date as June *(juin)* and *not* January *(jan* for *janvier).* (Collection of Norbu-Captier.)

The mountain range Jabal el Tarif, along the Nile River at Nag Hammadi, where the gnostic gospels were found. (Photograph by the author.)

The author with pottery he found at the Wadi Natrun site.

Arabet Alydos
nr. Balyana,
Egypt.
Dec. 16 1975.

Dear Mr. Simmons,
Just a line to wish you and your family all the very best for Christmas and the new Year. May 1976 be a better year for all of us.
Judging by the number of Tourists this year, things must be improving in Europe and America; I can't remember when we had so many, certainly not in the past ten years!
Again, all the best of luck and health to you, and yours.
Yours sincerely
Omm Sety.

Two letters to the author from Omm Sety (Dorothy Eady) who became a close friend of the author. Dorothy Eady, at the age of three, suffered a head injury from falling down the stairs. When she regained consciousness, she believed that she was reborn as an Egyptian priestess who had lived more than three thousand years earlier.

Arabet Alydos,
nr. Balyana.
Egypt.
May 11. 1973.

Dear Mr. Simmans,
How are you? I've been hoping to see you here this season, but up to now, no luck!
How did you get on with the Tourism Office project? I hope it is working out O.K.
Dr. Hani el Zeini, and I were mentioning you the other day, and we wondered if you had been able to do anything about our book on Alydos, as we are contemplating doing another book on some unsolved mysteries of ancient Egypt.
Lets hear from you when you can spare a minute.
All the best of luck,
Your's sincerely
Omm Sety.

Map of tribal migrations in late antiquity. (From the volume
L'Europe des Invasions, 1967, courtesy of Éditions Gallimard.)

Model of Jerusalem at the time of Jesus Christ.
(Courtesy of the Hotel Holy Land, Jerusalem.)

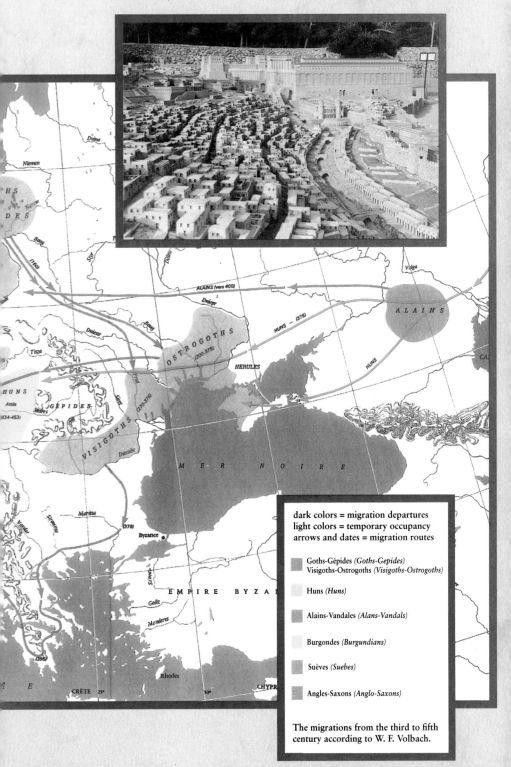

dark colors = migration departures
light colors = temporary occupancy
arrows and dates = migration routes

Goths-Gépides (Goths-Gepides)
Visigoths-Ostrogoths (Visigoths-Ostrogoths)

Huns (Huns)

Alains-Vandales (Alans-Vandals)

Burgondes (Burgundians)

Suèves (Suebes)

Angles-Saxons (Anglo-Saxons)

The migrations from the third to fifth
century according to W. F. Volbach.

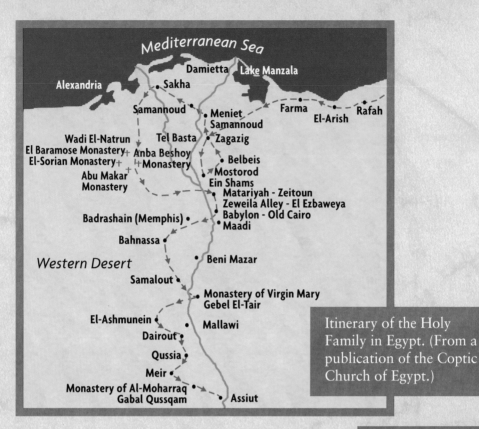

Itinerary of the Holy Family in Egypt. (From a publication of the Coptic Church of Egypt.)

Right: Muhammed Ali al-Samman (discoverer of Nag Hammadi codices). (Photograph by the author.)

Below: The Codex Syriacus dating to the fifth century, discovered in 1892. (Courtesy of the Monastery of St. Catherine.)

the authorship of Matthew soon became challenged. How? First, Mark shows considerable lack of knowledge of the geography of Judaea, with many errors such as that in chapter 7, which refers to Jesus going to Tyre through Sidon on the way to Galilee when in reality Sidon is in the opposite direction and there was no road to Galilee from Sidon at that time. Scholars found that the writer of Matthew drew so much material from Mark that he cannot but have been writing later than his inaccurate source. Therefore, Matthew cannot have been the tax collector turned apostle—and an eyewitness—for if he had been, he would not have needed to copy incorrect details from someone else's writing. This is just one small example, but it illustrates how difficult it is to rebut arguments based on such logic.

A vital work in this area, *The Four Gospels: A Study in Origins,* was produced by the English Canon Streeter, who put forward some remarkable reasoning. It had been recognized that the writers of the Gospels of Matthew and Luke, while relying on the Gospel of Mark, had also used a second Greek-language source referred to as "Q" (from *quelle,* the German word for "source"). But Cambridge Professor Cupitt thought that whoever wrote Luke was struggling with an Aramaic source he was determined to follow. Canon Streeter suggested that actually two other sources existed, both written in Aramaic, the language spoken by Jesus himself: "M" provided material to Matthew and "L" to Luke.

There are also instances of the gospel censors involuntarily betraying themselves. For example, according to Eusebius of Caesarea in his *History of the Church,* Bishop Papias of Hierapolis in Phrygia, who lived between AD 60 and 130, wrote: "Matthew completed the Sayings [of Jesus Christ] in the Aramaic language and everyone translated these as best they could." According to Irenaeus, Papias knew the apostle John. In other words, he was as close to a real eyewitness as we can find among the authors of known texts. Yet here is Eusebius himself, the first official historian of the Church, quoting him as writing something that vindicates the scholars' conclusions and gives the lie to the official version of how the gospels were produced!

The true dates of the writing of the four canonical gospels still remains undetermined. John A. T. Robinson placed them between AD 30 and 60 and Werner Kümmel suggested later dates, between AD 60 and 90. The difference is crucial, for the vital incident that evidently controlled most of the content of the gospels was the tragic and hopeless revolt of the Jews between AD 66 and 70 that ended in the total destruction of Jerusalem. In the aftermath of the tragedy, the early Fathers of the Church faced a terrible problem: Still reeling from the terror unleashed by Emperor Nero in AD 64, how could they present a new creed to a Roman world based on the horrible killing by Romans (for practically no reason) of the principal figure of Jesus, a member of the crushed Jewish community?

At about this time, the Gospel of Mark was written in Rome, though whether before or after the revolt is not known. Many scholars believe that Mark slanted his writing in favor of Rome and away from Roman guilt by placing total blame on the Jewish scribes, priests, Pharisees, and Sadducees. Pilate is shown as a reasonable figure—"What wrong has he done?"—finding no fault in Jesus and symbolically washing his hands of his death. Indeed, in Mark's gospel (15:39) a Roman centurion at the foot of the cross even says, "This man truly was the son of God!"

But Mark's gospel is not the only one to shift blame to the Jews. Matthew (27:25) went so far as to depict the whole of the Jewish people as accepting responsibility for Jesus' death with the terrible words "His blood be upon us and our children." Ironically, the Jews could have killed Jesus themselves by stoning if they had wanted to—they had no need to appeal to the Romans. On the evidence provided in the Bible, crucifixion was essentially the death reserved by Rome for its own direct enemies. Not many years later, for example, the Jews killed St. Stephen by stoning and did not involve the Romans at all.

Perhaps to encourage converts, Mark showed Jesus as rejected by his own people and placed his emphasis on this. We have already seen that references to Jesus as a Nazarene were taken to mean "from Nazareth" but more probably meant he was a Zealot (in modern parlance, a terrorist). Mark takes great care to avoid any reference to Jesus being in any way associated with those who created or managed the revolt. In fact, strangely enough, there is no reference to the Jewish revolt in any gospel.

If the gospels were written after the catastrophic destruction of Jerusalem, it seems strange that there is no mention of an event that in effect constituted the fulfillment of Jesus' prophecies in Matthew 24:1–3, Mark 13:1–4, and Luke 21:5. If, on the other hand, the gospels were written before the event, then why would the writers have shown such care in distancing the gospels from the rebellious Jews and absolving the Romans from any wrongdoing? These prophecies of Jesus in Matthew, Mark, and Luke could have been added later, but it seems unlikely. Their importance, in particular relating to the dating of the gospels, tends to be ignored.

The tragedy is that under Herod, the Romans had allowed much ostentation and opulence in the building of the Temple of the Jews. We can wonder just what the Jews might have achieved had they not revolted.

15

HOW IT ALL WENT WRONG

The first, almost immediate schism in the Judeo-Christian movement in the years following the Crucifixion was that between Peter and Jesus' brother James the Righteous on one side—the Jerusalem Church—and the followers of St. Paul on the other. This lasted for perhaps ten vital years before unity was reached. Paul, the antagonist of James, created a completely new doctrine that made Christianity no longer acceptable for Orthodox Jews. He, not Jesus, instigated the birth of a new religion.

Saul (later Paul) claimed he was a Jew from Tarsus with Roman citizenship and a Pharisee, though not all scholars today believe what he wrote in this respect. In his zeal, he originally persecuted the early followers of Jesus with the authorization of the Sanhedrin. After a vision of Jesus on his way to Damascus (very probably the Essene Damascus), followed by three days of blindness, he accepted baptism, became a devout Christian (some would say that he changed faith but remained a radical), and changed his name to Paulus (the Less), stressing his humility. His letters to disciples all over the Greek and Roman world give a vivid account of the brilliant thinking he overlaid on the teachings of Jesus. These epistles are the earliest documents of the Christian scriptures, having been written by Paul himself, whereas the gospels were written later (as much as half a century later, in the case of the Gospel of John) by disciples of the evangelists to which they are accredited.

Paul builds his philosophical construction on the idea of Original Sin: Because Adam sinned in the Garden of Eden, all humankind has inherited his Original Sin and its consequences. As he writes in Romans 5:12, "Wherefore, as by one man sin entered into the world, and death by sin; and so death passed upon all men, for that all have sinned." According to Paul, death and judgment cannot be avoided by living a pious life.

In Romans 3:25, for instance, he shows us the one path to salvation: the sacrifice of Christ, "whom God hath set forth to be a propitiation through faith in his blood." By his death, the Redeemer has taken away the sin of the world. As he writes in Hebrews 9:14, "How much more shall the blood of Christ, who through the eternal Spirit offered himself without spot to God, purge your conscience," and even more explicitly, in Romans 5:8–9, "In that, while we were yet sinners, Christ died for us. Much more then, being now justified by his blood, we shall be saved from wrath through him." But how could a mortal man redeem all humankind? The answer is really quite simple: Jesus was not a mortal man; he was God. According to Colossians 1:13–17, "[God] hath delivered us from the power of darkness, and translated us into the kingdom of his dear Son, in whom we have redemption through his blood, even forgiveness of sins."

These few passages express, in a nutshell, the idea that would develop into what we call Pauline Christianity. It must have been utter blasphemy to the Jews: The eternal and only God fathers a son with a mortal woman, and this son, who is also God, enters this world with the purpose of becoming a human sacrifice in order to save humankind from damnation. No wonder James the Righteous and his Jerusalem Church were horrified. Paul then declared that Christianity was for everybody, not just for Jews, and that did it—the line of separation was drawn. His ideas were in effect much more attractive to pagans than to Jews. Greek and Roman gods had many sons with mortal women. Alexander's claim to be the son of Jupiter Amon was quite acceptable to his Macedonians and Paul's preaching was immediately and widely successful, to the point that after the death of James, his doctrine was no longer seriously opposed.

Christianity, cast in his mold, entered the Roman Empire. At its beginning, from the time of Nero onward, its followers had to overcome more or less continuous persecution, killing, and torture of the most appalling kind. Perhaps even more terrible than Nero's were the persecutions of Decius (249–251), Gaius (251–253), Valerian (253–260), Diocletian (284–304), Galerius (305–311), and Maximus Daia (311–313). This so-called epoch of martyrs was followed at last by the Edict of Tolerance in AD 313, granting freedom for all religions, not just Christians. Sacred books and documents of all kinds were being destroyed continuously up to 313 and it is little wonder that so few early writings from this time have survived.

The true miracle of Christianity was not so much the speed of its spread over wide areas of the Roman Empire, but rather the astounding tenacity of purpose and penetration of its beliefs, even amid persecution. At this time, most early Fathers never met each other; they were limited to writing letters, which involved great delays. It is not hard to understand how, after such terrible troubles, they were determined that Christianity emerge finally as the great faith of the world. But at the time, they had no real assurance of the amazing success that the Christian faith would in fact achieve. Thus it was that unity of thinking became so vital to them in the events that followed, perhaps leading to a degree of intolerance of divergent opinions that would not be accepted today. Theology dominated thinking, which led to a tendency to overlook the way of life taught by Jesus himself. There was no supreme authority in the Church and each sector and locality developed a variety of inspiration and thinking.

To give my readers a better idea of how things went awry at this time, I can employ a parallel that some will find unusual, to say the least: a comparison between early Christianity and communism. I am not referring here to what some historians have rightly pointed out: that the party founded by Lenin and based on the teaching of Marx resembled a religion more than a political or economic movement.

What I'm talking about is the slide from the early communists' morally compulsive arguments for social justice to the repressive dictatorship of their official heirs not two generations later. This is the same mechanism that was likely responsible for the behavior of the early Church. Just as the communists of the first two decades of the twentieth century were convinced that violence was wrong but necessary to protect the Revolution from its many enemies, so did the Fathers of the Church in the first two centuries condemn heretics in an effort to save nascent Christianity from its many enemies. Just as people around the world still flocked to the promise of communist rhetoric while Stalin's secret police were already executing many of the original revolutionaries and their close associates, so did thousands of pagans flock to the ideals preached by early Christians while Iraeneus and others were already burning the books of gnostic Christians and chasing them out of town. We can remember, for example, how it later emerged that Stalin's NKVD had gone so far as to chemically remove ex-comrades from photographs taken before their downfall so that they would no longer appear in the official history of the Party. This is exactly how we may think of interpolations in ancient texts in the first centuries of the Church, efforts such as a copyist inserting a Christian view of Jesus into the lines that Josephus had written about Judaea in the first century.

There are two questions in this regard that must be considered. The first is whether we can, even with all our hindsight, judge the good faith of people who falsified writings and burned books in the first century or who denounced "revisionists" and touched up photographs in the twentieth. They almost certainly believed they were carrying out these acts for the advancement of a higher cause, but does this absolve them from tampering with the historical truth? The second question is perhaps more pertinent in the context of this book: A century after the first Russian popular uprisings against the czar, some people still claim that Leninism, Stalinism, and Maoism were actually betrayals of the original ideals expounded by Karl Marx or, in other words, that true communism has never actually been put to the test of history as its power-mad, corrupted versions have. We might ask, then: Was Jesus' true teaching ever put to the test of history, or were those struggling to be the leaders of the Church a mere two generations after him already betraying his lesson? If just one hundred years after the Crucifixion, someone had preached the very same things that Jesus had preached, might he or she not have already risked the second-century equivalent of the Siberian gulag?

DIVISIONS IN THE FAITH AND THE COUNCIL OF NICAEA

The Edict of Tolerance was recognized by Christians as their great chance. They seized it with vigor, but at that time there were still serious and often bitter divisions between those who had accepted mutilation and death rather than surrender and those who had betrayed them, who had mouthed pagan devotions to save themselves and allowed the destruction of the books that were held so dear. Other conflicts evolved over the territorial authority of bishops, mainly among Antioch, Alexandria, and Rome.

Very broadly, the first century was the great era of the apostles, with John dying in about AD 92. The second century saw great progress, yet a strange melancholy developed well into the third century, a loss of faith in the very idea of a Church when so many in Egypt and elsewhere went out into the deserts to seek individual salvation for their own soul in solitude and prayer. This period is not fully understood and there is much still to be learned. A kind of questioning emerged—so often entertained by humans—along the lines of "How can a good God allow such a terrible state of affairs to prevail on earth?" One likely explanation for this mood is that Jesus had said he would return soon. The persecutions were readily accepted by the martyrs in part because they knew they were experiencing the "last days" and were convinced that they would only be preceding their fellow believers into the Kingdom of God by a few years at most. In other words, it seems Jesus' resurrection was not fully understood, leading to a variety of heresies.

As an example of how subtle the differences in belief could be at that time between what are known as Christologies, consider this: By about AD 300, the concept that Jesus had existed more as a spirit than as a human, though not dominant, was still widespread. In Alexandria this thinking was known as Docetism. The great bishop of Alexandria, Clement, gave substance to the view that Christ was so near to being God that he did not require such earthly things as eating, drinking, and even going to the toilet, as mortals do, yet his actual words were (according to Stromateis 6:9), "It would be ridiculous to imagine that the body of our Redeemer, in order to exist, had the usual needs of mankind. He only took food in order that we should not teach about him in the fashion of Docetism." This might remind us of those creationists today who claim that God created the world in six days and planted fossils everywhere to confound faithless fools like the Darwinists.

In Alexandria this problem, which we could call Jesus' growing divinity, had developed to the point where it was believed that Jesus had always been God and was the equal of God from time immemorial. Thus in no way could he be less than God. The prevailing Christology in Antioch, however, was radically different, emphasising the unity of God, the importance of Jesus' way of life, his teaching, and his simple humanity. The great teacher Lucian strongly stressed this view. Among his first followers was Arius, who would later have authority in Alexandria itself. Arius's simplistic doctrines attracted wide support, so when he was suddenly excommunicated by the head of Egyptian Christianity, many bishops with views similar to his—including the bishops of Caesarea and Nicomedia—immediately supported him and called a synod to condemn the Alexandrian beliefs. This dispute—heavily influenced by what we could call the nationalisms of the time—was the seed of intense divergences that were to last several centuries and which survive in divisions among certain Eastern churches to this day. The basic argument was thus obsession with theology versus simplistic interpretations of Jesus' way of life.

The most important chapter in this history was without doubt the First Ecumenical Council of Nicaea in AD 325, where the foundations of the Catholic Church were laid. The Church of Rome had by then established the right to make decisions for the whole Christian world, but Eastern Churches refused to accept this and moved away, leading to the serious divisions that would result in the schism of AD 1054. Forgotten was the fact that the first head of Jesus' Church had been his brother, a Jerusalem Jew called James. After Nicaea, Rome would dominate Christianity until the sixteenth century, when Martin Luther affixed his ninety-five theses to the door of the Schlosskirche in Wittenberg, leading to breakaways from which the Catholic Church has never fully recovered.

The story of the Council of Nicaea is inextricably tied to its conceiver, moderator, and ultimate referee, Emperor Constantine the Great, a figure who cannot but have a central role in a chapter on how and when Christianity went wrong. Constantine was hardly a Christian in the true sense, having killed his wife by boiling her in her bath and putting his sons to death out of fear of any possible threat from them. Heavily built and bullnecked, he was probably ill educated but extremely shrewd. His great chance came in AD 312, when the Roman Empire radically changed. Following his terrible yet final persecution of Christians, Diocletian abdicated in AD 303, some say because of the proven ineffectiveness of his devastation.

Constantine had quickly captured northern Italy—and now Rome lay before him. To complete the conquest of the western half of the empire, he had to eliminate the son of Maximian, Maxentius. The Christian legend is that Constantine dreamed of a sign combined with the declaration: "By this sign you shall be victor" *(in hoc signo victor eris)*. The Chi-Rho symbol, the first two letters of Christ's name in Greek, had not been created by him but rather had been adopted by Christians long before and was known as their sign. It is said that his mother, Helena, convinced Constantine of the immense importance of this omen and that he subsequently gave orders for the sign to be painted on every soldier's shield. Yet we know that Constantine actually remained a believer and worshipper of the sun god Sol Minerva throughout his life. In fact, it is now believed that, for good measure, he had the Sol Minerva emblem painted on the reverse of the soldiers' shields!

The story of the battle at Milvian Bridge is well known. Constantine made a clever outflanking maneuver that upset Maxentius's plan to trap him on a bridge of boats constructed a few miles north of Rome. Maxentius's troops made a mad scramble for the boats, which were cut loose too soon, probably due to faulty communication. Many men fell into the Tiber in full armor and Maxentius himself died in this way. His decapitated corpse was found downriver. Constantine's victory was complete and he was sincerely grateful to Christ. This event proved to be a true turning point for Christianity.

Comparatively little is known about the life of St. Helena, his mother, though she became perhaps the greatest of all saints by establishing a firm foundation for Christianity through her son. Certainly it was she who influenced Constantine and explained Christianity to him. Yet the general belief that he was a fervent convert to Christianity is clearly wrong. He was baptized only on his deathbed in AD 337—but it is absolutely certain that he lavished huge funds on Christianity, spending on basilicas in Rome and all over the empire. There can also be no doubt that Helena played a great part in this work. No one knows whether Constantine became more convinced of Christianity in his later years, but it is possible that his mother swayed him somewhat in his beliefs.

With his Edict of Tolerance, issued in 313 (a year after the battle of Milvian Bridge), Constantine did not, contrary to traditional thought, make Christianity the official religion of Rome. At the time, the state religion of Rome was pagan sun worship and Constantine acted as its chief priest throughout his life. Before his victory at Milvian Bridge, Constantine was most assuredly not Christian. Commemorative medallions show him as Invictus Constantinus with the image of Sol Minerva. Later, he mixed Christianity with the Sol Invictus cult. This is clear from a second medallion issued within two years of the first and on which he is represented with a Chi-Rho emblem on his helmet and a leaping Sol chariot and horse below. There can be little doubt that Constantine was a superb opportunist, dominated as he was by the intense need to unite the divided Eastern and Western Empires. His political thinking seems to have been dominated by measures to bring together followers of every diverse religion in the Empire. The widely divergent plethora of faiths in Rome at this time were Mithraism, worship of Greek and Roman gods such as Apollo, emperor worship, Sol Invictus, and many others, among them Christianity.

At the time of the Council of Nicaea, Constantine had indeed, at great cost, secured unity between the Eastern and Western Empires. Now he realized the seriousness of the deep divergence of judgments between the Alexandrian and the Antiochian Christologies. The bishop of Alexandria was now Alexander, a fierce opponent of Arius's view of Christ as a "creature" and thus less divine than his Father. Constantine sent a letter to both Arius and Alexander to attempt a reconciliation, but the divisions were too deep by then and each bishop had full authority in his region while Pope Sylvester I in Rome exercised no real control.

As a result, Constantine took an unprecedented step: He called a council of delegates summoned from all parts of the empire to resolve the issue. All the dioceses into which the empire had been divided, with the exception of Britain, sent one or more representatives to the council, with the majority coming from the East. It is not known how much advance notice was given to all concerned and some had to cover immense distances for those days. Indeed, some delegates must have arrived very late, with journeys taking many months from as far away as Spain and Persia. Arius himself was there, while Pope Sylvester, too aged to be present, sent two presbyters as his delegates. The meeting was held at Constantine's palace and the emperor was impressively dressed in golden raiment.

The object of the council, we must remember, was not to pronounce what the Church ought to believe, but to ascertain as far as possible what had been taught from the beginning. No minutes exist of the council, but the decrees were written down and subscribed to by all. It seems that Eusebius of Nicomedia and Eusebius of Caesarea arrived early, strongly representing the Antiochian view. Believing they would achieve victory without serious challenge, they powerfully established the view of Arius. To provide a basis of acceptance, the following declaration, already in use for their baptisms, was offered for approval: "We believe in one God, the Father, the Almighty, Maker of all that is seen and unseen, and in one Lord Jesus Christ, the word of God, God from God, light from light, life from life, only begotten son, first born of all creation, before all ages begotten from the Father, who for our salvation was incarnate and lived among Men."

The words "first born of all creation" certainly bestowed divinity on Jesus, but nevertheless expressed the Arian view that he was the begotten son of the Father and not God himself. For the Alexandrians, this language was not sufficient or precise, making Jesus appear as less than God. A great decision was about to be made, the effects of which on the followers of Jesus would be felt right up to this day. Was Jesus a simple being (though clearly divine), brought into existence to serve God's design as the Word of God, or had he been God for all eternity from the creation of the world ("of one substance with the Father"), practically the same as God himself? These two alternatives are at an immense distance from each other.

We shall never know what caused Constantine to decide in favor of the Alexandrians. It may be that he could not precisely assess the differences and saw it as a fair compromise, which it was not. Eusebius's original declaration was heavily edited and all were obliged to sign it (for those who refused, there was immediate banishment) as a foundation on which future Christians would agree for all time. No gospel actually speaks of Jesus as God, but he had now been declared "Very God from all Eternity." All but two Arian bishops signed, but many later wrote to Constantine regretting their acquiescence in what they came to consider a blasphemy. It was too late, however—there was no way back for those who dissented later.

Today most Christians are no longer aware that there were several forms of Christianity before Nicaea. All recognized Jesus and the gospels as the basis of the faith. After the council, those that diverged were ruthlessly put down as heretical by the orthodox (Catholic) Church. Irenaeus had said there could be only one universal Church, with a doctrine relying on apostolic succession. This required a fixed and final list of authoritative writings that excluded all others. We may well wonder about this judgment, for the result of the selection is basically what we are left with today. Many believe Constantine's genius made possible the whole Christian empire that followed. Today we would be more tolerant, for recent studies show that though radically different from each other, the varied beliefs at that time were still all Christian.

No one has yet explained why Arianism spread at such great speed. What was it in that faith that so many accepted in place of orthodox Christianity? The main difference, as we have seen, lies in the view on the status and nature of Christ and his divinity. Arius's doctrine, that Christ had only a human body and was thus wholly mortal and did not even have perfect knowledge of the Father, ensured the permanent enmity of orthodox followers, which continues today in the Eastern Churches and at recent Ecumenical Council meetings. But this very "human" God became increasingly attractive to kings and princes, who could identify with such a God more readily than they could with a seemingly meek supreme being who submitted to martyrdom without resistance. It was the heresy of Arius that posed the most dangerous threat to orthodox Christian teaching during the first thousand years of its history. In fact, the God of Arianism enjoyed immense appeal in the West as Christianity came to acquire more and more temporal power.

Although Arianism was condemned at Nicaea, Constantine was always sympathetic to it, and became more so toward the end of his life. On his death, his son and successor, Constantius, became unashamedly Arian and under his auspices councils were convened that drove Orthodox Church leaders into exile. It seems possible that Constantius recognized that his father, by error or misunderstanding, had influenced the Council of Nicaea's decision in a wrong direction and tried to correct the situation. By AD 360 Arianism had all but replaced Roman Christianity, and although it was again officially condemned in AD 381, it continued to thrive and gain support. When the Merovingian kings rose to power in the fifth century, virtually every bishopric in Christendom was either Arian or vacant. The most fervent devotees were the Goths, who had converted from paganism during the fourth century. Lombards,

Vandals, Burgundians, Ostrogoths, and Merovingians were all Arians. So were the Visigoths who sacked Rome but spared the Christians churches in AD 410. As we learned in chapter 1, under the Visigoths, Arianism became the dominant form of Christianity in the Pyrenees, southern France, and Spain. It even seemed to be in better accord with the Muslims, to whom Jesus was a prophet.

Comparatively few people today realize how the divergent views at Nicaea and the attitude to the early heresies developed into later tragedies and persecutions, setting a regrettable pattern for the behavior of the Church. Some of the council's consequences were truly terrible. With regard to the Jews, for example, if Jesus was God, then the Jews had killed God, and in fact Constantine seems to have gradually withdrawn civil and other rights he had earlier granted to them. All alternative forms of Christianity, especially gnostic ones, were simply crushed after the council. We might wonder what Jesus himself would have thought of the decisions made in his name at Nicaea.

WHAT OF THE TEACHING OF JESUS?

Of course no one, in the heat of theological debate, seemed to notice that the final formula contained nothing of Jesus' teaching.

The idea of Jesus being God has always been rejected by Muslims and Jews, for whom there can be only one God. Agnostics, atheists, and many thinkers through the past two millennia have found it hard to believe that a young Jewish rabbi who taught for about three years should have been declared to be the Creator, with God, of the vast infinite cosmos. If we carefully consider what Jesus said about himself and what he taught his disciples, we can see that he regarded himself as a heaven-sent messenger, a being of divine inspiration and insight—but he also recognized that every soul in its very origin was one with the Divine. In John 10:30 he says, "I and my Father are one," implying that everyone should find this divine identity within himself, as he had done. Was the Church wrong in interpreting this statement as "He (Christ) and the father are one"? Jesus' true legacy was his commandment to "love each other," taken to the extreme of "love your enemies" in Matthew 5:44. He in fact loved people. The gospels give many examples of his healing, his compassion, and his understanding of his suffering fellow humans. When Peter asked Jesus how often he should forgive his brother—perhaps seven times?—the answer was a far greater figure, meaning "always" (Matthew 18:21–22). Jesus insisted that his followers not be content with obeying the Law and doing what is customary, but that they go beyond solid citizenship and strive for perfection of their souls. "Be ye therefore perfect, even as your Father who is in Heaven is perfect," he said in Matthew 5:48. In other words, he urged them to become divine beings. He knew many would not grasp this message, so he used parables that could be easily remembered and perhaps fully understood later, though, unfortunately, they were mostly misunderstood and misinterpreted.

GNOSTIC CHRISTIANITY

It is true that the heresy of Arianism was at the heart of the Nicaea watershed, but as we've seen, there were many other strands of Christianity competing for people's religious loyalty in the three hundred years from the Crucifixion to the Council of Nicaea, with the most widespread and dangerous for the orthodox Church being gnosticism. While it drew from and entered into many religious traditions, the effects of gnosticism were most keenly felt by emergent Christianity, so much so that some historians think the original function of the Canon, the Creed, and the Episcopal organization of the Church was to constitute a protective wall against gnostic Christianity. The limited knowledge we have of gnosticism derives mostly from the attacks and criticism of its opponents in the early Christian period. Irenaeus (d. 202), Hippolytus (d. 236), and Epiphanius (d. 403) are the best known, but there were countless others.

Perhaps the most important gnostic thinker of the time was Valentinus. Born in Alexandria, he spent the latter part of his life, from about AD 136 to 165, in Rome. He was very influential, had many important followers, and claimed to possess a quantity of secret teachings of

Jesus. Though he always refused to submit to any Roman authority, it is interesting to note that Valentinus very nearly became bishop of Rome, which could have had some most provocative consequences.

Another dangerous gnostic was Marcion, a shipping magnate and bishop who arrived in Rome in about AD 140 and was excommunicated four years later. It was to refute a list of biblical works created by Marcion (which excluded the Hebrew scriptures) that Irenaeus produced his famous list of heretics. Yet another heretical thinker of that crucial period (it sometime seems that the second century saw more heretics than "right thinkers") was Basilides, an Alexandrian scholar writing from AD 120 to 130. He knew both Hebrew and Christian gospels and was familiar with Egyptian and Hellenistic thought. He himself is supposed to have written a large number of gospels, which sadly have not survived. Irenaeus said that he put forward a terrible heresy, perhaps the most terrible of all. Interestingly for us, Basilides also claimed that the Crucifixion was a fraud—Jesus did not die on the cross and a substitute, Simon of Cyrene (who carried the cross), took his place. This rather unlikely belief nevertheless strangely persisted through the centuries at least as late as the setting down of the Muslim Quran.

In fact, though, many of the early Christian sects did not believe that Jesus had died on the cross. The Docetists believed that the Crucifixion was only apparent, that it did not actually occur. The Marcionite gospel claims the killing of Jesus could not have occurred because Jesus was never actually born but only appeared among us. The Gospel of St. Barnabas also contains the proposition of another being substituted for Jesus on the cross.

It has never been easy to produce a precise definition of gnosticism. Certainly the remarkable find of gnostic writings at Nag Hammadi allows us a better understanding. In gnostic belief, the self of humans, consubstantial with the Divine, fell from its heights into a world of unconciousness, deception, and evil. But humans can, by divine help and revelation, become conscious of their origin and their task to find their way back. Jesus may be describing this in his parable of the prodigal son.

Further, because the world is full of evil, it cannot be the creation of a good God but must be the work of a lower creator, the demiurge Jehovah or Yahweh, who is not the Supreme Being. In the gnostic view, the origin of all that is cannot be named or described; it is the unknowable, incomprehensible Godhead, the Silence, the Eternal, the Absolute, the Nothing bringing forth the All because an object is needed in order to express his eternal love. Manifestation begins with the Divine Trinity: Father (*nous*, the Creator), Mother (*ennoia*, the Holy Spirit), and Son (*logos*, the Word). Emanations from the Divine—that is, qualities such as love, truth, and power—are known as the *aeons* who become manifest as lightful entities, or angels. Having received the gift of free will, they were able to determine their own destiny, after which the Divine presence withdrew, making this world possible. Rebellious aeons, called archons, opposed the divine will and the results were matter, darkness, fate, and death.

Fallen angels and their leader, Satan, now ruled the world and the immortal soul of humans became a prisoner in an impure physical body and forgot about its divine origin. Only with the help and guidance of a Savior would it be able to find the way back to its true self. It was to bridge the gulf between eternal light and the world of man that the Logos, Christ, descended to show the way. Various myths adopting ideas from many traditional religions express these gnostic ideas. The allegorical method was used by gnostic schools of the second century to extricate gnostic meanings from Hebrew and Christian religious writings.

Gnosticism was essentially a creed of personal experience demanding continuous progression toward perfection and a direct relationship with the Divinity. This was not paralleled by orthodox Christianity, in which followers were required to give unquestioning faith, abandoning all thoughts of individual choice or responsibility. Gnostic revelation cannot be grasped by philosophical thinking and reason or by Christian dogma and scripture. It is understood only by the initiated seeker striving to find his or her divine self.

It is interesting to compare this to our way of thinking today. Despite the New Age and other forms of spirituality being defined as the modern version of gnosticism, do we in fact continually strive toward perfection?

16

THE GHOST GOES WEST

In the days when Jesus walked this earth, Jews were everywhere in the Roman Empire. They weren't just in the Eastern provinces—where Alexandria, Antioch, and Damascus had Jewish populations in the tens of thousands, accounting for a quarter or a third of the total—but in the West as well, including Rome itself. At the time of Caesar Augustus, there were over eight thousand Jews in Rome. The most diverse witnesses—Strabo, Philo, Seneca, Josephus, and the author of the Acts—all bear testimony to the fact that the Jewish people were dispersed over the known world, and archaeological discoveries constantly increase the number of known Jewish settlements. In a letter to Caligula, King Agrippa I names communities of the Jewish diaspora in almost all countries of the Orient. Josephus writes that after the land of Israel and Babylonia, Jews were most numerous in Antioch and Damascus. Philo estimates the number of Jews living in Egypt at one million, more than 10 percent of the population.

Alexandria was by far the most important Jewish community. In Philo's time, Jews inhabited two of the five quarters of the city. It seems inevitable that such a large community could not all be made up of emigrants from Judaea. Most likely a large fraction of them were converts to the Jewish religion. It is well known that in the time before the

destruction of the Temple, Jews engaged in vigorous and successful pros-
elytizing, favored by the pagan world's admiration for Judaism's moral
precepts and by its fascination with traditions reputed to be very old,
and the Jews' Torah was said to be among the oldest of holy scriptures.

All of this underlines how likely it is that when many gospels—the
four that would become canonical as well as dozens that would later be
forbidden—began to spread the tale of the resurrected son of God, Jews
would condemn and fight what they considered a Jewish heresy. Indeed,
apart from immediate accusations—starting on the very Sunday of the
alleged resurrection—that his followers had stolen the body themselves
in order to make just such a claim, condemnation of the followers of
Jesus kept on growing in Jewish circles, as we see from the story in Acts
9:1 of Saul being sent by the high priest, just a few years after the Crucifixion, to hunt "the disciples of the Lord in Damascus," and from much
other evidence right up to the second-century break between Judaism
and Christianity.

The *Encyclopedia Britannica* states:

> There were three major stages in the break between Christianity
> and Judaism: (1) the flight of the Jewish Christians from Jerusalem
> to Pella across the Jordan in AD 70 and their refusal to continue
> the struggle against the Romans; (2) the institution by the patriarch
> Gamaliel II of a prayer in the Eighteen Benedictions cursing such
> heretics (between AD 90 and 100); and (3) the failure of the Chris-
> tians to join the messianic leader Bar Kokhba in the revolt against
> Hadrian (132–135).

It seems likely that if the "Son of God" claim was blasphemous
and unacceptable to Jews, the most often repeated statement by Jewish
critics of early Christians must have been something along the lines of
"Jesus was just a man!" As we saw in the last chapter, the main debate
among Christians for three centuries after the Crucifixion was the one
on Christ's nature regarding the exact proportions of the human and
the divine in his person. This makes it almost inevitable that Jews every-

where would be supportive of Christians who considered Jesus a man and a teacher and who fought the Pauline version of Christ in which God sacrifices his only son to cleanse humanity of its sins.

Here, then, in a nutshell lies the essence of relations between Jews and Christians in the days of the early Church Fathers—that is, in the three hundred years between Jesus' disappearance (whether by resurrection or by flight to Egypt) and Constantine's convening of the Council of Nicaea, which outlawed any view of Christ that disagreed with Paul's. This would suggest that all Christian heretics who considered Jesus a man—gnostics, Judeo-Christians, Arians—must have had the sympathy of Jews throughout the Empire and beyond, and this at a time when Christianity was not yet the empire's official religion and Judaism and Christianity, in their quarrel, had to appeal to the emperor's justice as only two of the empire's innumerable faiths. It is telling, for example, that even Pelagius and Nestorius, two fourth-century monks who preached the wrong doctrines and were declared heretics after the Council of Nicaea, were accused by their excommunicators of "Judeizing" influences (preaching something too similar to Judaism).

It's true that Nestorius fled eastward and that communities established in his name spread from Persia to China, but it's fair to say that he was the exception and that heretics denying Jesus' divinity met with their greatest success in the West. After all, most Goths chose Arian Christianity and Celtic Christians were mostly Pelagian. Most important for this book's thesis, a strong aversion to the divinity of Jesus, the Virgin Birth, and especially the dogma of the Holy Trinity was displayed by early Christians in Gaul, Hibernia, and Iberia—that is, in France, Ireland, and Spain.

Why should this be? Why indeed should there be any geographical element among the factors that influenced pagans in choosing one form of Christianity over another? The obvious answer lies in preexisting traditions in a particular region. And what existing traditions were there in Gaul and Iberia that could influence the choice between two kinds of Christianity? Why, Jewish ones, of course. But we can add something to this: In the case of Gaul, not only were Judeo-Christian, gnostic, and Pythagorean traditions present in many places, but there was also something else that would make it natural to convert to a Christianity in which Jesus was a human teacher: the lingering memory of Jesus himself teaching there after the Crucifixion.

Because of this prevalence in the Western reaches of the empire of Christians who disliked that Paul had made a God of Jesus, let us look more closely at those crucial developing Christian communities in Gaul, Hibernia, and Iberia and discover how Christianity started in these lands, who their first martyrs and saints were, and what kind of Christianity they preached.

GAUL

As we discovered earlier, Jewish migration to the mouth of the Rhône began in the era of Greek colonization, and the flow increased in the late first century BC, encouraged by Emperor Augustus. After the destruction of Jerusalem in AD 70, the flow became a torrent, and this time some of the new Jewish refugees were Christians. The earliest Christian preachers in Gaul were the saints who arrived on the boat that bore Mary Magdalene. Most people are familiar with the tradition concerning the flight of Mary to the south of France. Some stories have Joseph of Arimathea organizing the escape of some disciples and family members of Jesus on one of his tin-trading ships, while others tell of a boat with neither oars nor sails being boarded by the fleeing saints and then safely borne by gentle winds to the coast east of Marseille. Churches dedicated to Mary Magdalene all over the Midi have images of this oarless boat that miraculously came ashore in the marshes of the Camargue, to be exact in the vicinity of a village called, after that event, Les-Saintes-Maries-de-la-Mer.

Today, tourists flock to the Gypsy (Roma) festival in this village that celebrates one of many so-called black Madonnas. These famous, much venerated, but hard to explain icons and statues, of which there are some four hundred in Catholic countries in Europe (almost two hundred in France alone), portray the Virgin with black face and hands (though usually without black African features), sometimes with the holy child and sometimes without. The commonly accepted origin of black Madonnas is that they are a leftover of the cult of Isis, which was extremely widespread in late antiquity. In the Camargue, however, a tradition survives that the Magdalene had a small child with her, a daughter named Sarah who was dark-skinned, and that black Madonnas were originally portrayals of that child (though some claim they represent the Magdalene herself). Sarah means "princess" in Hebrew, so it's not hard to see how this tradition contributed to the strangely persistent speculations about the child's father being Jesus.

Local traditions relate that soon after the Crucifixion, a boat full of Jesus' relatives landed near present-day Les-Saintes-Maries-de-la-Mer. By all accounts, the group included three Marys, covering the interwoven families of Jesus and John the Baptist. One of the three was Mary Magdalene, and also included were Martha and Lazarus, members of her family; some Romanized Jews, including Maximinius and Sidonius, the blind man from Jericho; and (whether she was Mary Magdalene's daughter or not) Sarah the Egyptian. Tradition relates that the group spread out through Provence and preached the good news with such success that by the time of the destruction of the Temple barely a generation later, Provence was at least partially converted to Christianity.

Two of the Marys along with Sarah remained in the seaside village where they landed, and when each died, she was buried in a small chapel in the center of the village, which became a church in the ninth century. Even today, the cool darkness of the church takes us back to another age, when faith was only superficially Christian but was actually illuminated from within by the antiquity of its goddess worship. A flight of stairs leads down to the crypt where the bones of Sarah and the two Marys were found in the 1440s. The atmosphere in the crypt, blackened by the candles of myriad pilgrims, most of them Roma who come to pray before the black statue of Sarah, is one of earthly mysteries. Here is a Christianity far different from the orthodox variety. Here the feminine is not excluded but is instead worshipped in a manner far more ancient than early Christianity itself.

The impression is heightened during the fête in May when the Roma gather to honor St. Sarah and the Marys. For several days prior to the festival Roma from all over Provence, southern France, and northern Italy pour into Les-Saintes-Maries-de-la-Mer, some still in their beautiful horse-drawn caravans. The three-day festival begins by taking down the reliquaries of the two Marys from their chapel in the local church. The relics are left on display while the black statue of Sarah, brought up from the crypt, is draped in many rich cloaks and paraded down to the sea. The next day, the two Marys make the same journey. Standing in a small blue boat piled high with roses and holding an urn full of healing balm—the Holy Grail?—the two Marys travel on the shoulders of their four guardians to the sea where they landed almost two millennia ago. In this simple ritual can be heard echoes of a goddess tradition going back to Egypt and beyond. After the Marys are returned to their chapel, the dancing and singing go on late into the night as the crowd prepares for bullfights, *bandido* runs, and the parties of the third day.

The small beach town of Les-Saintes-Maries-de-la-Mer, according to tradition, holds the key to the mystery of what happened to the Holy Family after the supposed resurrection of Jesus in Judaea. Yet why does this tradition not speak of the presence of Jesus on that boat? The obvious answer is that while Gaul may have been far from the troubles in Judaea, it was still a Roman province, so the pretender to the Judaean throne would have had to travel incognito. It must also be supposed that any writings pointing to Jesus being alive after the crucixion were destroyed by the Catholic Church as a lethal danger to its very existence. While we can't argue anything here *ex absentia,* as archaeologists call conclusions reached from the absence of something rather than from its presence, the fact that the Church has always considered the memory of Mary Magdalene in Gaul to be essentially harmless can mean only that right from the start it was not accompanied by a tradition about Jesus in Gaul. If he was there with her, then, as I suggest, the number of people aware of his real identity must have been very restricted.

Beyond tradition, can we conclude who exactly was on the boat? In his *Liber Pœnitentiae,* archbishop of Mayence Rabanus Maurus (AD 766–856) details those who were said to have traveled with Joseph of Arimathea, claiming that he was accompanied by "the two Bethany sisters, Mary and Martha; Lazarus; St. Eutropius; St. Salome; St. Cleon; St. Saturnius; St. Mary Magdalene; Marcella, the maid of the Bethany sisters; St. Maxium or Maximin; St. Martial; and St. Trophimus or Restitutus." It is interesting to note that Joseph of Arimathea is linked to both the Gallic and British traditions regarding the arrival, respectively, of Mary Magdalene and some of the apostles. We shall look more closely at the role of Joseph, a very wealthy Jew and a respected member of the Sanhedrin, but here we can look briefly at a passage in which Diodorus Siculus is writing of the tin trade. He says: "This tin metal is transported out of Britain into Gaul, the merchants carrying it on horseback through the heart of Celtica to Marseille and the city called Narbo." Effectively, if Joseph was a central figure in first-century tin trading, which he was, we may deduce that this would quite often take him both to the mouth of the Rhone and to Narbonne, a city whose Jewish community would become famous throughout the Middle Ages and which is also, not by coincidence, the nearest port to Rennes-le-Château.

Here is how the company's voyage is described by Cardinal Caesar Baronius, a sixteenth-century Vatican historian, who based his account on ancient manuscripts:

Leaving the shores of Asia and favored by an east wind, they went round about, down the Tyrrhenian Sea, between Europe and Africa, leaving the city of Rome and all the land to the right. Then happily turning their course to the right, they came near to the city of Marseille, in the Viennoise province of the Gauls, where the river Rhone is received by the sea. There, having called upon God, the great king of all the world, they parted, each company going to the province where the Holy Spirit directed them, presently preaching everywhere.

Most historians admit to a kernel of truth at the heart of this tradition, if only because of the abundance and antiquity of French churches dedicated to Mary Magdalene. Some of them (the basilica of Vézelay, near Avalon, among them) claim to be built on the site of the cave in which she meditated, in perfect protomonastic fashion, for the last twenty or thirty years of her life, while others (the basilica of St. Maximin, for instance) claim to be her burial site and to possess her remains.

Perhaps it was the danger entailed in moving around too much, as some of my psychic friends have often told me, that made Jesus decide to stay put and preach his message to only a select few disciples who knew who he was (gnostic teachers always had a limited number of initiates in their circle), while his wife, her presence not being considered a danger, moved around the country spreading the good news.

HIBERNIA

Whether Christianity reached Ireland or Britain first is a question of much debate, but there is no doubt that the tradition of Joseph of Arimathea traveling to Britain soon after the Crucifixion—alone or with some of the apostles—is very ancient and considered to be the original seed of so-called Celtic Christianity, the form of Christianity first received and practiced by communities in Britain and Ireland that spoke Celtic languages. Regardless of who was Christianized first, there is no doubt that early Celtic Christians observed practices divergent from those in the rest of Europe.

The debate about the antiquity of the Celtic Church and the influence it had on the Roman Catholic one is still lively, and is truly an important conversation, because if we could verify the existence of a Celtic Christian Church even before the authority of the Church in Rome was established by Constantine, this would seriously challenge the Catholic Church's claim to supremacy and seniority in Europe. At the heart of the theological clash between the two churches was the Roman claim that the Roman Church had been founded by the apostle Peter, while the Celts claimed that Jesus himself founded the Culdee Church by sending the apostles to Britain. Theologically, Jesus would trump Peter, of course, but how one apostle of Jesus would trump Peter, another apostle of Christ, is not clear. After all, the Catholic Church to this day argues that Jesus said to him, "You are Peter [the Rock], and on this rock will I found my church."

The earliest claim for the arrival of Christianity in the British Isles is that some of the apostles themselves or Joseph of Arimathea landed near Glastonbury. Known as the Tradition of Glastonbury, a number of manuscripts document the details of this tradition. The earliest support for the idea comes from Tertullian (AD 155–222), who wrote in his *Adversos Judeos* that Britain (and we can note that he actually mentions Gaul, Britain, and Spain) had already received and accepted the gospel in his own lifetime: "all the limits of the Spains, and the diverse nations of the Gauls, and the haunts of the Britons, inaccessible to the Romans, but subjugated to Christ."

Essentially, the claim is that Joseph and others followed the well-known Phoenician trade route to Britain and that upon arrival, according to *Hardinge's Chronicle,* the company was met by Arviragus, who later converted to Christianity and took the name Caractacus. There is evidence that Caractacus was indeed a Christian, for historian Dio Cassius describes him as a "barbarian Christian." Moreover, in the *Domesday Book,* Arviragus, or Caractacus, is recorded to have granted Joseph and his followers as Judaean refugees ("Quidam advanae-Culdich," which means roughly "certain Culdee strangers") "twelve hides of tax free land in Ynis-witrin," or the Isle of Avalon.

St. Gildas (AD 516–570) affirmed that "the Gospel arrived in Britain in the time of the Emperor Tiberius." Roman sources support Christianity's early arrival to Britain, Dio Cassius's reference being but one of them. In fact, the Roman Church itself accepted an early date for the arrival of Christians in Britannia. Eusebius (AD 260–340), bishop of Caesarea and father of Church history, wrote: "The Apostles passed beyond the ocean to the isles called the Britannic Isles." He is thought to have received his information from British bishops in attendance at the Council of Nicaea. There are even Eastern references to the Christianizing of Britain. St. John Chrysostom (AD 347–407), patriarch of Constantinople, wrote: "The British Isles which are beyond the sea, and which lie in the ocean, have received virtue of the Word. Churches are found there and altars erected."

Finally, in AD 1126, William Malmesbury, a scholar known for his accuracy and quoting certain ancient texts he found in Glastonbury Abbey, wrote:

> In the year of our Lord 63, twelve holy missionaries, with Joseph of Arimathea (who had buried the Lord) at their head, came over to Britain, preaching the Incarnation of Jesus Christ. The king of the country and his subjects refused initially to become proselytes to his teaching, but on consideration that they had come a long journey, and being pleased with their soberness of life and unexceptional behavior, the king, at their petition, gave them for their habitation a certain island bordering on his region, covered with trees and bramble bushes and surrounded by marshes, called Ynis-wytrin.

Though these references show that the tradition was known to early Church historians and accepted until later centuries, what modern scholars generally agree upon is only that the first conversion of the Celts was led by St. Columba (AD 521–597), who went from Ireland to Iona, an island in Scotland. Priests from Iona then led the Christianization of Northumbria and later of Mercia. The result of this: Britain seems to have now fallen back in the Christian seniority league, returning to the status of a land converted half a millennium after the Crucifixion.

The debate about the antiquity of the Celtic Church inevitably extends to how pagan Britain was converted. Official history holds that it was through a series of missions by Rome, a process that likely did not begin until the fourth or fifth century. Others, however, think there were two very different missions, one by pre-Roman Christians and the other by Roman Christians, that resulted in Britain being divided along ethnic lines, with the Celts accepting Christianity earlier than the pagan Anglo-Saxons and dominating the western part of Britain (Cornwall and Wales), Ireland, Scotland, and even Brittany and Galicia on the Continent. Historians also argue that even if early missionaries were not necessarily sent by Rome, they were far more likely to have been Roman than Greek, Assyrian, or Egyptian, though we here can refute this.

Celtic Christians saw themselves as independent of the Roman

Church, as evidenced by British bishop Diaothus's reply to St. Augustine on the authority of Rome in Britain:

> Be it known and declared that we all, individually and collectively, are in all humility prepared to defer to the Church of God, and to the Bishop in Rome, and to every sincere and Godly Christian, so far as to love everyone in perfect charity, and to assist them all by word and in deed in becoming the children of God. This deference we are ready to pay to him, as to every other Christian, but as for any other obedience, we know of none that he, whom you term the Pope or Bishop of Bishops, can demand. (*Concilia, Decreta, Leges, Constitutiones in re Ecclesiarum Orbis Britannici,* vol. 1)

In other words, Diaothus was saying that the Celtic Church's relationship to the bishop of Rome was the same as its relationship to any other Christian bishopric, and nothing more. Such independence is considered unusual only by those who claim that autocephaly (literally, "self-government") was not an ancient organizational principle of the Church. But Orthodox Christians hold the very opposite view, namely that autocephaly is the norm, which would lead to the conclusion that the ecclesiastical independence of the Celtic Church was not at all an unusual state of affairs, but takes on the appearance of uniqueness only if Christendom is automatically seen as dominated by Roman doctrine.

What were the actual differences between what Celtic Christians believed and practiced (presumably on the basis of what the apostles themselves had preached to them) and what Rome was spreading through the rest of Europe as the Word of Christ? Theologians would say these differences boil down to the rule of keeping Easter, the tonsure (the way a monk's hair is shaved), the manner of baptizing, and a few phrases in the Liturgy of the Mass. But if that were all, it's difficult to understand why it should have taken close to a millennium to reconcile the two churches. To understand these apparently insignificant differences, let us look at their context by examining the real, profound differences between Celtic and Catholic spirituality stemming from the influence on Celtic Christians of two preexisting traditions: Egyptian gnosticism and Druidism.

The Influence of Egyptian Gnosticism and Druidism on Celtic Christianity

Dom Henri Leclercq suggested that Celtic monasticism was directly derived from Egypt not least because "[t]he kind of asceticism associated with the Desert Fathers was especially congenial to the Irish." It is interesting that one of the most common names for Irish parishes is Disert, or "desert," a solitary place in which anchorites settled. (Presumably the same etymology gives us the Scottish Dysart and the Welsh Dyserth.) The ordinary explanation for this is that firsthand knowledge of the Desert Fathers was brought to the south of Gaul by St. John Cassian around AD 350, and that the especially strong links between the British and Gallic churches at the time did the rest.

But this is far too complicated. There is a great deal of evidence that the link between Egypt and Hibernia was a direct one. The Coptic Church has long known of the historic links between the British Isles and Christian Egypt (and I have been witness to this knowledge), but Western scholars have only recently contributed to the recovery of this piece of Christian memory. There are fascinating scholarly articles citing evidence of these ancient links (in particular *Coptic and Irish Art,* by Monique Blanc-Ortolan and Pierre du Bourguet, and *Coptic Influences in the British Isles,* by Professor Joseph Kelly). Shirley Toulson, in *The Celtic Year,* asserts that "rather than adhere to the ruling of the Council of Chalcedon (AD 451), some of the most dedicated adherents of Monophysism fled Egypt, some of them most surely traveling west and north to Ireland."

But that's by no means all on the subject.

- Scholars have interpreted an inscription on a fourth-century stone near St. Olan's Well, in a County Cork parish, as reading, "Pray for Olan the Egyptian."

- The Antiphonary of Bangor (dating from between AD 680 and 690) contains the text "Domus deliciis plena/Super petram con-structa/Necnon vinea vera/Ex Aegypto transducta," which translates as "House full of delight/Built on the rock/And indeed true vine/Transplanted from Egypt."
- The Martyrology of Oengus the Culdee, an early-ninth-century monk, in County Offaly has a litany that reads, "Seven monks of Egypt in Disert Uilaig, I invoke unto my aid, through Jesus Christ."

This last phrase is clearly a reference to seven Coptic monks said to be buried near the town of Ballymena, in County Antrim. They may have traveled to distant Hibernia after the Council of Chalcedon, as Shirley Toulson suggests, but on the other hand, they may have been gnostic monks from a place much like Wadi Natrun.

Let us now turn to Druids. Most people know that St. Patrick (AD 387–461) was a Scotsman who established himself in Armagh and became apostle of Ireland, but few are aware that he was the exception: Most saints traveled in the opposite direction, bringing Celtic Christianity from Hibernia to Britain. The most famous Irish saints to preach in Britain were St. Brigit, also spelled Bride, Brigid, or Bryd (AD 439–524), and St. Columba (AD 520–593), but there were many more and most had Druidic backgrounds, which they managed to reconcile with their newfound Christianity just as other "barbarians" were on the Continent.

Here is what the *Catholic Encyclopedia* writes about St. Patrick:

In his sixteenth year, Patrick was carried off into captivity by Irish marauders and sold as a slave to a chieftain named Milchu. . . . He acquired a perfect knowledge of the Celtic tongue in which he would one day announce the glad tidings of Redemption and, as his master Milchu was a Druidical high priest, he became familiar with all the details of Druidism, from whose bondage he was destined to liberate the Irish race.

We know that St. Illtud (425–505) was "by descent a Druid and a fore knower of future events," the writer implying that a Druid caste was still in existence, and St. Petroc (AD 468–564) was educated in Ireland, where he learned esoteric Druid wisdom as well as Christianity.

What influence did Druidism have on Celtic Christianity? As we saw in the chapter on Pythagoras, Druids embraced gnostic concepts such as mystical union with the Godhead, believed in reincarnation, accepted women in their caste, and practiced a shamanistic kind of magic based on music and sacred numbers. It should not surprise us, then, to find that in Celtic Christianity, women had a far greater role. In fact, the First Synod of Patrick (AD 450) excommunicated anyone who persecuted a witch. Article 16 of the synod reads: "A Christian who believes that there is such a thing in the world as an enchanteress, which is to say a witch, and who accuses anyone of this, is to be excommunicated, and may not be received into the church again until he has revoked his criminal accusation and has accordingly done penance with full rigor" (from Liam DePaor's *Saint Patrick's World*). In this respect, the Celtic Church could well be unique. Persecuting witches did not happen in Scotland until the teaching of John Calvin was introduced late in the sixteenth century.

The Differences between Celtic and Roman Christianity

Let us return to those seemingly minor differences between Celtic and Roman Christianity.

- *The method of tonsure practiced by monks.* The Britons were accustomed to shaving the whole head in front of a line drawn from ear to ear, instead of using the coronal tonsure of the Romans. The Celtic tonsure, perhaps because of evidence that it was practiced by Druids, was nicknamed *tonsura magorum.* (*Magus* was accepted as equivalent to *Druid* and to this day in the Gaelic Bible the *magoi* of Matthew 2 are *Druidhean.*) Later, the Roman party jeered at it as the *tonsura Simonis Magi* (the Simon Magus tonsure), in contrast to their "tonsure of St. Peter." This, then, was no small difference. It was actually a symbol of the Druidic culture Rome wanted to eradicate.

- *The baptismal rite.* There is plentiful evidence that the Celtic Church resembled the Spanish in that the faithful were baptized with a single immersion. In fact this form of baptism had been allowed for a long time by Rome in the case of Spain, so why was it frowned on for Britain? In a letter from Pope Zacharias to St. Boniface, written in AD 748, it emerges that an unnamed English synod had forbidden any baptism except in the name of the Trinity and had declared that whoever omits the name of any person of the Trinity does not truly baptize. Here, too, we find not some minor detail of the ritual but rather a fundamental theological disagreement—namely, on the Holy Trinity, which Celtic Christians refused to accept.

As I've said before, winners write history and the Roman Church won; thus the official version has become that there weren't any *real* differences between Celtic and Catholic Christianity, though nothing could be further from the truth. An attitude of indulgence, tolerance, and lovingkindness, a gnostic approach to personal divinity, and an unusual openness to women—each a reflection, after all, of Jesus' true teaching—are fundamentally what most distinguished Celtic spirituality from the repressive stance of Roman Catholic preachers.

An episode concerning the fate of children who die unbaptized may best serve to illustrate this most fundamental difference. St. Augustine of Hippo had decreed that children who died without baptism went to Limbo—a part of hell but not a place of punishment or suffering. The Celts rejected this view. While the rest of Christendom buried such children in unblessed ground along with suicides, criminals, and heretics, the Celts buried them right up against the walls of their churches. When a delegate from Rome objected, quoting scripture, a Celt suggested that "the rainwater falling from the eaves of the church would baptise them."

Seeking to expand its spiritual and political supremacy throughout

Europe, Rome made diligent efforts to bring the Celtic Church under its authority for many centuries. A series of synods, starting with the one in Whitby in 664 and ending with the one in Cashel in 1172, resulted in the theology and practices of the Celtic Church being brought into line with those of Rome. Although its cultural impact continued for a long time, Celtic Christianity officially ended in 1172, when its system was brought under the rule of the Roman Church.

IBERIA

Who was the first to bring the good news to Spain? As usual, historians give little credit to Catholic tradition on this point, denying that there is any evidence for the preaching of St. James there in the first century, but as in the case of the other two countries examined in this chapter, the Roman Church does not attempt to deny that the apostles preached the gospel there in person.

James the Elder was Christianity's first martyr. Some twelve years passed from the time of the Crucifixion to the time when he was imprisoned, scourged, and decapitated in the year AD 47 on the orders of Herod Agrippa. During those years, according to Catholic tradition, he spent much of his time preaching the gospel in Iberia, the first person ever to do so. The golden legend of Santiago (from Sancti Jacobi, or, in Spanish, Sant-Yago) relates how, led by the Holy Spirit, his disciples Theodore and Athanasius transported James's body across the Mediterranean in a dinghy, passing between the Pillars of Hercules (now the Straits of Gibraltar) to the Lusitanians' country. There the boat finally stopped on reaching the Celtic-Roman town of Ira Flavia, now called Padrón.

His tomb in the farthest northwestern tip of the Iberian Peninsula was miraculously discovered in AD 835 by Bishop Theodomir, who was led there by a star, thus the renaming of the place as Campus Stellae (Compostela). The apostle James is now buried in Santiago de Compostela's cathedral. Stories of the discovery of the apostle's tomb brought pilgrims from all over Europe, and the Camino de Santiago—the Way to Santiago—soon became the most important Christian pilgrimage of the Middle Ages.

I have always wondered who is really buried in Santiago. I've heard it said that it might be another James, the brother of Jesus who led the Jerusalem Church from the time after the Crucifixion until his own assassination in AD 62, which, according to many scholars, was the final spark that ignited the revolt against Rome and its collaborators.

Paul's Search

In his epistle to the Romans, St. Paul had expressed the desire to evangelize Spain. It seems possible, from the words of St. Clement of Rome (written in about AD 90) and the Muratonian Fragment (dating from about AD 200), that he actually carried out his plan, but if he did so, nothing is known about the specific place or the success of his labors.

Concerning this little mystery within the vast uncertainty that is early Church history there is one unusual idea that may provide a strangely plausible piece of information. Theologians have always wondered about the fact that Paul seems to possess no information about Jesus' life as a human being. He never once mentions Jesus as other than the Son of God, the Lamb, the sacrifice for our sins, the salvation of our souls. Though he writes as little as ten or twelve years after the Crucifixion, he seems to know nothing about a man born in Bethlehem and executed in Jerusalem: Jesus' family, his followers, the best-known episodes in his career, everything except the theological Jesus is absent from Paul's writings. Indeed, some scholars based the theory that a historical Jesus never actually existed on Paul's lack of references to the man. In other words, they postulated that Jesus was a mythical figure, a metaphor, just one more dying and rising god in a mystery religion like that of Osiris or Mithra or Dionysos, a figure who sometime in the late first century became a historical character through the misinterpretation of some of the earliest gospels, which were originally written for people who understood their symbolic meaning.

I don't share this view (nor is it as popular among biblical scholars as it was, say, fifty years ago) mainly because Paul did meet and have dealings with Peter, James, and other close associates of Jesus. In fact, the whole existence of a Jerusalem Church before the war with Rome is something such a theory would have a hard time explaining. Nevertheless, Paul does seem to have made a radical choice about Jesus the man: He never says a word about him.

We can imagine what might have happened while Saul (before he became the converted Paul) investigated and persecuted Jesus' followers and interrogated someone who knew that Jesus had survived the cross. One reaction he might have had was to become convinced that the Jewish heretics who spoke of resurrection were not just deluded, that they were liars and swindlers who had to be hunted down, as the Sanhedrin said. Or he might have reacted in the opposite way, suddenly understanding the meaning of the death and resurrection drama that Jesus had performed during those three days in Jerusalem a few years earlier. He might have seen the light, as it were, and converted to the gnostic lesson of the master of the sect he was hunting down.

If this was indeed the case and what Paul later described as "falling from his horse" on the way to Damascus was in fact the discovery that Jesus was alive somewhere, what would he have done after the discovery? He tells us that before returning to Jerusalem he spent three years in "Arabia"—and much speculation has taken place on just where this "Arabia" might have been—after which time he began his years as a wandering preacher and founder of Christian churches. Everyone has always remarked about the energy of his mission and the extent of his reach. At one point, according to legend, he even wanted to visit Iberia, literally at the other end of the Mediterranean.

Could it be that what Paul was really doing was looking for Jesus?

Evidence of Spanish Christianity

The story that St. Peter and St. Paul sent seven missionaries to Spain is pure legend. There are references to the existence of Christian churches in Spain in the works of Irenaeus and Tertullian, both of whom wrote between AD 180 and 200, but evidence for the places in Spain in which Christianity was actually practiced came only in the middle of the third century.

We can find this in accounts of the apostasy of two bishops in Iberia during the persecution of Christians by Emperor Decius in AD 249–251. When the situation improved, local Christians didn't want these bishops back and turned to St. Cyprian, bishop of Carthage, for guidance. In his reply, Cyprian declared that the apostates were indeed no longer entitled to the obedience of the laity. We do not know the sequel to this first embarrassing glimpse into the history of the Church in Spain.

Another piece of evidence of Iberian Christianity involves a Spanish heretic, still somewhat mysterious today, known as Priscillian (AD 334–393). The *Catholic Encyclopedia* writes, "[T]he Priscillianist heresy of the fourth century derived from the Manichaean doctrines taught by Marcus, an Egyptian from Memphis." (Again, we find mention of Egyptian gnostics going west.) Sulpicius Severus writes that his first adherents were a woman named Agape and a rhetorician named Helpidius, through whose influence Priscillian, "a man of noble birth, of great riches, bold, restless, eloquent, learned through much reading, very ready at debate and discussion," was enrolled. His high position and great gifts soon made him the leader of the party and an ardent apostle of the new doctrines, and through his reputation for extreme asceticism, he attracted a large following.

It is not easy to separate the genuine words of Priscillian from those ascribed to him by his enemies or from ideas later preached by groups labeled Priscillianist. Like most fourth-century Christians, he and his followers placed great emphasis on works later considered apocryphal that they regarded as helpful to the spiritually minded, who could discern truth from error. In 1889, G. Schepps published a series of eleven treatises that he had discovered at Wurzburg. The texts named Priscillian as their author and contained allegorical interpretations of scripture, calls to asceticism, and an emphasis on the unity rather than the Trinity of God. In these texts Christ is referred to as "unbegettable." Priscillianists were also said to teach that preexistent human souls were attached as a punishment to the body, which was the creation of the devil (a distinctly gnostic notion).

Priscillian and his sympathizers included many women, who were welcomed as the equals of men (always a sign that someone is following Jesus' original teaching). They were organized into bands of *spirituales* and *abstinentes*. (We note the similarity of these two groups found within both Therapeutae and Cathars.) Critics of Priscillian accused him of astrology, sorcery, dualism, Manichaeism, Sabellianism, modalism, and outright lying. His strong following of women also led to charges of licentious orgies. Though this was a particularly preposterous charge, given the rigorous nature of Priscillian's doctrines, it is one that the Roman Church has leveled against critics in every age. Priscillianism continued at least until AD 563, when it was condemned by the Council of Braga.

Priscillian, however, casts a long shadow in the north of Spain and the south of France, two areas where mystical asceticism has repeatedly been carried to extremes that the political mainstream denounced as heretical. Interestingly, some people claim that the remains found at Compostela belong not to the apostle James, but to Priscillian.

If we can conclude that Christianity was brought to France, Britain, and Spain not from Rome in the fourth and fifth centuries, but directly from Judaea and Egypt in the first century, then these three communities must have become a sort of time bubble safely outside the reach of the cultural dictatorship the Roman Church established after Constantine. It was within this bubble that the original gnostic teaching of Jesus survived for many centuries, although by now traces of it are so faint that the Roman Church has little trouble marginalizing those who find any of them.

17

SEPTIMANIA: THE DAVIDIC KINGS

As demonstrated in the last two chapters, contrary to what official scholarship suggests, Judeo-Christians, gnostics, and other critics of orthodox (as in Pauline) Christianity did not simply vanish after the Council of Nicaea. Instead, they gradually migrated from Egypt and Syria to the shores of the western Mediterranean and beyond because those shores—home to what was becoming Celtic Christianity—had been a safe haven for their view of Jesus for a long time, in fact from the time of Jesus himself.

As we've seen, too, the adage that history is written by the winners has particular relevance when it comes to the ups and downs alternately enjoyed and suffered by early Christianity in the three hundred years between the Crucifixion and the Council of Nicaea—and the history written is indeed rather selective. For example, the harsh persecutions of early Christians unleashed by some of the Roman emperors in that period are common knowledge, but not many people know that despite Constantine's edicts—and the political power they conferred on the Church—during the last two centuries of the empire's life (roughly the fourth and fifth centuries), the pagans who chose to become Arian Christians, Judeo-Christians, or even Jews were much more numerous than those who embraced the Roman Catholic brand of Christianity.

In his boastful *History of the Church,* completed after he attended the victorious council in Nicaea, Eusebius famously explains the sophistication of God's plan for humanity: The Lord first favored Rome's expansion, and only then, in the early decades of the Roman Empire, did he send his only son, for in order for the Word to spread to every corner of the world, it first had to be received by the ruling classes of the biggest empire in the world. This was of course propaganda—fighting rhetoric written at a time when Catholics in cities all around the Mediterranean still contended not only with countless internal enemies (the Christian heretics), but also with their rejected parent religion (Judaism).

The propaganda was not always successful. The direct apostolic line of authority of the Roman Church, for example, deriving from its supposed foundation laid by St. Peter and St. Paul, was denounced as a historical fake as early as the third century, and not surprisingly, those who denounced it most emphatically were the heirs of the first, true Church of the Christ—that is, the Church of Jerusalem. These Torah-abiding, circumcised Judeo-Christians, among whom were many close relatives of Jesus, were at first headed by James, the brother of Jesus, from the time after the Crucifixion until his own assassination in AD 62, and after him by Simon bar-Cleopas, a first cousin of Jesus.

Traditions such as the *Clementine Recognitions* and *Homilies* (the content of which scholars now consider Ebionite or Judeo-Christian in nature and have hence renamed *Pseudo-Clementines*—that is, attributed to Pope Clement I but written centuries later) tell of a delegation from the Disposyni, the descendants of Jesus' family, traveling to Rome in the first half of the fourth century to meet Pope Sylvester I and plead their case.

Traveling to Rome? Coming from where? To claim what, and in whose name?

In *James, the Brother of Jesus,* maverick scholar Robert Eisenman reconstructs the fate of the Jerusalem Church, seeking out all references to it in the documents that survived Catholic censorship, such as the *Clementines* and the *Testaments of the Twelve Patriarchs.* Eisenman's work is crucial to the search for the historical truth behind propaganda such as Eusebius's *History of the Church,* but he covers events only as far as the defeat of the second Jewish revolt, led by Simon Bar Kochbah in AD 132–135, after which Emperor Hadrian razed Jerusalem to the ground and expelled all Jews from Judaea.

Yet the most interesting period may be that immediately after Jewish expulsion both because of the variety of places where those exiled Jews and Judeo-Christians ended up and because of the religious "subversion" they participated in once there. For example, one of them, called Elchasai, founded a sect that later gave rise to the sweepingly successful movement known as Manichaeism (Mani was born into an Elchasaite family in about AD 210). Other Judeo-Christians fled to Alexandria, where they became a force for religious synchretism and used Pythagorean and Neoplatonic ideas to further develop Jesus' original gnostic teaching. Still others, as we saw in the last chapter, sailed west and settled in Jewish communities along the shores of the western Mediterranean.

What all these exiles had in common was that they never passively suffered the supremacy of Pauline Christianity in theological debate, either before or after Constantine. The fact that we so often find Jewish proselytism infuriating Catholic bishops everywhere—from St. Ambrose in Milan in the late fourth century to St. Agobard in Lyon in the early ninth century—is the sign of a lively opposition not at all resigned to fading from history and on the constant lookout for allies in the struggle against the eternal arrogance of Rome. The Jewish presence in politics in those centuries is a mosaic whose few surviving tesserae are scattered all over. The problem is that the period in question is examined only by specialist historians who are often reluctant to take a step back and look at the picture that is emerging from the fragments they have found. These fragments can give us reason to believe that the Jews of those centuries were indeed politically active.

A FIRST LOOK AT SEPTIMANIA

It is in this context that we must look at the faint traces of a Jewish principality called Septimania as they are presented by Arthur Zuckerman in his study *A Jewish Princedom in Feudal France.*

Septimania was the western part of the Roman province of Gallia Narbonensis, which covered more or less today's French region of the Languedoc. Its name derived from the fact that Emperor Augustus gifted most lands in the region to the veterans of his glorious Seventh Legion so that they could build villas and farms there for their retirement. As related in chapter 1, Septimania was taken by the Visigoths early in the fifth century, after Ataulphus had buried his brother-in-law Alaric I deep in the south of Italy. The Visigoths conquered practically all of Iberia as well, but their complete control of Septimania lasted less than a century, being almost immediately threatened from the north by Frankish tribes led by the Merovingians. In the end, the Visigoths were defeated by Clovis I in the Battle of Vouillé (AD 507), and though Aquitania passed into the hands of the Franks, Septimania, with its capital in Narbonne, and some other territories in Gaul remained in Visigothic hands for two more centuries. At one stage in that period so many Goths converted to Judaism that the terms Goth and Jew were used synonymously in southern France.

Let us diverge for a moment to look at the crucial role of the Merovingian kings in the theories, legends, and discoveries that swirl around what is hidden in Rennes-le-Château. Whether or not we find plausible the idea of the Merovingians marrying into the line of Jesus the Nazarene (*not* of Nazareth) and Mary of Magdala, it's hard to deny that the attitude of the Roman popes toward these eccentric, long-haired kings was one of reluctant recognition of a legitimacy they wished was not existent. We might sympathize with the Church, for if those uncouth Frankish warlords originally of the Arian faith really had mixed their blood with that of the Disposyni—if they really were descendants of the Lord—then the legitimacy of their claim to the thrones of Europe could indeed hold even Rome at bay, which it did, at least until Dagobert's assassination in AD 670.

The accusation that during the eighth century the Catholic Church betrayed its pact with Clovis and gave the Frankish crown to the Carolingians has been particularly enduring. The Priory of Sion may have been an invention, but Pierre Plantard's declared motivation—the Priory's raison d'être, as it were—was righting that wrong. The point we can gather here is that Clovis converted from Arianism to Catholic Christianity in AD 496 and immediately began attacking his Visigoth neighbors to the south not only to conquer more territory, but also because he was now the defender of the Church, and the Goths and Jews down there were enemies of the Church. Surely, however, the descendants of Jesus and Mary Magdalene, those who gave the Merovingians their supposed Davidic bloodline, were living in the very Jewish communities of Septimania that Clovis was assaulting. Thus, the Priory's claim, even in an imaginary history, doesn't hold water.

CHARLEMAGNE'S ORIGINS

Now let us fast-forward to AD 719. Muslim invaders had entered the Iberian Peninsula only eight years earlier and were laying the foundations of a civilization that would endure for almost eight hundred years. Bolstered by recently arrived troops from northern and southern Arabia—whom we would call Syrians and Yemenis—Muslims crossed the Pyrenees, probing deep into what they called the Great Land, al-Ard al-Kabirah. They quickly took most of Visigoth Septimania, including Narbonne, known in Arabic as Arbuna. The inhabitants of the city, mostly Arian Christians and Jews, were given honorable terms and allowed complete religious freedom by a treaty like the one granted to the Spanish Visigoths.

Then Charles Martel, the founder of the Carolingian dynasty, defeated the Moors at the battle of Poitiers (or Tours) in AD 732, and the Muslims retreated to Narbonne. Zuckerman tells how after a seven-year siege and in order to gain the allegiance of the Jews in Narbonne, Charles sent to Baghdad for a son of the Babylonian exilarch to come and lead the Jews of France.

Here are the details of this historical occurrence: Narbonne changed hands several times in the eighth century, and on one occasion, in AD 759, the Jews betrayed their Muslims allies, opening the city gates to Pepin the Short, son of Charles Martel. As a reward for helping him reconquer the city, Pepin granted them a Jewish principality in Septimania and installed Machir, a son of the Babylonian exilarch, as the Jewish king of Narbonne. The date of the arrival of two members of the exilarch family has long been debated, with some accounts such as the *chansons* (ballads focusing on the heroes of prechivalric France) placing it much later, in the reign of Charlemage, because some Jewish sources state that they arrived in the reign of King Charles, which people later interpretated as Charlemagne (Charles the Great). Other accounts place this arrival in the reign of Pepin because Machir married Pepin's sister Aude.

A third thought holds that Machir and his family in fact arrived in France under Charles Martel (Charlemagne's grandfather). Gershom ben Judah and his younger brother Machir arrived in Septimania in AD 739. Charles Martel made Gershom count of Vienne and Machir count of Narbonne. In the French chansons Machir was called Aimeri, but among the nobility he was known as Theoderic or Thierry, duke of Toulouse. Zuckerman writes that he was recognized by the caliph of Baghdad and by Pepin as "seed of the Royal House of David."

Impeccable genealogists such as Professor David Kelley have confirmed the Davidic origins of Machir of Narbonne and his descendants. The Jews of Babylonia had been administered by their own exilarchs, or "princes of the captivity," since their deportation by Nebuchadnezzar in the sixth century BC. These leaders, descended from King Jehoiakin of the Royal House of David, lived in great state in their own palace, and continued to rule over the Jews of Mesopotamia until overthrown by Tamerlane in the fifteenth century AD.

Machir married Charles Martel's daughter (Pepin's sister) Alda (also known as Aude, Olba, Alba, and Aldana) and gave his sister in marriage to Pepin. The son of Machir was Guillaume (William) and the son of Pepin was Charlemagne, so it would seem that the mother of Charlemagne was the sister of Machir. The fact that the great king was the son of a Jewess— something hardly acceptable to Catholic chroniclers—would explain the great uncertainty among historians as to who Charlemagne's mother really was. What we do know is that Charlemagne was friendly to the Jews. Even after Christmas night in the year AD 800, when Pope Leo III lowered the crown of the Holy Roman Empire onto his head, Charlemagne resolutely resisted pressure to persecute them and was sometimes referred to by the Jews of Frankia as King David.

JUDAISM IN SEPTIMANIA

Guillaume, son of Machir, was therefore Charlemagne's first cousin, and as king of the Franks from AD 771 and first Holy Roman Emperor from AD 800, Charlemagne was pleased to confirm his cousin's entitlement to dynastic sovereignty in Septimania. This appointment was also upheld by the caliph of Baghdad and, reluctantly, by Pope Stephen in Rome. All acknowledged King Guillaume of the House of Judah to be a true bloodline successor of King David.

Guillaume de Gellone, as he was also known, had many nicknames in the chansons, among them "Hook-Nosed Guillaume," and there can be no doubt whatsoever that he was Jewish. Guillaume was fluent in Arabic and Hebrew. The heraldic device on his shield was the same as that of the eastern exilarchs: the Lion of Judah. He refused to fight on the Sabbath and in one of his campaigns is recorded as celebrating the Jewish festival of Sukkoth during a September siege. Later historians tried to hide the Jewishness of this dynasty and remove all record of a Jewish kingdom in Europe—but modern scholarship is bringing much of this hidden history to light.

Jewish sources tell us that in AD 792, Guillaume established at Gellone a *yeshivah* (rabbinical college) later called, after him, St. Guilhem le Désert. There he gathered Torah scholars and created a Jewish library. In AD 806 he retired to this yeshivah for his final years. The official history of the place is somewhat different: It now tells of "St. Guilhem" (sic) founding not a yeshivah but a Benedictine monastery and retiring there as a monk—clearly another case of Catholic scribes and monks in later years bending the facts to their political convenience. A small, overlooked detail in this instance, however, gives the lie to the official version of events. Hanging on a wall in the remaining half of the cloister of the Abbey of St. Guilhem le Désert (the other half is now a part of New

York's Metropolitan Museum of Art and is known as The Cloisters) is a remarkable ninth-century painting on wood showing a Madonna wearing a breastplate studded with twelve precious stones, exactly like the breastplate worn by Aaron and the high priests in the Jerusalem Temple. What almost knocked me off my feet when I saw this painting was the writing on the icon itself: "Virgo Levitica," translated by the curators in the description of this work as Vierge Lévitique. Anyone familiar with medieval Christianity—or even simply with the gospels —can appreciate how shocking it is that the mother of Jesus could be portrayed—in the ninth century—in the attire of a Jewish high priest.

There are other surviving traces of a period of strong Jewish influence in this region, such as the recent discovery under a garage in Lunel (not far from Montpellier) of what seem to be the remains of a surprisingly large tenth-century synagogue. Clearly, Languedoc Jews in the early Middle Ages had a higher profile, more political clout, and more allies in their quarrel with Rome than later chroniclers were prepared to admit. But such wealthy and influential communities don't just spring up out of nowhere; they take generations to build. The scenario I suggest is that hundreds, perhaps thousands of Jews and Judeo-Christians, as well as gnostics of many denominations and assorted opponents of Roman orthodoxy, took refuge in a tolerant and heavily "Judaized" Languedoc in the fourth and fifth centuries. I suspect that between AD 350 and 850 the areas around Narbonne and Montpellier witnessed the flowering of an important Jewish political and cultural center. So famous were the scholars of Narbonne that Jews used to call the city Nerbina or, in Hebrew, Ner Binah, "light of understanding." (*Binah* is the third Sephirah in the kabbalistic Tree of Life.)

This new Alexandria had its good and bad times, swinging from possession of a mere third of Narbonne to the heights of a Jewish prince marrying the sister of Pepin the Short. Naturally, documents relating to this period of Jewish sovereignty were later destroyed by the chroniclers of the Holy Roman Empire and surviving traces are so few and far between that the picture they form is visible only to the eyes of heretical historians, visionaries, and novelists.

What might the behavior of the leaders of such a principality have been like? The kingdom of the Septimanian Jews was likely an enlightened kingdom for its time, a cosmopolitan society, just as Alexandria had been, made wealthy by trade with the East. It was probably a refuge for varieties of opponents of Roman orthodoxy and was likely the preferred destination of anyone running from the pope's watchdogs. Talmudic sources confirm that the Jews of Narbonne were in touch with the sages, known as Amoraim, of Sura and Pumpedita, the two Babylonian cities where the Gemarah—the later section of the Talmud—was being completed. They continued to be in touch with Jews in the Orient when these fellow faithful became the subjects of the most traumatic novelty of the seventh century—Islam. Later still, they must have corresponded with the Khazars of the Ukrainian steppes as the latter weighed the pros and cons of converting to Judaism (which they eventually did). Finally, they are sure to have been in touch with the Jewish communities in the two great "enemy" capitals, Rome and Byzantium.

Indeed, a promising avenue of research to emerge in the last decade for historians of the high Middle Ages is the previously neglected investigation of the Jewish community in Constantinople between the fifth and tenth centuries. The role of Jews in court politics, or in the eighth-century controversy over the worship of images, or in aiding and abetting the thousand heresies that plagued the polis, is slowly emerging from letters, homilies, and legal sentences never studied before. They present circumstances that are similar to those found in the mass of documents discovered in the nineteenth century in the *genizah* (a repository of manuscripts that cannot be destroyed because they bear God's name) of a Cairo synagogue and later thoroughly analyzed by Solomon Goitien. Only in the case of these more recently examined documents, they had been available in the sultan's library in Istanbul but no one had been interested enough to read them. (The work of two excellent scholars in this field, Professors Guy Stroumsa and Yuri Stoyanov, is enlightening in this area.) What is slowly emerging from this newly appreciated work is that Jews in Byzantium, like everywhere else, hindered and sabotaged the expansion of Rome's influence in every way they could.

Jewish leaders in Narbonne did so throughout late antiquity and the early Middle Ages—for example, by supporting various Visigoth tribes early on, when the Visigoths were heretical Arian believers, only to oppose them later once they gradually converted to Catholicism and joined the Roman camp. The Jews also at first aided the Muslims in conquering Spain in AD 711 as an anti-Christian strategy, but later, in 758, betrayed them and opened the gates of Narbonne to Pepin the Short in exchange for the legitimization of their principality. In a different context, the Jews requested that the yeshivot (Talmudic schools) of Babylon send emissaries to the king of the Khazar to make the case that upon being faced with the guile of two greedy contenders (Christianity and Islam), the wisest thing was to reject them both and become Jewish— which is exactly what the Khazar king did.

Another aspect of this hidden Jewish history that is of particular interest to our study here is that the presence of a Jewish cultural and political opposition to Rome—an active, well-connected, and influential opposition—would help to explain the gnostic, Pythagorean, and kabbalistic contents of the religious culture that evolved in this region over the centuries. The flowering of kabbalah (which Scholem, as we saw, called Judaism's gnostic tradition), of courtly and troubadoric culture, and above all of Catharism in the same towns and in the same decades, raises legitimate doubts about these movements being independent of each other. Scholars including Scholmen (see his *Origins of the Kabbalah*) regret that there are no documents proving that kabbalists and Cathars held theological debates or shared mystical awareness-raising techniques. That may be so, but the fact remains that these two groups of gnostic visionaries—both worshippers of the female aspect of the Deity, both considered heretics by their respective religious establishment, and both mortal enemies of Rome—flourished between AD 1170 and 1220 on these very hills. Could this be merely a coincidence?

As I mentioned in the introduction to this book, the standard explanation historians give of how Catharism arrived in the south of France harks back to a certain gnostic sect in Armenia, the Paulicians, whose name probably derives from their attachment to St. Paul's more openly gnostic pronouncements (and there are not a few). The Paulicians appeared around the middle of the seventh century and are thought to have derived from the Massalians, a previous Manichaean sect active in Syria. Constantine of Mananalis, calling himself Silvanus, began to teach a Manichaean form of Christianity at Kibossa, near Colonia in Armenia, and founded what appears to have been the first Paulician community.

Paulician thinking was repeatedly put down by the Byzantine emperors in the rest of the seventh century but was revived in the early ninth century, and its exponents were eventually deported to Philippopolis, in Thrace (now partly Bulgaria, partly Macedonia), where Byzantium thought it could better control them. To the empire's dismay, the Paulicians instead influenced the local populace to the point that in the tenth century a monk named Bogomil—literally "beloved of God"—started a new Manichaean sect, the Bogomils. It flourished in the Balkans from the tenth century to the fifteenth, notably in the Rila Mountains of Brinsa Dendu, in the Thrace area of Bulgaria. Even today there are traces of the creed in monasteries in the Rila area, but Bulgarian authorities say they believe the Bogomils to have disappeared, after their priests were probably massacred during the Turkish occupation.

It seems this last incarnation of a four-hundred-year-old gnostic movement sent its preachers ever westward until, it is surmised, they finally reached Provence in the late eleventh century. It does seem farfetched, however, that Cathar gnosticism came from the East—from Armenia through Bulgaria, and from there through Lombardy and Provence to the Languedoc—rather than grew out of a local tradition existing from antiquity and late antiquity. A compromise scenario could be that when the Bogomil Perfecti (more on the Perfecti in the next chapter) first reached what had been Septimania, they found traditions there, deriving from Pythagoras, Jewish gnostics, and Alexandrian Neoplatonists, to be the most fertile ground imaginable for the spread of their ideas.

We might agree that if this were the case, the legends of Mary Magdalene preaching a very different and not at all Pauline Christianity in the Camargue, the flowering of the kabbalah, and in fact the whole

Provençal courtly renaissance with its emphasis on the Sacred Feminine—would all find much simpler, more logical explanations that are more respectful of Occam's razor. But could the complex, intertwined traditions that have such deep roots here have reached this place only on the back of a handful of heretical Bulgarian monks?

THE BRIDE OF CHRIST

There is one last, seemingly insignificant detail that not only supports the scenario I have presented in this chapter, but also brings me back to the thesis running through this book: There is abundant documentary proof that the Cathars believed Mary Magdalene was the wife of Christ. In fact, this belief was openly recorded on more than one occasion by the Dominican monks of the Holy Inquisition who interrogated the heretics.

We know that the presence of Mary Magdalene in the region is a very ancient tradition accepted and perpetuated by the Church itself, but if we accept that Cathar ideas were introduced to southern France from the Balkans, we would have to envision this "marriage" tradition as not existing in the Languedoc before the arrival of the Bulgarian heretics, who never mentioned Mary Magdalene in any of their writings!

Let us suppose instead that Cathars didn't learn of the marriage of Jesus and Mary from Bogomil preachers; let us suppose they had that memory from way back when the oarless boat came ashore in the marshes at the mouth of the Rhône. Though the memory of Jesus himself arriving with his wife may not have survived in a direct fashion—for reasons that we examined earlier—the handful of people who were aware of that secret side of the story probably passed it on to other trusted followers of their faith, which was the original gnostic Christianity taught by Jesus himself. That handful of people, having come here with the "royal" couple, would have been mostly Jewish, so the likeliest place for us to find indirect traces of that memory is among the Jews who lived in this area in the first centuries after the Crucifixion. What we would have to look for, then, is a concealed message, an idea that seems on the surface to be perfectly normal Jewish thinking but under the circumstances cannot help but be connected with the secret knowledge of Jesus coming to this place.

We might then hear differently a phrase the Jews of Narbonne might well have said to Charles Martel when they asked for an exilarch from Babylonia to be sent to their community: "We want a descendant of King David to rule over us, for there was a descendant of King David among us when the Temple was still standing in Jerusalem."

18

THE CATHAR
MYSTERY

Another name for the crusade against the Cathar heretics is the Albigensian crusade, with the name Albigensian deriving from the town of Albi, one of the earliest Cathar religious and political centers in the south of France. Even by medieval standards, the war launched by the Roman Church against the gnostic Cathars in what had been Septimania was a shockingly violent one. It started in AD 1209, about halfway through the two centuries of Christian possession of the Holy Land and, perhaps not coincidentally, a mere twenty-two years after the loss of the Holy City of Jerusalem to Saladin's Jihad campaign.

The crusade against the Cathars was by no means the first or the last war waged by Christians on other Christians, but coming a mere five years after the ruthless sack of Constantinople by a fleet of cross-wearing marauders led by the Venetians, it made horrifyingly clear, once and for all, just how far the love of Jesus—abetted by adequate economic incentives—could actually go.

THE BEGINNING OF THE WAR
AGAINST THE CATHARS

Throughout the twelfth century, something sweet had been fermenting in the Christian soul. Almost everywhere there was an unprecedented love of knowledge, personal freedoms, music, even a love of love. Waves of mysticism, schools of philosophy, traveling minstrels, soaring new cathedrals that seemed to touch the heavens—Rome didn't like any of this one bit.

By the end of the century, an ignorant and corrupt clergy had pushed a multitude of Christians to the brink of spiritual rebellion against the Mother Church—a rebellion led, according to the Church, by heretics of all descriptions. Cathars, Poor of Lyon, Beguines, Humiliati—as one theologian put it, these were "penitents and visionaries to whose mysticism nothing is repugnant." No matter how it was denounced, in some way—and it was pointless to deny it—the spiritual spasm that had swept across Europe in the name of a more apostolic lifestyle and the definitive victory of love on earth had affected a worrying number of devout Catholics.

As if by a plot from hell, thousands of simple believers had been undermined by the apocalyptic, delirious preaching of prophetic monks, especially that of a certain Joachim of Flora, a self-styled reformer of the Cistercian Rule whose base was deep in the south of Italy. Joachim had announced the dawning of a "new age of the Spirit" that was about to enlighten the whole human race: Grace and love would soon replace doctrine and hierarchy. Perhaps even more damaging than the preaching of visionaries, however, had been the translation from Arabic of the writings of the ancient Greeks—which was not surprisingly carried out mostly at the hands of the ever-subversive Jews.

The Cathar heresy in particular had spread like a plague from Germany to Provence and from northern Italy to the Languedoc, where many nobles found the Cathar creed attractive for its tolerance, for they were often disillusioned by the great corruption of the Catholic Church. Above all, they had lost patience with its abuse of the tithe system; the money gathered simply disappeared to Rome. Surely Bertrand Russell had a point when he wrote that the early Renaissance in Provence, had it not been so ruthlessly repressed, would have anticipated by three centuries the rebellion that Martin Luther sparked in Germany. For that matter, it can hardly be a coincidence that in the fifteenth century vast sectors of the population in the Languedoc chose to become Huguenot

Protestants and perpetuate the break from Rome that their ancestors had attempted and paid for with their lives.

Eventually, news of sacked abbeys and violated churches began to reach Rome with alarming frequency. Innocent III, who had sat on St. Peter's throne at the incredibly precocious age of thirty-seven, seemed not to know what he wanted. One minute the entire Midi was a wasp's nest to be uprooted with fire, the next minute it was a wayward flock of helpless sheep that it was his mission to save. Romans joked that their pope could not stand by a decision long enough for his envoys to make it known. "He is like a blind dog in a meat market," they said.

Then suddenly, at dawn on a gray day in January AD 1208, hired assassins treacherously murdered Pierre de Castelnau, the papal legate to the Languedoc. The ineptly named Innocent launched a "just war" against the heretics, and from every pulpit in Christendom the cry had risen: "Arm yourselves! Go and bring back Christ's peace in Provence!" The indulgences for those who joined the campaign for at least forty days were the same as for taking up the cross against the infidels in Outremer: absolution from all sins, protection of their land by the Church when they left to fight, and—*dulcis in fundo*—the wiping out of any debts to the Jews, who were thus made to bear the cost of the massacre of their heretical friends.

Philip II Capetian, who by the grace of God was king of France (and found it so fitting that he styled himself with the name Augustus), declined to formally lead the ransacking of his neighbors to the south, alleging that the constant scheming of the English against his throne left him no time for chasing lunatics. Among the cream of French nobility, however (or at least among the families who hadn't been quick enough to grab a place in the sun in Greece or Syria), greed much more than righteous outrage against the heretics ensured an impressive attendance in the war. In fact, the call sparked the enthusiasm of the counts of Nevers, Châtillon, Saint-Pol, Auxerre, and Bar-sur-Seine; of the bishops of Autun and Clermont; and, naturally, of the papal legates to a man.

A year later the storm broke over the rich counties of Provence. The crusaders—French, German, Flemish, and Scandinavian—gathered in Lyon on and after St. John's Day at the end of June 1209. Soon the camp was a riotous city of some thirty thousand souls, each one proclaimed a divine executioner by Innocent's papal bull. The absence of any knights of the Temple inevitably fed the rumors about the order's intimacy with the heretics. By the beginning of July, the only wolf missing was the duke of Burgundy, the leader of the pack, who kept them all waiting for two turbulent weeks. Those who saw this group told of five thousand knights and for each knight at least five *ribauds,* feverish peasant zealots, many of whom had dragged along their whole families. Humble and fervent servants of Christ, they somehow knew that only in the blood that the Cathars would shed for their sins could they find mysterious absolution of their own.

Outraged by the news that most Cathars denied the divinity of Jesus, the ribauds made a disproportionate use of the name of Jesus Christ, the offended party, calling themselves Militia Jhesu Christi. Into that river of men—several times the number that had liberated Jerusalem—the clerics gleefully poured the accounts of the heretics' sacrilegious deeds. In a sermon held while the siege of Béziers was being laid, it was claimed that those dogs, not content with beating senseless a poor priest on his way to Mass, had pissed in his holy chalice! But behold, a ghost had appeared on the city ramparts and roared at the unrepentant heretics, "Who do you think will save you from God's wrath?"

Indeed, the way God chose to deliver Béziers to its executioners would put to the test the faith of many a Cathar. At first light on July 22, St. Mary Magdalene's Day, pyres and gallows were erected outside the walls, and radiant monks vied for the privilege of pronouncing the sermons that would commit the Cathar Perfecti to the fires of hell. A mission by the bishop of Montpeyroux that bore the offer to spare the city if it would give up the 222 Perfecti it was harboring left empty-handed from the Narbonne gate and some reckless burghers had come out to mock it. A handful of ribauds managed to get in the gate and keep it open until some knights rushed over to help them.

Thus had Béziers dishonorably fallen, in one day and without a siege. For the rest of that day the ribauds joyfully massacred men, women, and children: They had them drawn and quartered, burned them, boiled them, threw them from the towers. Not a single soul survived in Béziers, not even the Catholics who had fought the spread of heresy. After this, Arnaud Amaury, abbot of Cîteaux, papal legate, and leader of the crusade, who had uttered the phrase that would make him famous—"Kill them all, God will recognize his own!"—wrote a letter to Innocent, a missive undoubtedly inspired by God so that later generations could make no mistake about the man. In this letter he wrote: "Our forces, with no regard for rank, sex, or age, have exterminated twenty thousand corrupted souls, and after the massacre of our enemies the city was sacked and given over to the flames. Divine vengeance has surely done wonders in this place today!"

The crusaders moved on, leaving the still-smoking ruins behind them, and on August 3, the huge victorious army of Christ, waving banners bearing the Agnus Dei and singing out the Veni Creator Spiritus at the top of their voices, marched on Carcassonne in the hellish heat. As though the Lord were truly angry with the Cathars, that August was the hottest in heretical memory. Soon there wasn't enough water for men and cattle. Not a drop fell from the sky, so the animals had to be slaughtered. Within days the carcasses attracted a biblical plague of flies to the point that the few Catholics who remained—despite their solidarity with their heretical neighbors—began to call Carcassonne "the city of Beelzebub." Soon the flies brought the fevers, which halved the population in a week.

Carcassonne's resistance lasted twelve days. Abbot Amaury, sobered by the meager loot that had resulted from the frenzy at Béziers, consented to let the inhabitants leave the city—except, of course, the Perfecti—on condition that they take nothing with them but their sins. As in all wars, there were those among the vanquished, whether they were bought, blackmailed, or tortured, who pointed out the followers of the heresy to the victors. And as in all wars, when they couldn't think of any more names to offer, they resorted to their creditors and personal enemies.

There is a saying that rustic people don't have many ideas, but such as they have are hardy plants that seem almost to thrive in persecution. In Carcassonne it became clear for the first time that Perfecti and Perfectae would not seek to escape, mingling with the spared believers, but would instead affirm their faith on the stakes, mouths wide open, displaying the joy of true martyrs. On August 15, say the chroniclers, *"quadrigenti combusti sunt, atque quinquaginta patibulis appensi"*—forty were burned and fifty hanged.

WHO WERE THE CATHARS?

Most historians agree that the Cathars were admirable in their sincerity and heroism, and certainly their tragedy left a touch of melancholia in the Languedoc that is still felt by all travelers visiting the ruins of Cathar strongholds.

People called them Cathars, Cathares, and Cathari. In Italy they were called Patarini, but other names were applied to them, including Arians, Marsians, and followers of Mani. (In fact, the term Manichaeans was favored by their Catholic nemeses.) Yet none of these names was used by this group itself, who preferred to be called Good Christians, Good people (Bonshommes), or Friends of God.

Most existing knowledge of Cathar doctrines comes from the heavily biased records of their Catholic inquisitors. With very few exceptions, all their own writings were effectively destroyed. It is practically certain, however, that theirs was a heavily dualist version of Christianity, which arose from the distressing but quite inescapable fact that good and evil both have a share in this world. Like all gnostics, the Cathars asked why and how such an infinitely good and merciful—as well as infallible— God could have created such evil. Their answer, as it was for Zoroaster, Mani, and countless other gnostics, was that two principles—good and evil—are at odds in the universe. There is but one God, the God of good, Creator of the everlasting Kingdom of the Spirit, whose sparks of life are human souls. Evil is a lower principle that created the world, matter, and time. Evil is the lord of the world, the Rex Mundi. In his struggle to do away with the kingdom of good, he enclosed the soul in a material prison, the body, and invented time to affirm the principle of corruption and decay. Humans stand at the crossroads of these two principles. A human soul belongs to the kingdom of good, while the body belongs to the corrupted world below.

Salvation in the Cathar faith required that each person fully recognize this cosmic state of affairs in order to free him- or herself from this world of evil and reach the kingdom of good. Cathars did not, however, expect death to offer their souls automatic deliverance. The soul can enter the Kingdom of God only if it has regained its original purity, or, in other words, regained cognizance of its divine origin. For this reason the true God sent Christ to earth to reveal, through his mysteries, this key to the salvation of humans. This cognizance and knowledge of these mysteries could be received only from the Holy Spirit during a form of baptism performed by the laying on of hands. For Catharism, this spiritual baptism took on the three roles of revelation, ordination, and extreme unction and symbolized the entry into religious life and the recognition of the Holy Spirit by the soul, imprisoned within a body made flesh. This crucial sacrament, called Consolamentum, was administered to an individual only at an advanced stage of detachment from the material world, usually just before death. Those who had achieved a status of perfection and received the Consolamentum were known as Parfaits or, in Latin, Perfecti. Bound to lead a life of exemplary asceticism, prayer, and preaching, they became vegetarians, lived in celibacy, dressed in dark linen, and traveled in pairs, following the rules of their ethics to the absolute letter.

In AD 1145, more than sixty years before the Albigensian crusade, St. Bernard himself journeyed to the Languedoc to preach against the heretics, but when he arrived he was less appalled by the heretics than by the corruption of his own Church. In fact, he seems to have been quite impressed by the heretics. "No sermons are more Christian than theirs," he wrote, "and their morals are pure." The Perfecti were educated and often quite cultured, especially when compared to the moneyed but illiterate Catholic clergy. In addition, women played an important part in the Cathar "church": Many Perfectae ran orphanages and houses where Cathar girls were brought up and unaccompanied women could find shelter.

Yet the great majority of Cathars were not Perfecti but believers, *croyants,* which are laypeople who had joined the faith and were striving to attain the state of purity achieved by the Perfecti. Still under the sway of the evil in the material world, they were thus prone to sin. When the croyants died they would receive the Consolamentum of the dying, which offered believers only the reincarnation of their soul in a new human body and thus another chance for salvation. We can note how similar this is to both the Hindu and Buddhist cycle of reincarnations, which continues until enlightenment is achieved.

Other than a dualistic notion of life and death, Cathars seem to have had little fixed dogma. They rejected the Eucharist and the Mass and regarded both the Crucifixion and the Resurrection as totally irrelevant and probably untrue. They conducted their rituals in the open air and practiced a form of meditation. Their only prayer was the Pater Noster. (We might wonder if they knew it was a kabbalistic prayer.) They believed in Jesus as a gnostic teacher and placed special emphasis on the Gospel of John, whose mysteries they interpreted in conformity with their beliefs. They considered Catholic dogma a total perversion of Jesus' true teaching and consequently claimed to be the sole representatives of true Christianity.

In the eyes of Catholics (and of the Jewish rabbis they sometimes debated), the Cathars committed most serious heresy in regarding Creation as basically evil. At the turn of the twelfth century, a kabbalist in the almost completely Cathar town of Lunel wrote to one of his students that the student should not frequent the local Perfecti because "they claim that there is no blessing in this world." Nevertheless, despite powerful theological arguments against their worldview, the Cathars may perhaps have been the last exponents of a particular notion of perfection and freedom that is now lost to us.

THE FALL OF THE CATHARS

After Carcassonne, the crusading army gradually went through the whole of the Languedoc. Perpignan, Narbonne, Toulouse—all fell, one by one, with huge slaughter. The terrible massacres lasted forty years and it is believed that close to one million people died cruelly amid torture and mutilations. Even children were not spared: Some twenty thousand were exterminated in Béziers alone, most of them burned alive in St. Mary Magdalene's church. The full horrors will never be known. The cities suffered the worst of it, falling where they were, but many Cathars fled to their mountaintop castles, hiding out in them for years, waiting for the inexorable approach of their persecutors, who, at the end, dragged them out and burned them on the spot if these heretics would not recant.

It might seem strange that the Cathars didn't realize that so great a danger was approaching. We know that their culture was almost wiped out, but are we sure that we understand how such barbarity could come about? Was it really because the Roman Church was greatly alarmed by the danger that the Cathar movement might replace Catholicism in the Languedoc? We know of the Spanish fanatic Dominic Guzman, who had enormous hatred of what he called heresy. Some witnesses, though not all, say that his fanatical frenzy spurred on the ribauds, but this did not prevent him from becoming him who we now know as St. Dominic. He created a monastic order he called Praedicatores, or Preachers, but after his death in AD 1221, it was renamed after him and became the order of the Dominicans—the same order that was later put in charge of the Holy Inquisition. (Both critics and admirers of the order have made use of the pun on their Latin name, Dominicanes, which splits into Domini Canes, or the Lord's Hounds.)

Most modern historians prefer to explain what happened by pointing to the greed of the Cathars' neighbors to the north, who took advantage of a panicking Church to take possession of a rich and dangerously autonomous region. Whatever the true reason for the crusade—and I shall add my own speculations later on—the depredation of the Languedoc went on until 1244, when all organized Cathar resistance ceased. The crusade may have started out as a religious war, but it ended as mere political conquest.

Here we may return to the lingering mystery of the immense treasure the Cathars were said to have possessed. The Languedoc was extremely wealthy at the time of the crusade and rumors of a fantastic Cathar hoard spread as the Cathar destruction progressed. We know that the Cathars spent much money over the years to pay mercenaries to help defend them and also that little money was found in house-to-house fighting in the cities, but there is another intriguing story to consider.

By about 1244, all Cathar towns had fallen with the exception of some isolated mountaintop castles, included Montségur, Quéribus, Peyrepertuse, and Puilaurens, which can still be be seen today. Montségur had seemed impregnable and the people who took refuge in it seemed out of reach, but treachery allowed a group of Basque soldiers to climb halfway up the mountain, and on March 1, 1244, the Cathar defenders accepted capitulation terms. By that time they numbered fewer than four hundred, with about 150 being perfects and the rest being knights and men at arms and their families. These survivors were given surprisingly lenient terms: The fighting men were to be given full pardon for all crimes and would go free if they were prepared to confess their sins to the Inquisition. The defenders asked for a two-week truce to consider the terms. They gave hostages and it was agreed that if anyone attempted to escape the stronghold, the hostages would be killed. Not one of the Perfecti accepted the terms. Instead, all chose martyrdom. In addition, at least twenty occupants of the fortress, women and men, voluntarily received the Consolamentum and became Perfecti as well, thus committing themselves to certain death by fire.

On the night of March 15, four Perfecti and a guide, with the knowledge of their comrades, made a remarkable escape from the castle. They descended the sheer western face of the mountain on ropes, letting themselves down a drop of more than three hundred feet. This is well documented, and tradition holds that the four carried out the legendary treasure. It seems that any treasure had in fact been removed months before and in any event, these five could have carried very little on ropes. Perhaps this treasure was their sacred books and ritual objects. Perhaps the two-week truce was orchestrated simply to give these five time to secure what had to be kept out of hostile hands. But why did they act so late? Perhaps it is because on March 14 a sacred festival was held for which those treasured items were needed. Could they have located the Holy Grail, long believed to have been in Cathar possession? Wolfram von Eschenbach says that the Grail Castle was in the Pyrenees—but when Montségur fell, nothing was found. Archaeological work on top of Montségur in recent years located little even in the way of artifacts. Tradition says the treasure was taken to caves nearby at Ornolac, in the Ariège, but nothing has ever been found there either. Of course Rennes-le-Château is not twenty miles from the doomed fortress, as the crow flies.

On March 15 the truce expired, and at dawn the next day more than two hundred Perfecti were dragged down the mountain, but not one recanted his or her faith. There was no time for individual pyres, so all were locked in a wood-filled stockade at the foot of the mountain and were burned together while the remaining Cathars had to look on from the castle. A memorial now stands at the site of this dreadful scene.

To this day there abound all over the region stories of treasure smuggled out of Montségur and other mountaintop fortresses before surrender and hidden for a future rebirth of the faith. We may believe that these fine Christians who died with such courage rather than give up their precious secret knowledge to enemies in those heroic and bloody times would have ensured that later generations could regain this knowledge and wisdom, and that both are still to be found in this area.

Rennes-le-Château suffered brutally during the Albigensian crusade. The history and legends of the Cathars as well as the stories of the Grail were familiar to the young Saunière, who was born in the nearby village of Montazels.

CATHAR HERESY CONTINUES

To many modern historians, the Cathars represent little more than an unusual episode of dualist thinking in European religious history. Yet what is the origin of the Cathar phenomenon? I find it difficult to be content with the traditional Bulgarian explanation for the arrival of Cathar thinking in the Languedoc. In addition, there is the surprisingly stubborn survival in the region of the belief held by Cathars concerning the marriage of Jesus and Mary Magdalene.

As we have seen, the gnostic tradition in the south of France is primarily a Jewish and Judeo-Christian one dating back to the first centuries and almost certainly originating in Alexandria. Bearing this in mind, some French scholars now believe Catharism had its roots in heresies existing in France from the time of the gnostic beginnings of Christianity in Egypt. Some even believe there was a direct link between the gnostics and Arians in Egypt and the Cathars in France.

The idea is that a secret group of Egyptian gnostics survived for many centuries, establishing connections with European groups of Arians and gnostics. Certainly the close correlation between Catharism and Egyptian gnosticism is remarkable: Both make reference to the mysteries and secret teachings of Jesus and John regarding the secrets of the Kingdom of Heaven. Further, monks are known to have traveled between Europe and Egypt in the second, third, and fourth centuries AD. As we saw earlier, an Egyptian monk named Mark (or Markus) of Memphis introduced a form of gnosticism into central Spain, sparking the enthusiasm of the Spanish mystic Priscillian. From my own research in Egypt in recent years, I have come to believe that the origin of the Cathars was the strongly entrenched and widespread gnostic faith of Egypt. But there is another possible trail.

An article on the Web site of the Société Périllos recently argued for the arrival of Manichaean preachers on the coast near Perpignan during the lifetime of Mani, the founder of the most successful dualist religion since the time of Zoroaster. It also posits, as scholars have long been aware, that after Mani's execution in about AD 274, his followers spread westward along the Roman Empire's commercial arteries into Spain, Gaul, and Britain. But the article then elaborates the thesis to suggest that two local Perpignan saints, St. Abdon and St. Sennen—originally Persian princes and officers in the army of Shapur I, second emperor of the Sassanid dynasty—were in fact followers of Mani who declared themselves Christian but continued to preach in the French region his Zoroastrian vision of two powers in heaven.

Abdon and Sennen were condemned as Christians in AD 250, during the fearful persecutions by the Roman emperor Decius, and were beheaded in the Coliseum, but as it turns out, they had been close to Shapur I and had witnessed him granting Mani's teachings the status of primary religion among all the Persian empire's religions, officially replacing the old Zoroastrian belief and the Magoi's cult of Sacred Fire. The story is a long one, but suffice it to say the saints' bodies are buried in Arles-sur-Tech, a village in the eastern Pyrenees close to the Spanish border, and they were brought there by a Perpignan-based Catholic society, the Archiconfrérie de La Sanch, established in 1416 by the Spanish saint Vincent Ferrer. In their article, the researchers of the Société Périllos bring much evidence to show that this fraternity was in fact, since its very inception, a secret repository of Manichaean lore and beliefs.

Interestingly, La Sanch members often appear in the ups and downs of Saunière's life, and the idea proposed by the article is that the abbé may himself have been a secret follower of this local gnostic tradition. What I find more interesting is how the story relates to the question we posed earlier about Jesus' destination after fleeing to Egypt: Why would two followers of Mani come to southern France, of all places, as early as two hundred years after the Crucifixion? Was it because the place already had a reputation as a center of gnostic and neo-Pythagorean thought? Catholic priests throughout the Middle Ages accused the people in this area of being Manichaean heretics—what if this was true, and from a long time before any Bulgarian dualists ever set foot in the region?

An Egyptian gnostic monk converts Priscillian, followers of Mani arrive in Perpignan, Jewish kabbalists migrate to the region from Babylonia—what is it about this place that seems to attract dualist thinkers who reject Paul's version of Christ and his teaching? Could the Bulgarian heretics who came to the Languedoc in the eleventh century have arrived not to bring their gnostic vision, but instead because this is where they knew they would find teachers more versed in the teachings of the gnostic Jesus than Bogomil himself?

I am certain that Catharism in Europe—including its often stated conviction that Jesus and Mary Magdalene were married—evolved from all these beginnings. The region's excitement over Mary even after the Cathar extermination caused the Church to clarify strenuously that Our Lady, the Bride of Christ, was Mary the mother of Jesus and not Mary Magdalene. Yet songs, art, and even religious paintings hinted at more than the Church was letting on. Even in sanctioned art, Mary Magdalene is shown mourning over the body of Jesus and clinging in the way only a spouse or lover might, and depictions of a pregnant or nursing Mary Magdalene can be found in many examples of Church art.

There are several sources for this tradition, almost all of them descriptions of Cathar beliefs set down by their critics and persecutors, with the best known being the *Summa Contra Haeriticos,* ascribed to Praepositinus. Scholar Yuri Stoyanov writes about it in his excellent study on religious dualism, *The Other God:*

> According to the same tract, another teaching that these Albigensians regarded as esoteric and that again was taught in their "secret meetings" claimed that Mary Magdalene was in reality the wife of Christ. . . . She was also recognized as the Samaritan woman to whom he said, "Call thy husband." She was the woman whom Jesus freed when the Jews were trying to stone her, and she was his wife because she was alone with him in three places—in the Temple, at the well, and in the garden. This Albigensian belief in Mary Magdalene as Jesus' wife is confirmed by two additional Catholic tracts on the Cathar heresy.

Later in the same chapter, Stoyanov writes: "The origins of the teaching of Mary Magdalene's marital status appear rather obscure. It appears, moreover, to be an original Cathar tradition which does not have any counterpart in the extant evidence of Bogomil Christology and New Testament exegesis." But as I asked at the end of chapter 17, if the Cathars didn't learn of this sacred marriage from the Bogomils, from whom did they learn about it?

We know full well that Mary Magdalene played a very prominent role in earlier gnostic traditions, especially in the Egyptian gospels found at Nag Hammadi, such as the Gospel of Mary, the Gospel of Philip, the Pistis Sophia, and the Dialogue of the Savior, in which she is often extolled as the chief disciple of Jesus, a visionary, and the mediator of gnostic revelations. She is praised as "the woman who knew the All" and "the inheritor of light." The Gospel according to Philip actually recognizes her as the *koinonos* (companion or consort) of Jesus, whom he loved more than all other disciples, and the spiritual union between Jesus and Mary Magdalene is described in slightly erotic terms. It would seem, then, that the Cathars invented nothing and were instead the inheritors of either a tradition that came from Egypt or one that was local and that perpetuated the memory of that couple as local people remembered them.

A researcher in this area of southern France, a member of a prestigious cultural association, recently showed me his collection of remarkable paintings and prints portraying Jesus and Mary Magdalene. Most of them date to the eighteenth and nineteenth centuries—in other words, they are devotional art produced before Saunière was born! This scholar claims they perpetuate the popular Cathar tradition about the couple that is still present beneath the surface and is strongly believed by many Huguenot families in the region. This fascinating phenomenon is also found in many Christian families in Spain and Portugal, which, to this day, retain some Jewish symbols and rituals such as the lighting of candles on Friday evening, remnants that identify them as Christians who, after converting from Judaism, spent some time as *marranos*—that is, converts secretly practicing their old faith.

If only I had been allowed to reproduce some of these devotional portraits in this book (but rest assured, they will be published in the United States soon, I'm told), I feel sure my readers would have agreed that their emotional impact speaks volumes about the depth of the locals' belief in the couple having lived out their love story in these hills.

19

THE KNIGHTS
TEMPLAR

Thousands of books have been written about the most famous of all chivalric orders, known as the Order of the Temple, or Knights Templar. Perhaps the most glamorous and enigmatic figures of Western culture, the Knights Templar in their white robes with splayed red crosses certainly had secrets that they managed to retain. We have no idea what those secrets were, nor will we ever know unless we should one day find some of their secret documents.

Were they just warrior knights, fanatically fierce mystic fighters and soldiers, a militia of Christ—or were they also a secret society with heretical, gnostic principles and aims? Were they deeply devoted Christians, protectors of pilgrims, and firm believers in the gospels and in Jesus himself or, as charged in the trials that led to their annihilation in the early fourteenth century, were they sympathizers with Islam, heretics who did not accept the truth of the Crucifixion and who, in their secret ceremonies, "spat on the cross" and worshipped an idol they called Baphomet? Historians to this day seem unable to reach a consensus on the seven-hundred-year-old conundrum presented by the knights.

If it's true that they didn't believe Jesus died on the cross, what was it that influenced them toward this view? Did they get their unorthodox ideas on the Crucifixion from the Arabs, with whom they developed close relations in the course of their history, or did they find documents relating to the incident during their lengthy searches under the Temple Mount in Jerusalem (which, incidentally, amounted to the first ever methodically conducted archaeological dig)? This is just one of the questions we shall attempt to answer in this chapter.

A BRIEF HISTORY OF THE TEMPLARS

The Templar order was founded in 1118 (some say AD 1119), a mere nineteen years after Jerusalem had fallen to the Christian armies, by nine European noblemen who took a vow to protect the route followed by pilgrims climbing from the ports on the Mediterranean shore (Tyre and Jaffa, mainly) to the Holy City. Our most important source is Guilleaume of Tyre, who wrote between AD 1175 and 1185, at the peak of Crusader conquests and Templar power. He was therefore writing of events that took place before he was born, and unfortunately, he doesn't mention his sources or other firsthand records. A great historian of the Crusades, Sir Stephen Runciman, says that Guilleaume's writings are vague and often factually incorrect, but with little else on the subject, they are still invaluable. This is intriguing in itself: Our understanding of the Templars is limited by the lack of documents from their early period. In other words, there seems to have been total secrecy from the beginning—but why?

Guilleaume says that the Order of the Poor Knights of Christ of the Temple of Solomon was founded in AD 1118 by Hugues de Payen, a nobleman from the Champagne area who was born in 1070. The story is that one day Hugues arrived, quite unsolicited, with eight comrades at the palace of Baudouin I, king of Jerusalem, whose elder brother, Godfroi de Bouillon (Godfrey of Bouillon), had captured the Holy City nineteen years before. (The tombs of both men, defaced but intact, are still in the Church of the Holy Sepulchre, their original location.) Baudouin seems to have received them well and immediately placed an entire wing of the Royal Palace at their disposal. In spite of their declared oath of poverty, the knights moved into these lavish accommodations.

Their quarters were built on the foundations of the ancient Temple of Solomon, the present-day site of the Al-Aqsa Mosque. It was from this location that the new order took its name. Guilleaume tells that for nine years no new candidates were accepted into the order, which seems most odd under the circumstances, for how could nine men do much to help pilgrims attacked by bandits on the roads? Surely recruits were needed right away. That there are no records of the Templars' early years is even more bizarre if we consider that the king employed an official royal historian by the name of Fulk de Chartres, who wrote at the very time in question. Fulk makes no mention whatsoever of Hugues de Payen or the Knights Templar and their supposed mission to help the pilgrims. Still, word spread rapidly about them back in Europe. By AD 1128, St. Bernard, abbot of Clairvaux and probably the foremost spokesman for Christendom at that time, issued a document, *In Praise of the New Knighthood,* which extolled their virtues and declared them Christian monks of the highest possible order.

At the Council of Troyes, also in AD 1128, the Templars were officially incorporated as a religious and military order and Hugues de Payen was given the title of grand master. St. Bernard himself drew up most of their Rule, which began with poverty, chastity, and obedience. Official Templar seals show two knights riding on a single horse as an indication of their poverty. Curiously enough, this was also the picture carved into the stone that Saunière discovered facedown in front of the altar in the church of Mary Magdalene in Rennes-le-Château (although, as mentioned earlier, some people claim that the carving shows not two knights on one horse, but the child Sigisbert being rescued by a rider following the murder of his father, Dagobert II). Yet there is no doubt the Templars adopted this exact emblem, which they later depicted on their seal.

In an age when Western men were normally clean-shaven, the Knights were obliged to cut their hair but were forbidden to cut their beards. Diet, dress, and most aspects of their daily life were tightly controlled by monastic and military routines. Military conduct was strict: Templars were compelled to fight to the death and they were not permitted to retreat unless the odds were greater than three or four to one. If captured, they were not allowed to ask for mercy or to ransom themselves.

After Troyes, an order was issued by Pope Innocent II, a former Cistercian monk at Clairvaux and a disciple of St. Bernard, stating that Templars would owe allegiance to no ecclesiastical power other than the pope himself, and certainly to no king of any country. From that time onward they were therefore totally independent from both political and religious interference. In the subsequent twenty years, the order expanded very rapidly and came to exist on a large scale. Recruits joined in great numbers, signing over to the order all their possessions. Interestingly, though the knights themselves were sworn to poverty, this did not prevent the order from amassing wealth on an immense scale. The Templar order owned land in France, England, Scotland, Flanders, Spain, Portugal, Italy, Austria, Germany, and Hungary, as well as in the Holy Land. When Hugues de Payen returned there in 1130, it was with an entourage of three hundred knights.

In AD 1146 the Templars accompanied King Louis VII of France on the Second Crusade, where they established their reputation for martial skill and fighting zeal. The king himself said afterward that only the Templars prevented the Second Crusade from collapsing. After this, the knights developed great influence everywhere in Europe, having close links, for example, with both Henry II and Thomas à Becket, which two they tried to reconcile. It is known that a master of the order even stood beside King John at the signing of the Magna Carta. They also developed close links with the Muslims, who respected them. They even associated with the Ismailic sect known as the Assassins (Hashishin), who paid tribute to Templars.

Through land acquisitions, commercial trading, and hiring out its ships, the order's wealth and strength became so great that it is credited with creating the concept of modern banking. Having preceptories throughout Europe and the Levant, the Templars devised reasonable rates and organized safe and efficient transfers of money for merchants, who slowly became dependent upon them. By drawing money in one country from another, the Templars became the money changers of the age and their Parisian base becoming the center of European finance. It is said that even the check was devised by them. Eventually they started to lend large sums to destitute kings and became bankers for every throne in Europe and for some Muslim ones as well. Historians believe that this dependence of kings on the Templars' willingness to finance their countries' military campaigns was what eventually made them more enemies than even they could handle.

At the peak of the Knights' power, the situation in the Holy Land seriously deteriorated. In AD 1185, King Baudouin IV of Jerusalem suddenly died. In the quarrels that followed, the master of the Temple, de Ridefort, betrayed his oath to the previous master and brought the community to the edge of civil war. He also stupidly disturbed the close relations with the Muslims and in July 1187 led his knights, along with most of the Christian army, into a disastrous battle against Saladin at Hattin in Galilee. The Christians were annihilated and two months later Jerusalem itself fell after almost a century in Christian hands.

It is during this period, the last twenty years or so before Innocent III launched his crusade against the Cathars in AD 1208, that the Templars, whose presence in southern France had always been strong, began to associate with the Cathars. During the Albigensian crusade, however, they remained neutral, limiting themselves to the role of witnesses (though it is also known that they provided a haven for many Cathar refugees). It is interesting to note that in the decades after the fall of Jerusalem, the order began to accept Cathar nobles (*seigneurs faidits*) into its ranks, something forbidden by its Rule up to that time. There is much circumstantial evidence indicating that at least some important Templars became close to Catharism in this period: the role of black cats in secret ceremonies that the Church's inquisitors accused both Cathars and Templars of performing; the role in the beliefs of both groups played by the Gospel of John was the only part of the Christian scriptures that the Cathars used in their liturgy); and the intense devotion both groups exhibited for John the Baptist and Mary Magdalene.

In the century that followed the fall of Jerusalem, the situation in the East gradually became hopeless for the Christians, and by AD 1291 virtually the whole of Outremer, as Christian possessions in Syria were known in France, had fallen. The Holy Land was once again under Muslim control—only Acre remained in Christian hands, and in May 1291 that last bastion was lost, too. In the final fight, the Templars showed great heroism: With space in the order's galleys being very limited, women and children were evacuated while the Knights, even the wounded, chose to remain behind. In the end, the walls collapsed on both attackers and defenders in a holocaust of ruin.

The Templars then established themselves in Cyprus, which they had bought from Richard the Lionheart a century earlier, but with the loss of the Holy Land, their prime reason for existence had gone. They looked for new fields of activity, such as fighting with the Teutonic Knights in the northeast of Europe, and also turned their attention to the Languedoc, where they developed existing *commanderies* (preceptories) and founded new ones—among them, as we shall see, Le Bézu, very close to Rennes-le-Château.

The thinking of the Templars at this time is not known. They certainly had the power to seize control of France, and we may well wonder why they did not do so. Perhaps this level of power was the reason why, in AD 1306, King Philip IV of France, known as Philippe le Bel (Philip the Fair), decided to crush the order. Their economic and military power could have achieved anything, and there was a real risk of the Templars declaring a separate state in the south. Perhaps the king saw the danger and simply preempted their action. Despite squeezing every last Louis d'or out of the realm's Jews before expelling them, Philip's coffers were quite empty. He owed the Templars a great deal of money and he was convinced that they had stolen part of his grandfather's ransom in AD 1250. As if all that were not enough to incite his bad feeling for the Templars, he had once applied to join the order and the grand master had unwisely humiliated him by refusing to admit him.

Philip laid careful plans, using spies to construct charges against the Knights. First he sought the help of the pope, to whom the Templars owed allegiance, however modest it had become by then: The ruthless

French king had already arranged the death of one pope, Boniface VIII, and probably poisoned another, Benedict XI. In AD 1305, Philip finally managed to fix the election of his own pope: The bishop of Bordeaux assumed the papacy with the name Clement V. He was Philip's man and could not refuse the king's demand to suppress the Templars. Philip issued sealed orders to his marshals for the simultaneous seizure of all Templars in France.

Early on Friday, October 13, 1307, along with the arrest of the Knights themselves, all their assets were to be seized, but we can imagine the king's complete surprise when none of the great treasure was found. No one else has been able to find it either, and the whereabouts of the treasure of the Templars has remained a mystery ever since. There is clear evidence that the Templars had prior warning of the seizure: Grand Master Jacques de Molay had many of their books and documents burned well beforehand and preceptories in France were warned that no secret or document was to be revealed. Those arrested went quietly into custody, but it is known that the Paris treasure was removed. Indeed, the whole of the Templar fleet seems to have escaped; certainly there is no record of its capture. Those in La Rochelle and Port Bacares, the Templar seaport near Rennes-le-Château, saw the Knights moving Templar documents and funds about that time, with many galleys involved. Some researchers believe that a large part of these precious possessions was hidden in the mountain area of Rennes-le-Château, where it remains.

In France many (but not all) Templars were tried and tortured. Strange confessions were extorted from some and there were rumors of the confession of weird Templar ceremonies. In their questioning, the Knights were persistently accused of repudiating and spitting on the cross. Many men were imprisoned and some were burned at the stake as heretics. In AD 1312 the pope agreed to dissolve the order officially. Finally, in March 1314, on the island in the Seine at the heart of Paris where Notre Dame Cathedral rises, Jacques de Molay, the grand master, and Geoffrey de Charnay, preceptor of Normandy, were burned to death most cruelly over a slow fire.

In spite of all this persecution, the Templars did not cease to exist, and in fact many escaped Philip's vengeance. The king tried to eliminate Templars abroad, but the Knights had considerable strength in England and Scotland. Edward II of England defended them at first, but threatened with excommunication by the pope, he disbanded them, though without persecution. They were never disbanded in Scotland, however, and almost certainly took part in the campaign of Robert the Bruce against England in 1314. In Alsace-Lorraine, then part of Germany, they were supported by the duke and all were exonerated. In Germany the Templars defied the judges, who later decided on their innocence. The same occurred in Spain and Portugal, where, after an inquiry cleared them, they changed their name to the Knights of Christ, continuing as an order until about 1700. Vasco da Gama was a knight of this order and Henry the Navigator was a grand master.

Indeed, Christopher Columbus's ships carried the Templar red cross on their sails. A book has been written by Italian researcher Ruggero Marino on the role of the Templars in the discovery of the New World. In it the author shows that the Templar fleet, probably enabled by Arab maps and navigational technology, reached America during the thirteenth century, before the time of Columbus. This gives credence to the hypothesis that the fleet that escaped from La Rochelle headed for Templar bases across the Atlantic, which in turn would explain the mystery on Oak Island, off Nova Scotia, where for more than a century people have been searching for a treasure apparently buried beneath insurmountable traps: It seems that sophisticated hydraulic mechanisms flood with seawater any excavation effort as soon as a certain level of digging is reached. Interestingly, the Templars were famous for using just this kind of technology to protect crypts and passageways.

QUESTIONS ABOUT THE TEMPLARS

Of course the most common interpretation of the real nature of the Templar order in the circles of Rennes-le-Château enthusiasts—a view famously proposed by Lincoln, Baigent, and Leigh in *Holy Blood, Holy*

Grail—is that the Templars were the military arm of the Priory of Sion. According to this theory, the Merovingian kings, betrayed by the Church with the murder of Dagobert, spent the next thirteen centuries plotting their revenge (albeit somewhat ineffectually). Being the legitimate descendants of Jesus and Mary Magdalene, they had a pressing need to search for documents that would either prove their divine lineage or give the lie to the Roman concept of the apostolic line—or possibly succeed at proving both. Where could such documents ever be found if not in Jerusalem?

What this meant for the devisers of the Plantard hoax was that if a genealogical link could be found tying the noblemen who accomplished the First Crusade (who were, in effect, mostly French) to the Merovingians . . . then voilà! The Crusades themselves could be shown to have been not about recovering the Holy Sepulchre (a convenient pretext), but about the Priory's need to dig in Jerusalem at a time when the city was most inconveniently in the hands of ferocious Muslims who could be dislodged only through an all-out war. But was it possible to prove that the Merovingian line had been preserved all the way to prominent lords such as Raymond IV of Toulouse and Godfrey of Bouillion? After all, the Merovingians had been gone for only four hundred years, and if Sigisbert had really survived, anything was possible. . . .

In this heavily conspiratorial view of medieval history, the lack of documents from the early years of the Templars is admittedly easier to explain. That they spent their first nine years frantically digging where the Temple had stood while refusing to admit any new knights into the order actually seems logical. If we stick to logic, however, it seems that given that the Merovingians were not reinstated as kings of Europe in the twelfth century, the diggers in Jerusalem found nothing.

As I've said, debunking Pierre Plantard and de Chérisey's hoax does not prove, however, that something powerful and hidden has not been a part of the history of the village of Rennes for close to two thousand years. While there may not be secret societies that have manipulated world history through the centuries, it is possible that many people, throughout the generations, can be aware of a particular secret and can both contribute to its transmission and make sure that it remains a secret. What I suggest is that such knowledge—the mystery hidden in plain sight, known to Gypsies and common folk but not to historians in their libraries, the true history of that underground stream, the gnostic Christianity of the West—can be traced back through the centuries to a seemingly unthinkable truth: the natural death and burial of Jesus, Mary Magdalene, and Joseph of Arimathea somewhere below the Pyrenees village of Rennes.

So if it wasn't on the orders of the Priory of Sion, then why did the Templars spend their first decade digging under the Dome of the Rock? If they found anything, what was it, and when the nine knights emerged from the tunnels King Solomon built a thousand years before the time of Jesus, was what they found in any way linked to the astounding success their order enjoyed for two centuries? It's not easy to even formulate hypothetical answers to these questions without leaving the realm of historical facts and starting to embroider a tapestry of historical fantasy. Thus I introduce a relatively recent philological discovery that gives us something concrete on which we can base speculation.

The Power of the Baphomet

A few years before his death in 1988, Hugh Schonfield came across *Holy Blood, Holy Grail* and was intrigued by what its authors related about the idol that the Templars were accused of worshipping in their secret rites: a head variously described in the confessions of the poor tortured knights as "half golden and half black" or "half male and half female" or "half bearded and half clean-shaven." The one point every Templar agreed on was the name given to the head: the Baphomet, a name that has intrigued historians of the order for a long time. All sorts of interpretations have been given for its origin and meaning, from the early supposition—put forward by the inquisitors themselves—that it was a corruption of Mahomet (that is, Muhammad), and perhaps the first syllable was changed precisely so that should the secret of their worship ever be discovered, they might deny worshipping the prophet of the Muslims. Other interpretations have included that a numerical code might be hidden in the mysterious word.

Schonfield was a leading expert on the languages of late antiquity and particularly on the kinds of Hebrew and Aramaic that were spoken just before and after the first century, the time when the Dead Sea Scrolls were written. Because of his years of work on those scrolls, he was also aware that the Essenes used ciphers to hide the contents of their communications from Romans, Temple priests, and other enemies who may have even been hiding in their fold. One such cipher was of kabbalistic origin and its use had been identified in several scrolls discovered at Qumran. It was called the Atbash cipher and it made use of a relatively simple stratagem: If we write the Hebrew alphabet from the first to the twenty-second letter in the usual way (that is, from right to left), we have this:

א ב ג ד ה ו ז ח ט י כ ל מ נ ס ע פ צ ק ר ש ת

If we now simply write it backward—that is, from left to right—we have this:

ת ש ר ק צ פ ע ס נ מ ל כ י ט ח ז ו ה ד ג ב א

The Atbash cipher consisted of simply replacing the letter in the first line with the one directly below it in the second line—or, in other words, the first letter becomes the last, the second one becomes the one before last, and so on. In Hebrew, Alef becomes Tav, Bet becomes Shin, and so forth, which is how the cipher acquired its name.

While working on the Dead Sea Scrolls, Schonfield used the Atbash cipher to decode some words that scholars had found impossible to translate. In the Essene work *The Assumption of Moses,* there appears a meaningless name, Taxo, applied to a saintly Levite who, with his seven sons, retires from the corrupt city of Jerusalem and sets up residence in a cave. Credit is due to Schonfield for having applied the old cipher of Hebrew scripture (whose previous use in the Book of Jeremiah was known) to discovering that Taxo is a coded disguise for Asaph.

Asaph ben Berechiah is described in several books of the Bible as a

Levite at the time of King Solomon. In both Jewish and Islamic lore he is regarded as a master of occult and miraculous arts, a wizardly figure who advises King Solomon in theurgic practices and possesses knowledge of the true and ineffable Name of God. These qualities, combined with the notion that he was said to have fled to live in a cave, were sufficient to establish him as a forerunner of the Teacher of Righteousness in the eyes of the Essenes.

Like anyone who has applied a cipher to thousands of words, Schonfield happened to write the word Baphomet in Hebrew, then absent-mindedly ciphered it using the Atbash cipher. As he later told Michael Baigent, his jaw dropped when he contemplated the result of the experiment:

T EM O F AB

ת מ ו פ ב

א י פ ו ש

A Y F O S

Yes, Schonfield had accidentally discovered the real meaning of the word Baphomet: It was the gnostic Sophia, the goddess of Wisdom, encoded with a cipher used by the Essenes at Qumran more than a millennium before the Templars were founded!

This concrete detail not so much tells us that some Templars worshipped an androgynous idol they called Sophia (though that is perhaps interesting enough), but begs the question: Where did the Templars learn the Atbash cipher? If we believed Pierre Plantard's Merovingian fantasy, the immediate answer would be that Jesus and Mary Magdalene, being Essenes themselves, knew the cipher, so their Merovingian descendants presumably did too. Why, then, should the supposed military arm of the Priory of Sion not be aware of it? This would seem to be a faulty explanation, but that the Templars knew the cipher is a black-and-white fact, so what are the alternatives?

I can see only two other possible explanations: One is that knowledge of the Atbash cipher came to the Templars from the Jewish nobility of Septimania, which had married into French aristocracy as late as the ninth century, only two hundred years before the First Crusade. Perhaps one of the Templar founders hailed from such a family. The other possible explanation, and the one that is perhaps more likely, is related to Cathar and Templar traditions and was described by the inquisitors (and confessed to by several Templar Knights) as spitting on the cross.

A SHARED TEMPLAR AND CATHAR BELIEF

It would seem that this gesture of spitting on the cross was tied to the Templar (and Cathar) belief that the cross was an irrelevant, ignominious episode in Jesus' life that should never have become a symbol of his mission or an object of worship. The possibility I raised earlier that the Knights acquired this opinion through frequenting their Muslim adversaries—for we know that the Quran does not accept that Jesus died on the cross—doesn't of course rule out that they may have come into contact with other groups who didn't believe he died on the cross—or who knew he didn't because they were in fact descendants of those Judeo-Christians who were aware of this secret from the beginning.

These were the various Judeo-Christian sects that continued to preach their Jewish brand of Christianity in a region spanning Jerusalem, Damascus, Antioch, and Mesopotamia—indeed, the same sects that gave rise to Manichaeism and a score of other gnostic schools over the first three centuries and that taught Muhammad what he knew of the Bible. These groups took no notice of what Pauline Christianity had become in the meantime or of the deliberations in Nicaea or of the creation of the Holy Roman Empire and they sometimes even continued to speak Aramaic, the language of Jesus, not caring to express themselves in Greek or Latin. And some of them certainly would have known about the Atbash cipher.

One such sect, the Mandeans, still survive in the marshlands of southern Iraq, where they worship John the Baptist rather than Jesus and actually consider Jesus an upstart who tried to usurp the Baptist's role as the rightful Messiah. Nine hundred years ago, the Mandeans may have been living much closer to the Holy Land than they do now—and who's to say that Templar Knights didn't come across them or were not influenced by them (or others like them) into taking up their almost obsessive worship of the Baptist? Naturally, these sects would all have spoken of Jesus as a man and not a God, and some of them, given that the Essenes had a central role in Jesus' staged "resurrection," could even have retained the knowledge that he came down from the cross alive.

But why would Templar Knights seek out such apparently heretical groups? Could it be that they were actually looking for those who might possess knowledge and practice of early Christian traditions? Perhaps this search would help to explain their highly unusual "archaeological" activities in Jerusalem. Templar chaplains were known for their erudition, especially in the field of ancient languages, and some of them seem to have been mystical initiates. Their knowledge appears to have extended beyond Christianity, with their mysteries including alchemy, kabbalistic lore, and arcane wisdom.

Some people believe that among the important centers of the order were Rennes-le-Château and a number of other places in the vicinity, such as Alet-les-Bains, Le Bézu, and Campagne-sur-Aude. It is suggested that in these centers teachings were passed on to initiates, including those who were to go out as teachers themselves to spread their ever-widening knowledge and understanding among the growing Templar ranks.

But is there any real evidence of a connection between Rennes-le-Château and the Templars? *Holy Blood, Holy Grail* almost takes for granted such a connection, arguing that the castle at Le Bézu, not three miles from Rennes as the crow flies, was a Templar commandery. In addition, the three authors go as far as to claim that its commander at the time of King Philip's roundup was a close relation of the French pope:

Alone of all the Templars in France, they were left unmolested by Philippe le Bel's seneschals on October 13, 1307. On that fateful day the commander of the Templar contingent at Bezu was a Seigneur de Goth. And before taking the name of Pope Clement V, the archbishop of Bordeaux—King Philippe's vacillating pawn—was Bertrand de Goth. Moreover, the new pontiff's mother was Ida de Blanchefort, of the same family as Bertrand de Blanchefort, the fourth Grand Master of the Order of the Temple. Was the Pope then privy to some secret entrusted to the custody of his family?

In truth, I had never even been able to ascertain if the Templars had in fact possessed the castle at Le Bézu—until recently, that is. Abbé Mazières, a respectable historian of the Aude region, who died in 1988, was always convinced that the order indeed owned the castle of Albedun between 1292 and 1307. He wrote that Pierre de Voisins asked a group of Templars to settle in Albedun Castle to look for the treasure of the Visigoths in the region of Bézu. Mazieres's story was of course used by the authors of *Holy Blood, Holy Grail.* Recently, however, a well-documented article on the castle of Albedun offered this: "Near the end of the thirteenth century, a separate detachment of Templars was sent from the Aragonese province of Rossillon to the Rennes-le-Château area in southern France [the old Cathar stronghold]. This fresh detachment established itself on the summit of the mountain of Bezu, erecting a lookout post and a chapel."

So the Templars actually were in Le Bézu around the turn of the fourteenth century. What's more, it's possible that a member of the family of Pope Clement V was with the Templars of Le Bézu, for I looked at the coat of arms of the pope's family and was surprised to find that it contained definite elements of Templar heraldry. It is likely, then, that there was a Templar in the de Goth family, though whether he headed the group at Bézu remains to be proved.

Just as Jesus would not have advertised his presence in these parts, if the Templars had discovered something extremely important about Rennes-le-Château, it's likely they would not have drawn attention to the place by installing themselves in its castle. Yet they might have tried to control the area at some safe, defendable place close by—and that's just what Bézu was.

To sum up what this chapter suggests, the Templars may well have sought ancient documents in the ten years they spent searching the premises of the Temple in Jerusalem, but what they found likely sent them right back to the region from which many of their founding members hailed: the Languedoc. What they found there, probably guided by parchments encoded with the Atbash cipher, was a tomb that resulted in the fatal blow that their Catholic faith suffered, leading them to respect and associate with Muslims, whose Holy Book explicitly denied that Jesus had died on the cross; to respect and associate with Cathars, whose traditions claimed that Jesus and Mary Magdalene had been husband and wife; and to respect and associate with Muslim Hashishin (Assassins) and Jewish kabbalists—in other words, with the heirs of the gnostic tradition in those religions. They had knowledge of a secret and managed to retain this secret despite paying the highest price for their forbidden knowledge.

Knowing that in the gnostic gospels Jesus constantly refers to secret teachings (in fact, even in the canonical gospels he says that some of his wisdom is meant only for "those who have ears to hear") and knowing the workings of the Atbash cipher, we may wonder who Jesus was addressing and what he meant when he pronounced, as recounted in Matthew 19:30: "But the first will be the last, and the last will be the first."

20

WHO KNEW THE
TRUTH?

"In the early thirteenth century, the Church was in danger of a revolt scarcely less formidable than that of the early sixteenth," writes Sir Bertrand Russell in his *History of Western Philosophy*. The two threats were similar not just in the extent of the potential revolt but in other ways, too. Of course by that I don't mean that Martin Luther was a gnostic—the good Augustinian monk would have recoiled from any association with "Manichaean" ideas. Nor am I referring to the outrage that both Luther and thirteenth-century nobles in Provence felt for the greed and corruption of the Catholic clergy. The similarity I refer to as I continue to highlight the Jewish role in the unceasing struggle against Rome is best seen in the other revolution that unfolded during the three decades before Luther pinned his ninety-five theses on the church door in Wittenberg in October 1517.

We know that other revolution by the largely positive and admiring name of the Renaissance and consider it an artistic and cultural movement that was, in hindsight, the harbinger of modernity and the beginning of the end of the Middle Ages. It began in Italy, home both to the Catholic Church and to some of the richest and most innovative cities in the Western world. The Renaissance effected far-reaching changes in fields as diverse as painting, architecture, economics, warfare, and exploration and had its most intense expression in the Medici's Florence, a fact surprisingly agreed upon by all historians.

But whereas Luther's reform had nothing to do with gnosticism, this other revolution was thoroughly imbued with and took its earliest inspiration from it. I'm not referring here to the alchemy of Paracelsus or the secret messages encoded by Leonardo in his paintings, for these things came later and were part of the effort to spread the new awareness with which Florentine intellectuals and artists had been endowed. Instead we can look at the early manifestations of that spiritual awareness, which began not long after the destruction of the Cathar heresy and involved mystics such as St. Francis, Dante, Raymond Lull, and Meister Eckhart. Theirs was indeed a gnostic and Neoplatonic worldview that all through the thirteenth and fourteenth centuries prepared the ground, culturally speaking, for the quiet explosion that took place in the late fifteenth century, triggered by two determining factors.

"Quiet explosion" is one way of defining the flowering of the hermetic tradition in Florence, which can be said to have started in Marsilio Ficino's academy through several projects patronized and financed by Cosimo de' Medici, first among them the translation by Ficino of the *Corpus Hermeticum,* a collection of Greek writings from the early Christian centuries attributed to the legendary Hermes Trismegistus but most of which, not surprisingly, were actually penned by Egyptian gnostics.

Gnosticism, as we have seen, places great emphasis on personal responsibility for individual choices and actions, a far cry from St. Paul's idea of inescapable Original Sin and the consequent need for the redeeming sacrifice of the Son of God. The threat to the Church of Rome posed by gnosticism was always obvious, but how it actually precipitated a cultural revolution can be seen only with hindsight. Recognizing the divine spark within them, gnostic adepts developed the confidence—today we would call it self-esteem—that is the key to realizing personal potential, to making the most of individual talent. This confidence is what made the Renaissance possible. The fearlessness that fueled this time can be seen in its artistic revolutions, in its exploration of the whole planet, in the birth pains of science. It is no exaggeration to say that Rosicrucianism—which early in the seventeenth century affirmed the divinity each person can and should strive to attain—amounted to a philosophical *summa* of the entire Renaissance.

Perhaps the three defining moments of the Renaissance were the invention of a more efficient press by Johannes Gutenberg (1447), the "discovery" of America by Christopher Columbus (1492), and the publication of *De revolutionibus orbium coelestium* (On the Revolutions of the Celestial Spheres) by Nicolas Copernicus (1542), all of which encapsulated the hundred years that saw Catholic dogma begin to lose its grip on the Western mind. Gutenberg's invention increased dramatically the speed with which ideas—orthodox as well as heretical—could spread to the four corners of Christendom: Ideas could no longer be stopped by controlling the copyists. The discovery made by Columbus and the publication of *De revolutionibus* by Copernicus dislocated the very cosmology emanating from Rome: Columbus showed everyone that the world was much bigger than they thought, and subsequently Copernicus went a step farther and showed that the earth was not at the center of the universe. How sublimely in tune these actions were with the fearlessness of the time. We might find it symbolic that the day Martin Luther chose to make his rebellious statement came exactly in the middle of the half-century that separated the day Columbus landed in the West Indies from the day Copernicus's tractate saw the light.

Undoubtedly a crucial part in the birth of this spiritual rebellion to Catholic dogma was played by the Renaissance hermeticists, whose quest for Sophia and belief in the divine nature of human beings had their roots in Egyptian gnosticism. Giordano Bruno taught that the Egyptian religion was far superior to Christianity in every way. In this chapter we may see that hermeticism, alchemy, and gnosticism, whether found in the schools of Florence, in the writings of Paracelsus, or, later still, in the works of Jakob Boehme, inevitably lead us back to the Alexandria of Jesus' time, that veritable spiritual melting pot in which the ideas fermented that we find in the Pistis Sophia, in the works of Philo, in the *Corpus Hermeticum,* and in the sacred texts of the Nag Hammadi heretics.

THE IMPORTANCE OF
THE CHRISTIAN KABBALAH

Let's return to the topic of Florence in the 1480s. Why might the translation of gnostic writings from Egypt be crucial to the development of this new attitude toward knowledge on the part of Europeans? What is the relevance to this phenomenon of stubborn, continuing Jewish opposition to the Church? The answer to both questions: Christian kabbalah.

We saw earlier how Jesus was very probably an early exponent of the Jewish gnostic school of thought that would become known as kabbalah. These ideas, originating from the time of Ezekiel and Pythagoras, had by the first century grown into a system based on personal enlightenment through gnosis, but also included a monastic lifestyle and a Neoplatonic cosmology with evident dualistic overtones. The footsteps of this Jewish tradition—or, more important, of the Judeo-Christian version of it that Jesus may well have taught—have been followed in this book to illustrate how the south of France had become a center of dualistic traditions in the West, a veritable powerhouse of gnostic thinking that attracted early Christians from Judaea, neo-Pythagoreans from Egypt, and Manichaeans from Mesopotamia and eventually gave rise to both medieval kabbalah and Catharism. But while Catharism was virtually destroyed in the middle of the thirteenth century, we know that most kabbalists escaped across the Pyrenees to Spain, where crucial texts such as the *Zohar* (Book of Splendor) were produced in the fourteenth century.

Two hundred years later we suddenly find respectable Christians in Italy and Germany approaching rabbis and asking to be taught Hebrew so they could better understand the true meaning of the Hebrew scriptures. Some of them, especially in Florence, sought out rabbis who were known to frequent kabbalistic circles and pleaded with these men to be initiated in the secret teachings of the *Zohar* and other reputedly "magical" texts of that tradition. This Florentine school developed the belief that kabbalah was an indisputable source for the validation of Christianity in Neoplatonic and Pythagorean terms and believed that in kabbalah the long-lost secrets of the original Christian faith had been rediscovered.

Perhaps the first and best-known Christian kabbalist was Count Pico della Mirandola, a close friend of Marsilio Ficino and famous all over Italy for his fantastic erudition and miraculous memory. This young genius began his kabbalistic studies in 1486 at the age of twenty-three and had a large number of kabbalistic tracts translated into Latin for him by Samuel ben Nissim and Raymond Moncada (better known as Flavius Mithridates), two Jewish converts to Catholicism. Pico's famous nine hundred theses, publicly displayed for debate in Rome, included the statement "No science can better convince us of the divinity of Jesus Christ than magic and kabbalah," thus exposing the kabbalah to many Christians for the first time.

Predictably, the reaction of the Church to this and other propositions made by Pico was one of fierce rejection, but the public debate Pico wanted was granted and kabbalah, an otherwise unknown esoteric doctrine that had been overlooked or thought to be completely lost, now became the principal topic of discussion in Christian intellectual circles. Here are Vicomte Léon de Poncins's thoughts on Pico in his *Judaism and the Vatican:*

> Pico, who died in Florence in 1494, was a "hebraiser" who devoted himself to studying the kabbalah under the direction of Jewish masters, Jehuda Abravanel among them. It was in Pico's princely house that Jewish scholars used to meet. *The discovery of the kabbalah, which he imparted to various enlightened Christians, contributed far more than ancient Greek sources to the extraordinary spiritual blossoming known as the Renaissance* [my italics]. Pico della Mirandola understood that the indispensable purification of Christian dogma could be effected only through a profound study of the authentic Jewish kabbalah.

Christian Platonists in Germany, Italy, and France quickly attached themselves to Pico's school. Another Renaissance Hebraist, a German lawyer and linguist who met Pico in Florence, was Johann Reuchlin (1455–1522), and his *Rudimenta Hebraica* was the first Hebrew grammar book written by a non-Jew. Kabbalah was already quite popular in Germany, but after Reuchlin published his *De Verbo Mirifico* (On the Wonderful Word) in 1494, in which he spoke of the power of Hebrew words and their numerological values, it became a craze. Just like Pico, Reuchlin tried to find justification for Christianity in Jewish texts. Here is an example: YHVH, the unpronounceable Jewish name of God known as the tetragrammaton (four-letter word) and usually read as Jehova or Jahwe, is expanded and, of course, completed in Reuchlin's work by adding a symmetrically central *S*, which transforms it into YH S VH—that is, Jehoshua, or Jesus Christ.

It took Reuchlin twenty years to complete his much more famous *De Arte Cabalistica* (On the Art of the Kabbalah), which came out in 1517, the same year that Luther launched his rebellion against the papacy, and quickly became the bible of Christian kabbalists.

It would seem, then, that the Florentine fascination with the hermetic tradition had a strong Jewish component—and this should not surprise us, for we have followed Jewish thinkers' decidedly subversive attitude to Pauline Christianity all through late antiquity and the early Middle Ages. But as mentioned in the beginning of this chapter, two events explain how orthodox Christians (as opposed to Cathar heretics, who didn't need Jewish friends to set their hearts against Rome) became followers of a gnostic tradition, leading them to feverishly translate both Egyptian and kabbalistic texts, and explain why this happened when it did, in the second half of the fifteenth century. These two events were the fall of Constantinople in AD 1453 and the expulsion of Jews and Moors from Spain in AD 1492, both of which resulted in a massive migration of Jews into the heart of Europe. Thousands of families who had lived in those two places for centuries ended up in France (such as Nostradamus's grandparents), Holland (such as Spinoza's great-grandparents), Germany, and Italy. Of course, many Jews in Constantinople waited as long as they could to see just what consequences would befall their lives after the replacement of the last Byzantine emperor with Muhammad II, the conquering caliph, before deciding whether to join their relatives in the Christian West.

Similarly, many Jewish families in Spain could see what was coming as the last few Moorish possessions on the peninsula were reconquered by their most Catholic majesties, Ferdinand and Isabel, and thus made arrangements to transfer their not inconsiderable wealth and households to Amsterdam or Mainz or Leghorn before the dreaded threat—"Convert or be gone!"—actually materialized. These two events resulted in the flow of Jewish immigrants continuing ceaselessly during the forty years between their occurrences, with large families arriving and new synagogues being established almost every year.

Most relevant to our discussion here is the fact that thousands of Jewish books—rare and sometimes ancient—came with their owners into the cities where the Renaissance was blossoming. The kabbalah had been spreading through Jewish communities in both East and West, so when these new immigrants were approached by Christian intellectuals who usually asked them for help in determining the meaning of the original Hebrew of some passage in the Hebrew scriptures, the kabbalists among them inevitably alluded to the esoteric exegesis of Jewish scriptures. We know, for example, that a young Martin Luther, in his efforts to produce a German translation of the Bible, engaged in lively discussions with some of these rabbis from Spain and came away with a stinging inferiority complex, for the Jews mocked the *goyim* for their inability to penetrate the hidden meanings of the Torah.

Thus what the rebellion in the early thirteenth century and that in the early sixteenth century had in common was Christians practicing excessive intercourse with Jewish gnostics—that is, with kabbalists—and it is likely that every friar in the Holy Inquisition of those years would have agreed with this assessment. Yet this Jewish context or background to events in the thousand years we call the Middle Ages, roughly from the fall of the Western Roman Empire in 476 to the years up to the Renaissance, is a dimension of which history books seem blissfully unaware, but which adds immeasurably to our understanding of those thousand years and why occurrences did or did not happen.

TWO FIGURES THAT CARRIED GNOSTICISM IN THE MIDDLE AGES

In the two centuries that passed between the extermination of the Cathars and the flowering of the Florentine hermetic revival, kabbalistic networks were surely not the only context in which gnostic ideas survived. Historians have identified the influence of Catharism and kabbalah, as well as Sufism, on some of the most famous—and seemingly most Christian—figures in the century immediately following the crusade against the heretics in the Languedoc. Two of these famous figures from whom emanated a whiff of gnostic heresy were St. Francis of Assisi and Dante Alighieri.

Francis of Assisi

St. Francis was a true mystic. Historians credit him (and his far less romantic contemporary St. Dominic) with channeling the spiritual fervor of the late twelfth century into safe, orthodox expressions by founding their respective "lesser" orders. (Franciscans and Dominicans are known as Fratres Minores, or Lesser Brothers.) Naturally, the Church has always stressed Francis's submission to the pope and to Catholic dogma and has rightly pointed out that however widespread the Cathar heresy may have been in Italy at the time (and there were certainly a lot of Patarini in Tuscany and Umbria), Francis would never have approved a theology that considered this world the creation of an evil demiurge. As the disarming simplicity of his poetry shows, he loved nature in a way that could not have coexisted with a dualist view of matter as impure. Yet many writers have convincingly shown the influence of southern France on St. Francis, who was well aware of both Cathar spirituality and the songs of the troubadours. We know that in his teens he accompanied his cloth merchant father on many fabric-buying expeditions to the Languedoc. He was known to sing troubadour songs in French in his hometown of Assisi. Of course, we mustn't forget that Francis began his movement in 1209, the same year in which the bloody Albigensian crusade made martyrs of thousands of Cathar preachers in a region he knew very well. Some have seen Francis's worship of poverty as a lesson learned from the Cathars' *endura*, or fasting to the death, and there is certainly something akin to Cathar disdain for the material world in Francis's attempt to starve evil into submission. To him, the voluntary destruction of the body's appetites and desires was an act of severance: The soul was finally separated from matter. To love God was to love the possibility of dying.

Francis came close to being condemned by the Church, but he had strong supporters in Rome. In 1215, at the First Lateran Council, convened by Innocent III (where he met Dominic for the first time), Francis finally and reluctantly (for he feared that his movement would be drawn into the politics of the wealthy and the powerful) agreed to bring his order under Church discipline to avoid being declared a heretic.

In AD 1219, Francis traveled to Damietta, in Egypt, crossed the lines of the Fifth Crusade in between battles, and preached to Sultan al-Malik al-Kamil for three full days without succeeding in converting him to Christianity. The sultan nevertheless sent him safely back to the Crusader camp and chroniclers make clear that the sages of Egypt had no doubt in their minds that they were dealing with an exceptional man who radiated love for humanity. It may be, as Sufism scholar Idries Shah has suggested, that when Francis traveled to Egypt, he actually wanted to question Sufi teachers there about their method known as *dhikr*, the ritual act of remembering that was so similar to the technique of holy prayer developed by Francis himself (and to the "art of memory" that would later be held in such esteem by Pico and Giordano Bruno).

The words of Francis and his Sufi contemporary Mevlana Jalalludin Rumi show strong similarities. Like Francis, Rumi revered his religion as pointing the way to experience God but decried blind practice and routine observance, declaring them useless to obtaining knowledge of God. It may be no accident that Franciscan garb, with its hooded dress and wide sleeves, is the same as that of the Sufi dervishes of North Africa and Spain. In another point of similarity, Francis never became a priest but sought to spread his message among all people, which is how Sufis operate even today. Francis's salutation, like that of the Sufis, was "The peace of God be with you!" And finally, Francis rejected personal salvation as the primary object of asceticism, just as do Sufis, who regard salvation as an expression of vanity because it places too much emphasis on our personal spiritual expectations.

Whatever its motivations, Francis's journey to the Middle East was a pivotal point in his life, changing him for the remainder of his days. Once he had returned from Egypt, it seems that a new level of consciousness entered his thinking: We must learn to withdraw from the supersubstance of being in order to realize our essential nature. We must learn how to grapple with our love and longing for the perfect and complete discovery of God. This is a Sufi insight and, of course, a mightily gnostic one. Francis had already proposed a radical departure from the commonplace Catholic idea that individuals approached God through the Church and its clerics, but by abandoning the reins of the order he had himself founded and retiring to meditate on Verna Mountain, he took the final step, which was perhaps the clearest indication of his spiritual greatness.

Dante Alighieri

The fraternity of which Dante was a member, the Fedeli d'Amore (Faithful of Love), was a group of poets practicing an erotic spirituality. They formed a closed brotherhood devoted to achieving harmony between the sexual and emotional sides of their natures and their intellectual and mystical aspirations. Theirs was an attempt to regenerate society through the application of chivalric ideas, including courtly love.

The group's doctrine was set forth by their leader, Guido Cavalcanti, and their practice included training the imagination to hold the image of the Beloved in the form of a loved Lady, for the pure light of the One would be too much to bear. Ficino and others in the Platonic Academy considered their poetry to be a supreme Neoplatonic statement of love. Dante Gabriel Rossetti (1828–82) originated the idea that the poetry of the Fedeli contained heresies disguised to hide them from the Holy Inquisition.

In time, Dante and the Fedeli transformed the troubadours' symbolism into their Dolce Stil Novo (Sweet New Style), which was intended to embody the beautiful doctrines of the Fedeli in correspondingly beautiful words and meters. They were always explicit in stating that the Lady should be interpreted symbolically. There are many similarities in style and content between the poetry of the Fedeli and that of the Sufis, especially in the idealization of the Beloved as Holy Wisdom or Intelligence. This has led some to suggest that the Fedeli were a Western *tarika*, or secret order of Sufi dervishes.

There were, of course, other potential sources of Islamic influence for the Fedeli, including the troubadour tradition and pilgrims returning from the Holy Land. The Templars may also have brought the Fedeli some of these ideas, as well as the tradition of Solomon's Temple as the dwelling place of Wisdom. Some have even claimed there may have been an alliance between the Fedeli and the Templars. These first surfaced in the seventeenth century and were later defended by Rossetti, who went as far as claiming that *The Divine Comedy* represents Dante's own initiation into La Fede Santa (Sacred Faith), a Templar tertiary order of laypeople. Certainly *The Divine Comedy* contains considerable symbolism connected with the Temple. Given that the Templars were destroyed on grounds of heresy in 1307–12 (about the time Dante was writing *The Inferno*), secrecy and obscurity of connections would have been subsequently necessary because any defense of Templar ideas could likewise be interpreted as heresy. This theory is considered exaggerated by modern scholars, but some Dante experts such as Luigi Valli and René Guénon have defended it.

Dante was educated by Franciscan monks and was greatly influenced by philosophers and poets. He began writing poetry before he was twenty and became associated with the Dolce Stil Novo, in which, as we saw, poets exalted their love and their Lady in philosophical verse. The focus of Dante's love was Beatrice. Today, we would have little trouble understanding Beatrice as Dante's inner feminine, which becomes obvious in *The Divine Comedy*, in which traces of gnostic cosmology can be found everywhere. There was very likely a real Beatrice to whom Dante dedicated his *Vita Nuova*, a sequence of poems with prose comments in which he describes his fleeting contacts with her, from their first meeting when they were both nine years old until her death at twenty-four. It may be, however, that too much has been made of this earthly love and too little of the mystical significance of their relationship.

As conductor of souls, Virgil's function in *The Divine Comedy* is to bring Dante to the point where his initiator—that is, Beatrice—takes over. It is significant that Dante's initiator is feminine for reasons that go beyond the Jungian idea of the outer masculine being balanced by the inner feminine, or the notion of the poet getting in touch with his feelings. Beatrice clearly fulfills the role of Isis, queen of heaven and savior of the gnostic mysteries. Dante's formidable knowledge of the classics should not be underestimated. *The Vita Nuova* is not merely a childhood romance writ large. As Joseph Campbell writes in *Creative Mythology,* "The Beatific Vision beheld by Dante in the radiant celestial bowl of the rose of Paradise and that seen, finally, by Galahad within the mystic vessel of the Grail are one and the same."

OTHER WAYS GNOSTICISM SURVIVED

So it would seem that the Church's actions in the thirteenth century, far from removing the gnostic threat from the European spiritual landscape, simply drove it underground, where its ideas survived in countless ways during the two hundred years that separated Cathars and troubadours from Pico and his friends in Florence.

Sometimes the clues are almost shocking in their precision. Such is the case of the mysterious but perfectly documented anachronisms in the tract called *Schwester Katrei* (Sister Catherine), written around 1330 by a female disciple of Meister Eckhart, perhaps the best-known German mystic of the Middle Ages. Its portrayal of a woman's spiritual experience contains references to Mary Magdalene that clearly link it to Cathar traditions—and one hundred years after the Albigensian crusade, this hardly raises any eyebrows. Yet it also contains phrases about Mary that are otherwise found only in the Nag Hammadi texts! The Magdalene is portrayed as superior to Peter in her understanding of Jesus' mysteries, and the tension between her and Peter is described in the exact same terms. We might wonder how on earth a fourteenth-century author would have access to texts that were discovered six hundred years later. There is only one possible explanation: Knowledge of those texts existed in European gnostic circles throughout the eight centuries that passed between the burying of the heretical gospels in the Egyptian cliffs and the appearance of the Cathar heresy in France. *Schwester Katrei,* then, is one more piece of evidence of the direct links between early Christianity in Egypt and the gnostic tradition in the south of France.

There is another mysterious text that seems to link most heretics: the Gospel of John. In fact, the idea that John's gospel conceals mysteries and secrets—or that a secret version of it exists—is nearly always found in gnostic movements. The Cathars are said to have possessed such a heretical alternative (indeed, Isaac Newton was obsessed with the search for it) and some hold that the cabal of gnostics hiding in the heart of the order of the Temple possessed one as well. Bernard Raymond Fabré-Palaprat, founder of the best known of the many self-styled Templar orders that sprouted in Paris during the occult revival at the end of the nineteenth century, claimed to possess—and often quoted—a strongly gnostic version of John's gospel, a document he called the Levitikon.

One possible explanation for all these secret versions of the Gospel of John is that Jesus bestowed his secret teaching on the young John—the beloved disciple—and that it was later set down and passed on through generations of heretics. Perhaps not surprisingly, all the groups who shared and kept this secret clearly believed to be in possession of knowledge about the true origins of Christianity. Strangely enough, closer investigation of what this secret knowledge might be often leads to the other John, the one who baptized Jesus at the start of his mission and was then killed by Herod Antipas. In fact, it sometimes seems that confusing the worship and roles of the two Johns is a hallmark of many heretical traditions.

In their excellent book *The Templar Revelation,* Lynn Picknett and Clive Prince describe the traces of a clandestine Church of John that they found hiding in the darker corners of European art, religion, and literature. Starting from the paintings of Leonardo da Vinci, they argue that knowledge of a secret concerning John the Baptist was the most unsettling thing gnostic heretics shared. Toward the end of the book, Picknett and Prince postulate that the rivalry between John the Baptist and Jesus that could be deduced from several passages in the canonical gospels may be all that's left—after the evangelists' careful editing—of an uglier, almost blasphemous story of Jesus' usurpation of John's role as the true Messiah. After all, they suggest, John had a wide following that hindered Paul's mission decades after the Baptist's death. Herod must have known that having him killed would risk a popular uprising, yet he did so anyway. The authors ask how much historical plausibility there might be in the gospels' theatrical version of the story that Herod decreed John's death just to humor a cruel whim of his stepdaughter, Mary Salome.

Whether the idea is one of the real role of the two Johns or the role of the Magdalene or the real relationship between Jesus and John the Baptist or the truth about the Crucifixion—that is, that Jesus came down from the cross alive—what emerges again and again in the history of Christian heresies is that the heretics never content themselves with telling the Catholic Church that it preaches the wrong message or that its theology is not what Jesus taught or that God's plan is not what they claim it to be. Instead, they always seem to say one thing to Rome: You're not telling the truth about what happened!

WHO KNEW THE TRUTH?

Every mysterious event in the history of the Church since the day Jesus was taken down from the cross seems somehow connected to knowledge of the truth about that day. What were the Templar knights looking for under the Temple Mount? Why was the destruction of the Cathars so vital to the survival of the Church? What did Saunière find that enabled him to extort money from someone? It is quite doubtful that any of these mysterious events have ever been connected to a material treasure. The idea that Saunière, for instance, found precious and valuable objects doesn't pass the simplest of tests: It did not solve his recurring cash-flow problems. A large trove of valuable items can be sold when you run out of money. The source of cash is deep. It is only when you have a paymaster—when someone is handing over money to you for whatever reason—that the source of wealth may run dry.

We can surmise that the Church has always known the truth of those first-century events. As Nietzsche wrote, using his merciless concision: "The priests don't err, they lie." There is the real implication that the Church possesses documents safely buried in the Vatican's vaults (with God knows how many other supposedly "lost" treasures) that it would no doubt destroy rather than show the world. Also implied is that the Church has been silencing all possessors of any evidence concerning those events ever since it became a political power through the Donation of Constantine, a document that was proved to be a forgery in AD 1440 by Lorenzo Valla, an Italian Renaissance humanist hailing from Piacenza.

In the now debunked *Dossiers Secrets,* which Pierre Plantard placed in the Bibliothèque Nationale in the 1950s, the Priory of Sion gives a list of grand masters of the secret society. Let us imagine for a moment whom we might have included on that list had we been in Plantard and de Chérisey's place. In other words, if we were going to attribute possession of a secret about the true story of Jesus, the Baptist, and Mary Magdalene to at least one person in every generation, how would we go about choosing our attributions?

We might include Nicolas Flamel, the most famous alchemist of the entire Middle Ages, who traveled to Spain to learn the secrets of kabbalah from the Jewish masters in Andalusia and who was the only one to allegedly succeed in transmuting lead to gold, which, thanks to the philosopher's stone, led him to become fabulously rich. We might also include Leonardo, whose paintings are full of mysterious symbolism and show, among other figures, the infant Jesus seemingly praying to the infant John the Baptist as if the Baptist was God's true messenger *(The Madonna of the Rocks),* and a beloved disciple whose likeness is so much like a woman's that many think it is the portrayal of Mary Magdalene herself *(The Last Supper).* Some might include Robert Fludd, the famous

English Rosicrucian, physicist, astrologer, and mystic who frequented every master of the occult sciences in Europe, who had a famous exchange with Johannes Kepler concerning the hermetic approach to knowledge, and whose memory system was on a par with that of Pico and Giordano Bruno. And we might add Sir Isaac Newton, whose occult studies in alchemy and astrology and research into the Bible's hidden meanings (especially in John's Apocalypse) were more important to him than any of the mathematical or physical experiments that made him famous and won him the presidency of the Royal Society.

The perpetrator of a hoax assemblying the false hidden history of an order (the Priory of Sion) that supposedly protects a vital secret giving its holders power over the Church in Rome would obviously choose names either from royal families (who might have access to such a secret through hereditary privilege) or from those with links to occult traditions, heretical circles, or a legacy of opposition to the Church, the more ancient the better. I think most of us, with the use of some imagination, could have put together a list at least as good as the one in the *Dossiers Secrets*—except for a name near the end of the list: Jean Cocteau.

We may well ask what could possibly link this French poet, novelist, playwright, boxing manager, and filmmaker who lived from 1889 to 1963 to the line of keepers of such a secret. All answers point to the erudition and privileged esoteric connections of our two hoaxers, Plantard and de Chérisey, but there is a particular link between Cocteau and our story—one that everyone can see on the wall of a small church just off Leicester Square in the West End of London.

In the church known as Notre Dame de France, when it was restored in 1960 after being bombed in the Blitz, Cocteau painted a famous mural. The subject of the fresco is the Crucifixion, and our attention is immediately caught by the fact that we see only the legs of the person on the cross. It is perhaps the only painting of the Crucifixion in the world in which the artist has refused the challenge of painting Jesus' face. This is not the only unusual aspect of the painting, however: There is also an unsettling figure in the right foreground who is not easily recognized as one of the characters traditionally present at the foot of the cross. The figure's only visible eye is unmistakably fish-shaped—the symbol most directly associated with Jesus in the early centuries. Is Cocteau trying to tell us that Jesus was there, at the foot of the cross, watching someone else writhing in his place? And who might that someone else have been?

Perhaps Jean Cocteau really was a grand master of the Priory of Sion. Some people claim that the whole Rennes-le-Château mystery came to the surface only as a consequence of a schism in that secret society, precipitated by controversial changes to its rules that Cocteau introduced in the 1950s that drove Plantard and others to found a new, breakaway group. Whatever the circumstances, the Cocteau mural shows us one fascinating possibility: If part of the truth the Church has been hiding—the truth to which heretics have constantly alluded and of which they've constantly reminded each other—is the fact that Jesus did not die on the cross, then even today, or as close to the present as 1960, this secret is guarded and obliquely transmitted by different people in all walks of life, some of whom are quite above suspicion.

Who knew the truth? Many did, and perhaps some still do.

21

FULL CIRCLE

An interesting aspect of the Rennes-le-Château mystery, one that many people seem to have forgotten, is that it was only with the publication of *Holy Blood, Holy Grail* in 1982 that the story of Rennes-le-Château and its *curé aux milliards* (millionaire vicar) began to involve Jesus, Mary Magdalene, and their supposed descendants. Before that, Plantard and his cohorts had spoken and disseminated clues only about a treasure in the traditional sense of gold or precious items, albeit wrapped in legends of Merovingian kings. Saunière's link to knowledge of a "tomb of Jesus" was actually projected onto him in the quarter century since the best seller came out, transforming a mystery about a local treasure (rumors of which had long preceded the vicar's sudden wealth) into the stuff of *The Da Vinci Code*.

If my research was always concerned with the true content of original Christianity and this mystery was really about a treasure some local priest found a mere century ago, why did I come to live in this village? The answer lies in my conviction that it was the Knights Templar who found the secret. A series of historical circumstances, some of which I have included in this book, led me to think—long before the Priory of Sion ever surfaced in any book, at least in English—that the Order of the Temple had spent the first ten years of its existence digging under the Dome of the Rock because the nine knights who first formed the order had, from the very beginning, been looking for *something* in Jerusalem. All along, their mission to protect pilgrims on the roads to the Holy City was nothing but a pretext. The notion that searching for something in this way was the reason for which the Templars came together was in my mind a logical and nearly inescapable conclusion, given the facts.

As to whether the Knights found anything, many have held that the incredible wealth the order accumulated over the first century of its existence cannot be explained by mere donations. Theories of the source of their wealth have included alchemical secrets that supposedly enabled them to turn lead into gold; the blackmailing of the Church, Saunière-style, through documents they found in the thousand-year-old ruins in Jerusalem; and gold from the Americas, which they are said to have discovered more than two centuries before Columbus. Of course there is no evidence for any of these ideas, but in the light of the censored Jewish history we have discovered here, I think the fact that most of the original nine knights came from the south of France—some of them from the very region that, until two hundred years earlier, had been called Septimania—should make us wonder about why the Templars decided they had to dig in Jerusalem.

Their meetings with surviving Judeo-Christian sects (as strongly indicated by their knowledge of the Atbash cipher as well as the clearly gnostic contents of the heresies of which they were later accused, including the Cathar-like denial of and contempt for the symbol of the cross) have led me to believe that they somehow discovered the secret of Jesus surviving his crucifixion—unless of course they knew that secret to begin with and were digging for some kind of proof.

Then, in the trail of my own search, came the finding of the tiwas, the Muslim talisman I discovered in Villa Bethania in 1992. The scholars who examined it in Cairo confirmed that the Arabic writing indicated a date of composition sometime in the thirteenth century. One thing is certain: Saunière had no connections to the Islamic world. Not only were Muslims few and far between in France in his days, but also he was the sort of reactionary royalist who would have had no use for interfaith activities, as they are referred to nowadays. In the last thirty years, people have searched every nook and cranny of the poor priest's life, but nothing has turned up to support the idea that Saunière somehow procured a medieval Arabic talisman himself, which means he must have found it somewhere.

We might ask, then, who the Frenchmen were who would have had the closest links with Islam at the time of the Crusades—connections that ran even to cultural exchanges with mystical, esoteric branches of Islam such as the Sufis and the Assassins. The answer: the Knights Templar. After obtaining the translation of the booklet I found and a date for its likely composition, I searched for alternative explanations, but could find none. The tiwas must have been hidden somewhere on the church grounds by Templar Knights and then, some six hundred years later, found by Saunière, who in turn hid it behind a skirting board in his brand-new villa. I wondered if he knew what it was. He likely could see that it was very old and may have recognized that some of the symbols inscribed in it were of a magical nature. Saunière may have had no knowledge of Islam, but he was certainly no ignoramus.

Something the Templars found in Jerusalem led them to this place, where I believe they found a large tomb in a subterranean cave under the village. As we've learned, the whole area is littered with natural limestone formations: caves, shafts, and sudden crevasses. The tunnels under many points in the village, as I mentioned in chapter 3, may also have been natural but may well have been enlarged, especially those in the proximity of the lost church of St. Pierre.

I believe the Templars found a natural cave containing the graves of Jesus, Mary Magdalene, and Joseph of Arimathea, which they subsequently enlarged, restored, and embellished. This location became a heavily guarded secret. In fact, any member of the Templars' inner cabal of initiates would have given his life before revealing its location. I suspect that in this cave, writings by Jesus have been preserved, though I'm well aware that conditions in southern France are not like those in the Egyptian or Judaean deserts, where parchments can survive two millennia with practically no damage.

In the introduction to this book I wrote that one possible interpretation of the Parousìa or Second Coming of Jesus is the idea that he survived the cross and is buried, from whence, in the fullness of time, he will rise again as a living being of power and wisdom. I have long been fond of the idea that this prophecy may be fulfilled in finding writings by Jesus himself, which would indeed constitute a form of resurrection. Through his autographed words, undeniably the expression of his genuine thought, he would rejoin the conversation, in a way—be here with us again.

Throughout my years of research, reading, and reflection, I have become profoundly convinced that Jesus did indeed survive the Crucifixion and that he escaped first to Egypt and later to the hills near Rennes, either with Mary Magdalene or alone, at a later stage. If he did live out the rest of his days here, for obvious reasons he must have done so without revealing his true identity beyond a very small circle of trusted family and friends. This was a remote village, to be sure, but it was not that far from important imperial roads, and rumors of a famous refugee from Judaea would not have been long in spreading once people came to know who he was. Given these circumstances, we might well ask if Jesus would have continued to teach about the Kingdom of God or practice spiritual healing. Would he and Mary Magdalene, as the Priory of Sion claims, have raised a family? The Cathar tradition about them contains no references to offspring, although some of the local devotional pictures collected by local researchers do show Mary Magdalene with a child, and then of course there is that stubborn memory of a girl named Sarah (Princess) who is said to have landed with Mary at Les-Saintes-Maries-de-la-Mer.

Nevertheless, the Jesus bloodline made famous by Dan Brown's novel is not what I want to focus on here, nor has it been the issue that has most intrigued me in all my years of research. Instead, we can surmise that if Jesus lived to be seventy—not unusual for an Essene initiate—the terrible news about the war in his homeland must have reached him from Jerusalem in his old age. With the predictable defeat and devastation, the massacres, the destruction of the Temple, his prophecy had tragically come true. I have often wondered how Jesus reacted to the final act in the long drama in which he'd had such a crucial role.

Even this, though, two thousand years after the event, is not really the heart of the matter. What may still hold relevance for our own future is, if he indeed lived to be seventy, how Jesus reacted to what had become of his message, of his disciples' mission—in a word, what had become of his religion. By the time Jerusalem had fallen, all the events that produced the Christianity that was to be the Roman Catholic religion had taken their destined path. Paul had founded his churches and gospels were being written in Judaea, Alexandria, Antioch, Anatolia, even Rome. The split between the Jewish Church of Jerusalem and the Church of Rome had already become inevitable, and (unacceptable to Jews everywhere), the Messiah from Galilee was by now the risen Son of God.

Jews moved around the empire constantly and the city of Narbonne, as we have seen, was already a thriving commercial port. Is it likely, then, that the group of anonymous Jews living in this region would have heard about the followers of a new religion spawned by Judaism, those who were starting to be called Christians after their risen messiah? Surely if Jesus lived to be an old man, he would have heard about the grave and ominous distortions of his message that were spreading like wildfire among Jews and pagans alike, but what—if anything—would he have done about it?

He was a rabbi, a kabbalist, an Essene, and a neo-Pythagorean thinker. As such, I think he would have written an epistle, a memorial, a spiritual testament. He couldn't simply reenter the world's religious scene and denounce the idolatrous perversion of his gnostic teaching. Therefore, he must have put down in words what he truly believed. A mere hundred years after Jesus' death, Bishop Irenaeus of Lyon—at the other end of the Midi—formulated rules that made the likely content of Christ's writing un-Christian, yet I cannot help but think that Jesus must have written his version of the historical and spiritual truth—the Gospel of Jesus. And he must have tried to make sure that it would survive the likes of Irenaeus.

The world-shaking impact lies not in the fact that if Jesus survived the cross, there could be no real resurrection and, as Paul said, that if there was no resurrection, the whole Christian faith would be in vain. Rather, the earthquake is that his tomb is where his gospel lies hidden, waiting for his Parousìa.

AFTERWORD

Sadly, Graham left us on August 20, 2005. I was his closest friend for the last twelve years of his life. Many expected him to live much longer, for he had always been so full of energy, ideas, and plans for the future.

People, friends from all over the world, used to come to our home in Rennes and listen to his experiences and opinions, basking in his wisdom and enjoying his English sense of humor. At his funeral, somebody said, "You know, he just loved people." How very true.

During his many journeys to every corner of the world, he met people of all races, cultures, and religions. His life was full of miraculous encounters, wonders, and adventures. The monks of the Himalayas called him a seeker, and that is how he liked to think of himself. As he offers more than once in this book, Graham was convinced that many more documents dating from early Christian times would be discovered, one day including perhaps the writings by Jesus himself.

In the year since his passing, his prediction has turned into a prophecy of sorts, for as we all know, a gospel of Judas has been published that throws a new light on Jesus, his teaching, and his true intentions that no one would ever have suspected. I hope that the coming years will fulfill his expectations that the full truth about Jesus would come to light.

In the last months of his life, Graham seemed to be on a new search. This time he was looking for the passage we call death, and after making that passage, there was a distinct air of accomplishment on his face. There is only a thin veil between his world and ours, and through that veil—I am sure—he is smiling at us with his kind smile, the one you can see in the photograph on the back cover of this book, which is, in a way, his testament.

INGRID RIEDEL-KARP
RENNES-LE-CHÂTEAU
AUGUST 2006

BIBLIOGRAPHY

Adler, Elkan Nathan. *Jewish Travellers in the Middle Ages*. New York: Dover Publications, 1987.

Ahmad, Khwaja Nazir. *Jesus in Heaven on Earth*. Surrey, England: Woking Muslim Mission and Literary Trust, 1952.

———. *Truth about the Crucifixion*. London: London Mosque, 1978.

Allegro, John M. *The Dead Sea Scrolls*. Harmondsworth, Middlesex, England: Penguin Books, 1956.

Baigent, Michael, Richard Leigh, and Henry Lincoln. *Holy Blood, Holy Grail*. New York: Harper and Row, 1983.

Barth, Karl. *The Theology of Schleiermacher*. Edited by D. Ritschl. Translated by G. Bromiley. Grand Rapids, Mich.: Eerdmans, 1982.

Berrigan, Daniel. *Ezekiel: Vision in the Dust*. New York: Orbis Books, 1997.

Beskow, Per. *Strange Tales about Jesus: A Survey of Unfamiliar Gospels*. Philadelphia: Fortress Press, 1985.

Brent, Peter. *The Mongol Empire*. London: Weidenfeld and Nicolson, 1976.

Bullit, Orville. *Search for Sybaris*. London: J. M. Dent, 1971.

Bulst, W. Heinrich. *Das Turiner Grabtuch und das Christusbild*. Vol. 1 and 2. Frankfurt am Mein: Knecht, 1987–1991.

———. *Betrug am Turiner Grabtuch*. Frankfurt am Mein: Knecht, 1990.

Cannon, Dolores. *Jesus and the Essenes*. Bath, England: Gateway Books, 1992.

Cardini, Franco. *Francesco d'Assisi*. Milan: Mondadori, 1989.

Chambers, James. *The Devil's Horsemen*. London: Cassell, 1988.

Charlesworth, James. *Jesus and the Dead Sea Scrolls*. New York: Doubleday, 1992.

Churton, Tobias. *The Gnostics*. London: Weidenfeld and Nicolson, 1987.

Cohen, Jeremy. *The Friars and the Jews*. Ithaca, N.Y.: Cornell Univerity Press, 1982.

Craig, William Lane. *The Historical Argument for the Resurrection of Jesus during the Deist Controversy*. Lewiston, N.Y.: Edwin Mellen Press, 1985.

Crossan, John Dominic, and Jonathan L. Reed. *Excavating Jesus*. San Francisco: HarperSanFrancisco, 2001.

Deardorff, James W. *Jesus in India*. Bethesda, Md.: International Scholars Publications, 1994.

Denon, Vivant. *Travels in Upper and Lower Egypt*. New York: Arno Press, 1973.

Derrett, J. D. M. *The Anastasis: The Resurrection of Jesus as an Historical Event*. Shipston-on-Stour, England: P. Drinkwater, 1982.

Docker, E. B. *If Jesus Did Not Die on the Cross: A Study of the Evidence*. London: Robert Scott, 1920.

Duquesne, Jacques. *Le Dieu de Jésus*. Paris: Desclée de Brouwer, 1997.

Eisenman, Robert. *James, the Brother of Jesus*. New York: Faber and Faber, 1997.

Eisenman, Robert, and Michael Wise. *The Dead Sea Scrolls Uncovered*. New York: Penguin, 1993.

Eusebius. *The History of the Church from Christ to Constantine*. Translated by G. A. Williamson. Baltimore: Penguin, 1965.

———. "Against 'Apollonius of Tyana'" by Philostratus. In *The Life of Apollonius of Tyana, the Epistles of Apollonius and the Treatise of Eusebius*. New York: Macmillan, 1912.

Evelyn-White, Hugh. *The Monasteries of the Wadi 'n Natrun*. 3 vols. New York: Arno Press, 1973.

Feather, Robert. *The Mystery of the Copper Scroll of Qumran*. Rochester, Vt.: Inner Traditions, 2003.

———. *The Secret Initiation of Jesus at Qumran*. Rochester, Vt.: Inner Traditions, 2005.

Ferguson, Everett. *Backgrounds of Early Christianity.* Grand Rapids, Mich.: Eerdmans Publishing, 1993.

Fox, Robin Lane. *Alexander the Great.* London: Allen Lane, 1973.

Frugoni, Chiara. *Vita di un uomo: Francesco d'Assisi.* Turin: Einaudi, 1995.

Funk, Robert W. *Honest to Jesus.* San Francisco: HarperSanFrancisco, 1996.

Gibbon, Edward. *Decline and Fall of the Roman Empire.* London: Chatto and Windus, 1960.

Graves, R., and J. Podro. *Jesus in Rome.* London: Cassell, 1957.

Habib, Rouf. *The Holy Family in Egypt.* Cairo: Ministry of Tourism in Egypt, 1998.

Hancock, Graham. *The Sign and the Seal.* New York: Crown Books, 1992.

Hassnain, Fida. *A Search for the Historical Jesus.* Bath, England: Gateway Books, 1994.

Hertzberg, Arthur. *Jews.* San Francisco: HarperSanFrancisco, 1998.

Hesse, Herman. *Franz Von Assisi.* Frankfurt: Insel, 1988.

Hodge, A. Trevor. *Ancient Greek France.* London: Duckworth, 1998.

Holy Bible, The. King James Version.

Huber, Jean, Jean Porcher, and W. F. Volbach. *L'Europe des Invasions.* Paris: Gallimard, 1967.

Idel, Moshe. *The Mystical Experience in Abraham Abulafia.* Translated by Jonathan Chipman. Albany: State University of New York Press, 1988.

Introvigne, Massimo. *Il Ritorno dello Gnosticismo.* Milan: Sugar Edizioni, 1993.

Irenaeus. *Against Heresies.* In *Ante-Nicene Fathers,* vol. 1. Boston: Adamant Media Corporation, 2001.

Josephus, Flavius. *The Jewish Antiquities.* The Loeb Classical Library. London: Heinemann, 1929.

———. *The Jewish War.* Translated by G. A. Williamson. Harmondsworth, Middlesex, England: Penguin, 1981.

Joyce, Donovan. *The Jesus Scroll.* Melbourne: Ferret Books, 1972.

Kamil, Jill. *Coptic Egypt.* Cairo: The American University in Cairo Press, 1993.

Kenyon, Kathleen. *Digging Up Jericho.* New York: Praeger, 1957.

Kersten, Holger. *The Jesus Conspiracy.* Dorset, England: Element Books, 1992.

———. *Jesus Lived in India.* Dorset, England: Element Books, 1986.

Kletzky-Pradère, Tatiana. *Rennes-le-Château—Guide du Visiteur.* Atelier Empreinte, 1992.

Klinghofer, David *Why the Jews Rejected Jesus*. New York: Doubleday, 2005.

Knight, Gareth. *A Practical Guide to Qabalistic Symbolism*. London: Kahn and Averill, 1965.

Kochan, Lionel. *Jews, Idols, and Messiahs—The Challenge from History*. Oxford: Blackwell, 1990.

Larson, Martin A. *The Essene-Christian Faith*. New York: Truth Seeker, 1989.

Leet, Leonora. *The Secret Doctrine of the Kabbalah*. Rochester, Vt.: Inner Traditions, 1999.

Le Goff, Jacques. *Saint François d'Assise*. Paris: Gallimard, 1999.

Lister, Richard. *The Travels of Herodotus*. London: Gordon and Cremonesi, 1979.

Lockhart, Douglas. *The Dark Side of God*. Dorset, England: Element Books, 1999.

———. *Jesus the Heretic*. Dorset, England: Element Books, 1997.

Maccoby, Hyam. *Judas Iscariot and the Myth of Jewish Evil*. New York: Free Press, 1992.

———. *The Mythmaker: Paul and the Invention of Christianity*. New York: Harper and Row, 1986.

———. *Revolution in Judaea*. New York: Taplinger, 1980.

Martin, Geoffrey. *The Sacred Animal Necropolis at North Saqqara*. London: The Egypt Exploration Society, 1981.

Meier, Eduard, ed. *The Talmud of Jmmanuel*. Mill Spring, N.C.: Wild Flower Press, 1996.

Mitchell, Janet Lee. *Out of Body Experiences: A Handbook*. New York: Ballantine Books, 1981.

Moorehead, Alan. *The Blue Nile*. London: Hamish Hamilton, 1962.

Morton, H. V. *Through the Lands of the Bible*. London: Methuen, 1938.

Neher, André. *Jewish Thought and the Scientific Revolution of the Sixteenth Century*. Oxford: Oxford University Press, 1986.

Neusner, Jacob. *Jews and Christians The Myth of a Common Tradition*. Philadelphia: Trinity Press International, 1991.

Omm Sety and Hanny El Zeini. *Abydos: Holy City of Ancient Egypt*. Los Angeles: L. L. Company, 1981.

Ouaknin, Marc-Alain. *Mystères de la Kabbale*. Paris: Editions Assouline, 2000.

Pagels, Elaine. *The Gnostic Gospels*. London: Weidenfeld and Nicolson, 1980.

Patai, Raphael. *The Jewish Alchemists*. Princeton, N.J.: Princeton University Press, 1994.

Patton, Guy, and Robin Mackness. *Roots of Egyptian Christianity*. Philadelphia: Fortress Press, 1986.

———. *Web of Gold*. Edited by Pearson Birger and James E. Goehring. London: Macmillan, 2000.

Philo. *The Complete Works*. London: Heinemann, Loeb Classical Library, 1929.

Philostratus. *Life of Apollonius*. Edited by G. W. Bowersock. Translated by C. P. Jones. Baltimore: Penguin Books, 1970.

Picknett, Lynn, and Clive Prince. *The Templar Revelation*. London: Bantam Press, 1997.

Pliny. *The Complete Works*. London: Heinemann, Loeb Classical Library, 1929.

Prophet, Elizabeth Clare. *The Lost Years of Jesus*. Gardiner, Mont.: Summit University Press, 1984.

Riley, Gregory J. *One Jesus, Many Christs*. San Francisco: HarperSanFrancisco, 1989.

Robinson, James M., ed. *The Nag Hammadi Library in English*. New York: Harper, 1990.

Robinson, John A. T. *Honest to God*. Louisville, Ky.: John Knox Press, 2006.

———. *Redating the New Testament*. Eugene, Ore.: Wipf and Stock, 2000.

Rosenberg, Shalom. *Good and Evil in Jewish Thought*. Tel Aviv: MOD Books, 1989.

Sabatier, Paul. *Vie de Saint François d'Assise*. Paris: Librairie Fischbacher, 1904.

Schaff, Philip. *History of the Christian Church, vol. III, Nicene and Post Nicene Christianity*. Grand Rapids, Mich.: Eerdmans Publishing, 1989.

Schanks, Hershel, ed. *Christianity and Rabbinic Judaism*. Washington, D.C.: Biblical Archaeological Society, 1992.

Scholem, Gershom. *Major Trends in Jewish Mysticism*. New York: Schoken Books, 1946.

———. *Les Origines de la Kabbale*. Paris: Aubier-Montaigne, 1966.

Schonfield, Hugh J. *The Essene Odyssey*. Dorset, England: Element, 1993.

———. *The Passover Plot*. London: Hutchinson, 1966.

———. *The Pentecost Revolution*. London: Macdonald and Jane, 1974.

———. *Those Incredible Christians*. Dorset, England: Element, 1991.

Scott, Jonathan. *The Search for Omm Sety*. New York: Doubleday, 1987.

Shorto, Russell. *Gospel Truth*. New York: Riverhead Books, 1997.

Silberman, Neil Asher. *Heavenly Powers: Unraveling the Secret History of the Kabbalah*. New York: Penguin Putnam, 1998.

Simmans, Graham, Marilyn Hopkins, and Tim Wallace-Murphy. *Rex Deus*. Dorset, England: Element Books, 2000.

Sipra, Jean-Alain. *La Cité du Chariot*. Paris: L'Aquatinte, 1965.

Smith, Morton. *Jesus the Magician*. New York: Harper and Row, 1978.

Spong, John Shelby. *Liberating the Gospels*. San Francisco: HarperSanFrancisco, 1996.

Stoyanov, Yuri. *The Other God*. New Haven: Yale University Press, 2000.

Strauss, David. *A New Life of Jesus,* vol. 1, second ed. London: Williams and Norgate, 1879.

Tacitus. *Annals of Imperial Rome*. Harmondsworth, Middlesex, England: Penguin, 1956.

Thiering, Barbara. *Jesus and the Riddle of the Dead Sea Scrolls*. San Francisco: HarperSanFrancisco, 1992.

———. *Jesus the Man*. New York: Doubleday, 1992

Vermes, Geza. *The Complete Dead Sea Scrolls in English*. London: Penguin, 1997.

———. *Jesus the Jew*. Philadelphia: Augsburg Fortress Press, 1981.

Walker, Benjamin. *Gnosticism*. Dartford, Kent, England: The Aquarian Press, 1983.

Weinman, Aryeh, ed. *Mystic Tales from the Zohar*. Philadelphia: Jewish Publication Society, 1997.

Williams, Michael. *Rethinking "Gnosticism."* Princeton, N.J.: Princeton University Press, 1996.

Wilson, Ian. *The Blood and the Shroud*. London: Orion Books, 1998.

———. *Jesus: The Evidence*. Washington, D.C.: Regnery, 2000.

———. *The Turin Shroud*. London: Victor Gollancz, 1978.

Yadin, Yigael. *The Message of the Scrolls*. New York: Crossroad, 1992.

Yates, Frances A. *The Rosicrucian Enlightenment*. London: Routledge and Kegan Paul, 1972.

Zacharias of Sakhâ. *An Encomium on the Life of John the Little,* vol. 18, numbers 1 and 2. Translated by Maged S. Mikhail and Tim Vivian. East Brunswick, N.J.: Society of Coptic Church Studies, 1997.

Zuckerman, Arthur. *A Jewish Princedom in Feudal France.* New York: Columbia University Press, 1973.

INDEX

BOOKS OF RELATED INTEREST

The Woman with the Alabaster Jar
Mary Magdalen and the Holy Grail
by Margaret Starbird

Montségur and the Mystery of the Cathars
by Jean Markale

The Church of Mary Magdalene
The Sacred Feminine and the Treasure of Rennes-le-Château
by Jean Markale

Gnostic Philosophy
From Ancient Persia to Modern Times
by Tobias Churton

Forbidden Religion
Suppressed Heresies of the West
Edited by J. Douglas Kenyon

The Sacred Embrace of Jesus and Mary
The Sexual Mystery at the Heart of the Christian Tradition
by Jean-Yves Leloup

The Gospel of Mary Magdalene
by Jean-Yves Leloup
Foreword by Jacob Needleman

Gnostic Secrets of the Naassenes
The Initiatory Teachings of the Last Supper
by Mark H. Gaffney

Inner Traditions • Bear & Company
P.O. Box 388
Rochester, VT 05767
1-800-246-8648
www.InnerTraditions.com

Or contact your local bookseller